The Clinician's Guide to Anxiety Sensitivity Treatment and Assessment

The Clinician's Guide to Anxiety Sensitivity Treatment and Assessment

Edited by

Jasper A. J. Smits
Michael W. Otto
Mark B. Powers
Scarlett O. Baird

ELSEVIER

ACADEMIC PRESS
An imprint of Elsevier

Academic Press is an imprint of Elsevier
125 London Wall, London EC2Y 5AS, United Kingdom
525 B Street, Suite 1650, San Diego, CA 92101, United States
50 Hampshire Street, 5th Floor, Cambridge, MA 02139, United States
The Boulevard, Langford Lane, Kidlington, Oxford OX5 1GB, United Kingdom

Notices

Knowledge and best practice in this field are constantly changing. As new research and experience broaden our understanding, changes in research methods, professional practices, or medical treatment may become necessary.

Practitioners and researchers must always rely on their own experience and knowledge in evaluating and using any information, methods, compounds, or experiments described herein. In using such information or methods they should be mindful of their own safety and the safety of others, including parties for whom they have a professional responsibility.

To the fullest extent of the law, neither the Publisher nor the authors, contributors, or editors, assume any liability for any injury and/or damage to persons or property as a matter of products liability, negligence or otherwise, or from any use or operation of any methods, products, instructions, or ideas contained in the material herein.

Library of Congress Cataloging-in-Publication Data
A catalog record for this book is available from the Library of Congress

British Library Cataloguing-in-Publication Data
A catalogue record for this book is available from the British Library

ISBN 978-0-12-813495-5

For information on all Academic Press publications visit our website at https://www.elsevier.com/books-and-journals

Publisher: Nikki Levy
Acquisition Editor: Nikki Levy
Editorial Project Manager: Ruby Smith
Production Project Manager: Bharatwaj Varatharajan
Cover Designer: Miles Hitchen

Typeset by SPi Global, India

Contents

Companion site for this book is available at https://www.elsevier.com/books-and-journals/book-companion/9780128134955

Contributors

Nicholas P. Allan Ohio University, Athens, OH, United States

Gordon J.G. Asmundson University of Regina, Regina, SK, Canada

Dylan A. Braun University of Miami, Miami, FL, United States

Scarlett O. Baird The University of Texas at Austin, Austin, TX, United States

Dan Capron University of Southern Mississippi, Hattiesburg, MS, United States

Jill Ehrenreich-May University of Miami, Miami, FL, United States

Hayley E. Fitzgerald Boston University, Boston, MA, United States

Lorra Garey University of Houston, Houston, TX, United States

R. Kathryn McHugh McLean Hospital & Harvard Medical School, Belmont, MA, United States

Brooke Y. Kauffman University of Houston, Houston, TX, United States

Ashley A. Knapp Dartmouth College, Hanover, NH, United States

Kara Manning University of Houston, Houston, TX, United States

Janine V. Olthuis University of New Brunswick, Fredericton, NB, Canada

Michael W. Otto Boston University, Boston, MA, United States

Mark B. Powers Baylor University Medical Center, Dallas, TX, United States

Norman B. Schmidt Florida State University, Tallahassee, FL, United States

Jamie A. Sherman University of Miami, Miami, FL, United States

Jasper A.J. Smits The University of Texas at Austin, Austin, TX, United States

Steven Taylor University of British Columbia, Vancouver, BC, Canada

Michael J. Telch The University of Texas at Austin, Austin, TX, United States

Michael J. Zvolensky University of Houston, Houston, TX, United States

Anxiety sensitivity as a transdiagnostic treatment target

1

Jasper A.J. Smits, Michael W. Otto†, Mark B. Powers‡, Scarlett O. Baird**
*The University of Texas at Austin, Austin, TX, United States, †Boston University, Boston, MA, United States, ‡Baylor University Medical Center, Dallas, TX, United States

As illustrated by the 1979 film, *When a Stranger Calls*, a classic horror-story meme involves repeated, threatening calls at night to an isolated babysitter. The babysitter notifies the police, and is subsequently informed, "we've traced the call, it's coming from inside the house." Threats arising from within the secure walls of a home are terrifying. Likewise, threat arising from stimuli within one's own body can be both terrifying and disabling. This is the type of fear captured by the concept of anxiety sensitivity, which has been defined as the fear of anxiety and related sensations (Reiss, Peterson, Gursky, & McNally, 1986).

Why a book about anxiety sensitivity? We have four specific answers. The first is that anxiety sensitivity is a strong predictor of both psychopathology and negative health behaviors. Anxiety sensitivity is elevated in individuals with anxiety and depressive disorders, and particularly in panic disorder and posttraumatic stress disorder (Naragon-Gainey, 2010; Olatunji & Wolitzky-Taylor, 2009). Individuals who report disordered eating also evidence heightened anxiety sensitivity (Anestis, Holm-Denoma, Gordon, Schmidt, & Joiner, 2008), which predicts overeating in response to negative emotions (Deboer et al., 2012; Hearon, Quatromoni, Mascoop, & Otto, 2014). Anxiety sensitivity also is related to a striking breadth of negative health behaviors and related medical conditions Otto et al., 2016). In a recent review of this area of study, Horenstein and colleagues (Horenstein, Potter, & Heimberg, 2018) identified 160 studies on the association between anxiety sensitivity and chronic illness, disability, and negative health behaviors. Horenstein and colleagues provided convincing evidence that anxiety sensitivity is linked to fear of pain, fear of cardiac symptoms, fear of respiratory symptoms, and fear of gastrointestinal symptoms relevant to the disability in a wide range of chronic medical conditions. Similarly, anxiety sensitivity predicts the avoidance of health behaviors, including exercise (Farris et al., 2016, 2017; Moshier et al., 2013; Moshier, Szuhany, Hearon, Smits, & Otto, 2016; Smits, Tart, Presnell, Rosenfield, & Otto, 2010), and also certain preventive procedures, like dental treatment (Horenstein et al., 2018). Indeed, the association between anxiety sensitivity and both exercise avoidance and mood-induced eating (Hearon et al., 2014) provides a particularly concerning "1:2 punch" to health. These negative health effects are further strengthened by the association between anxiety sensitivity and coping motives for drug use (Lejuez, Paulson, Daughters, Bornovalova, & Zvolensky, 2006; Leventhal & Zvolensky,

The Clinician's Guide to Anxiety Sensitivity Treatment and Assessment. https://doi.org/10.1016/B978-0-12-813495-5.00001-2

2015; Stewart & Kushner, 2001), including greater difficulties discontinuing smoking (Leventhal & Zvolensky, 2015). In sum, anxiety sensitivity serves as a highly useful, transdiagnostic predictor of distress and disability across a wide spectrum of mental health and physical health disorders (Otto et al., 2016; Otto & Smits, 2018).

The second reason is that the Anxiety Sensitivity Index (ASI; Peterson & Reiss, 1992) has proven its mettle relative to alternative measures of distress tolerance. In the last decade, distress tolerance has emerged as an increasingly studied construct for understanding the development and maintenance of psychopathology (Leyro, Zvolensky, & Bernstein, 2010). Distress tolerance is defined both by (1) the perceived capacity to withstand negative emotional or somatic states, and (2) the behavioral act of withstanding these internal states, as elicited by particular stressors. Distress tolerance is presumed to have both general factors as well as domain specificity, and accordingly measures have been developed to try to measure distress tolerance within specific domains such as the intolerance of uncertainty, the intolerance of frustration, the intolerance of emotion, as well as intolerance to pain or other induced physical states (Zvolensky, Bernstein, & Vujanovic, 2011). The original ASI is the most widely used instrument of the construct. This self-report measure, which has sound psychometric properties both for use in clinical and nonclinical samples (Peterson & Reiss, 1992), lists 16 statements reflecting either distress about anxiety symptoms (e.g., "It scares me when I feel shaky") or concern about negative consequences of anxiety symptoms (e.g., "When I am nervous, I worry that I might be mentally ill"), and asks respondents to indicate the degree to which they agree with each statement (0 = "very little"; 4 = "very much"). The total score can range between 0 and 64. A revised version of the ASI, the ASI-3 (Taylor et al., 2007), has been developed in addition to a modification of the instrument for assessing anxiety sensitivity in children (CASI; Silverman, Fleisig, Rabian, & Peterson, 1991). Chapter 2 provides an overview of these measures and discusses how to best use them in practice.

Not only is there an impressively large literature regarding the ASI relative to other measures of distress intolerance (Horenstein et al., 2018), the ASI has done well in one-to-one comparisons with other measures of distress tolerance. For example, McHugh and Otto showed that the assessment of distress tolerance does indeed appear to rely on both general and domain-specific components, and that anxiety sensitivity, as measured by the ASI, has value in showing linkages across both self-report and behavioral persistence indices of distress tolerance (McHugh et al., 2011; McHugh & Otto, 2011). Why might anxiety sensitivity be so valuable as a broad-based predictor? We believe that it is not because of the domain specificity of the ASI (to anxiety-related physical, social, and cognitive symptoms), but because measures of anxiety sensitivity evaluate the fearful and anxious responses to these symptoms (e.g., all items of the 16-item Anxiety Sensitivity Index start with the phrase, "It scares me when…"). As illustrated in Fig. 1, we believe that it is this anxious response to symptoms of anxiety that underlies the value of anxiety sensitivity for assessing the amplification of anxiety and motivation to escape/avoid these target sensations (Otto et al., 2016). In short, anxiety sensitivity amplifies the aversiveness of a wide range of somatic experiences, and thereby motivates avoidance and escape, including the use of maladaptive strategies for avoidance such as drug use, stressful events, mood

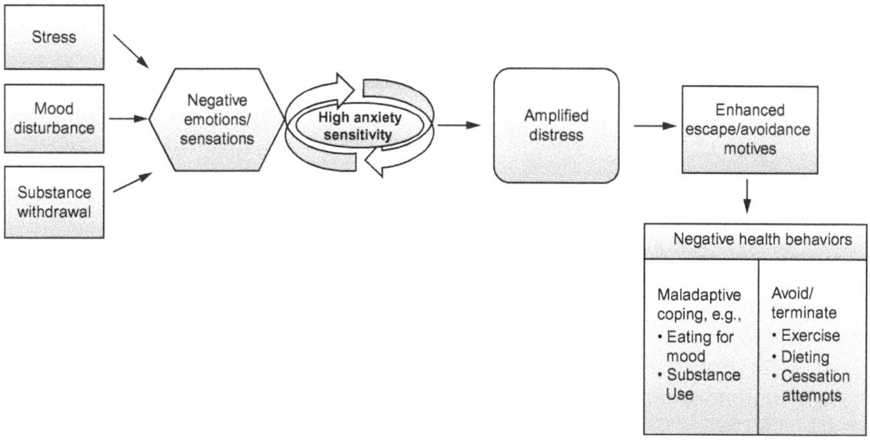

Fig. 1 Anxiety sensitivity in the maintenance of psychopathology and negative health behaviors.
Reprinted by permission from Otto, M. W., Eastman, A., Lo, S., Hearon, B. A., Bickel, W. K., Zvolensky, M., … Doan, S. N. (2016). Anxiety sensitivity and working memory capacity: risk factors and targets for health behavior promotion. *Clinical Psychology Review, 49*, 67–78. https://doi.org/10.1016/j.cpr.2016.07.003.

disturbances, or other physical provocations such as substance withdrawal, which all produce anxiety-like sensations. The role of anxiety sensitivity is to amplify the aversiveness of these sensations and drive maladaptive avoidance responses. We believe it is this essential pattern that underlies the value of anxiety sensitivity as both a predictor of maladaptive behavioral patterns and as a potential treatment target for ameliorating these maladaptive behaviors (Otto et al., 2016).

The value of anxiety sensitivity as a treatment target is the third reason for this book. Anxiety sensitivity is a malleable risk and maintaining factor. Indeed, meta-analytic review of 24 studies (1851 participants) showed that cognitive-behavior therapy results in very large reductions in anxiety sensitivity relative to a control condition (Hedges' $g = 1.40$; Smits, Berry, Tart, & Powers, 2008). Interoceptive exposure procedures provide a particularly focused intervention for fears of emotions and associated bodily sensations—providing stepwise exposure to these sensations as induced by a range of physical procedures provides patients an opportunity to (re)establish a sense of safety around anxiety and related sensations (Boswell et al., 2013; Otto et al., 2012). Similarly, aerobic exercise has been shown to be efficacious in rapidly reducing anxiety sensitivity (Broman-Fulks, Berman, Rabian, & Webster, 2004; Smits et al., 2008), presumably following the same mechanism as interoceptive exposure (Smits et al., 2016; Smits, Powers, Berry, & Otto, 2007). Cognitive procedures also show value in reducing anxiety sensitivity, through either education (Schmidt et al., 2007) or computerized training aimed at modifying threatening interpretations of feared sensations (Capron & Schmidt, 2016).

There is also evidence that reducing anxiety sensitivity is a core mechanism of change for cognitive behavioral interventions for panic and other disorders

(Boswell et al., 2013; Gallagher et al., 2013; Smits, Powers, Cho, & Telch, 2004). Likewise, targeting high anxiety sensitivity in smokers has the expected effects on promoting smoking cessation (Smits et al., 2016; Zvolensky et al., 2018, 2018). Lastly, there is evidence for successful prevention of anxiety sensitivity-related disorders by targeting anxiety sensitivity in at-risk individuals (see Chapter 4; Schmidt et al., this volume).

Our final motivation for editing this book is to promote the broader conceptualization of the role of anxiety sensitivity in emotional regulation. The wealth of evidence implicating anxiety sensitivity as a mechanism for disorder onset, maintenance, and successful treatment encourages broader consideration of anxiety sensitivity as a crucial emotional-regulation factor. Emotion regulation research (Gross & Thompson, 2007) typically focuses on strategies to minimize the impact of negative emotional content through minimizing the intensity of exposure (i.e., through distraction), modifying its meaning (i.e., through reappraisal), or trying to behaviorally minimize its effects (i.e., emotional suppression). We believe the modification of the amplification of emotion deserves attention as an associated strategy. This strategy is directed not at modifying the impact of external stimuli, but by modifying the impact of internal stimuli. That is, we believe that emotional regulation strategies can be divided into: (1) ways to modify the impact of external stressors (distraction and reappraisal) as well as (2) ways to modify the impact of internal stimuli (through suppression or the modification of anxiety sensitivity). An abundance of research shows that suppression is a poor strategy for long-term wellbeing (John & Gross, 2004). In contrast, the available research, much of which is reviewed in this book, suggests that modification of anxiety sensitivity is a particularly useful strategy to enhance emotional regulation. After all, low anxiety sensitivity is associated with greater resilience to stress (Schmidt, Lerew, & Jackson, 1997), lower psychopathology (Naragon-Gainey, 2010; Olatunji & Wolitzky-Taylor, 2009), and greater adaptive health behaviors (Otto et al., 2016). Lowering anxiety sensitivity appears to break the link between the experience of negative emotional and physical stimulation and maladaptive responses to these sensations. As such, low anxiety sensitivity should share characteristics with both the disidentification with and reduced reactivity to negative emotional content that helps define decentering interventions (Bernstein et al., 2015). Indeed, mindfulness training lowers anxiety sensitivity (Tanay, Lotan, & Bernstein, 2012), consistent with the notion that anxiety sensitivity helps define aspects of healthy emotional regulation.

Given these four motivations, we have assembled an authorship team of experts in different aspects of anxiety sensitivity. We asked them to contribute brief and focused chapters that can facilitate the targeting of anxiety sensitivity reduction in clinical practice. McHugh reviews assessment strategies for anxiety sensitivity and provides guidance on how to use these measures for treatment planning and assessment of treatment progress. Telch introduces a framework and a set of strategies for refining case formulation and treatment planning by attending to the patient's anxiety sensitivity level and his anxiety sensitivity profile—i.e., the specific threat perceptions associated with somatic arousal. Schmidt and colleagues review a body of work that supports anxiety sensitivity reduction as a target for prevention and discuss a range of clinical strategies to achieve this aim. Taylor introduces established interventions (e.g., interoceptive exposure, cognitive restructuring) for targeting anxiety sensitivity as applied to patients who present with anxiety disorders. The set of chapters that follow involve adaptations of these strategies for (1) common clinical problems in practice, including pain (Olthuis & Asmundson, this volume) and smoking cessation (Zvolensky & colleagues, this volume), and (2) treatment with children and adolescents (Sherman and colleagues). Each of these chapters is clinically focused, aiming to provide a resource for clinicians as they plan for their clinical practice. To this end, the chapters provide clinical case examples, figures, and worksheets. Figures and worksheets have also been made available on the book's companion website (https://www.elsevier.com/books-and-journals/book-companion/9780128134955). We hope that this book provides a useful resource for clinicians who wish to target core transdiagnostic mechanisms in order to optimize outcomes for their patients.

References

Anestis, M. D., Holm-Denoma, J. M., Gordon, K. H., Schmidt, N. B., & Joiner, T. E. (2008). The role of anxiety sensitivity in eating pathology. *Cognitive Therapy and Research*, *32*(3), 370–385. https://doi.org/10.1007/s10608-006-9085-y.

Bernstein, A., Hadash, Y., Lichtash, Y., Tanay, G., Shepherd, K., & Fresco, D. M. (2015). Decentering and related constructs: a critical review and metacognitive processes model. *Perspectives on Psychological Science: A Journal of the Association for Psychological Science*, *10*(5), 599–617. https://doi.org/10.1177/1745691615594577.

Boswell, J. F., Farchione, T. J., Sauer-Zavala, S., Murray, H. W., Fortune, M. R., & Barlow, D. H. (2013). Anxiety sensitivity and interoceptive exposure: a transdiagnostic construct and change strategy. *Behavior Therapy*, *44*(3), 417–431. https://doi.org/10.1016/j.beth.2013.03.006.

Broman-Fulks, J. J., Berman, M. E., Rabian, B. A., & Webster, M. J. (2004). Effects of aerobic exercise on anxiety sensitivity. *Behaviour Research and Therapy*, *42*(2), 125–136. https://doi.org/10.1016/S0005-7967(03)00103-7.

Capron, D. W., & Schmidt, N. B. (2016). Development and randomized trial evaluation of a novel computer-delivered anxiety sensitivity intervention. *Behaviour Research and Therapy*, *81*, 47–55. https://doi.org/10.1016/j.brat.2016.04.001.

Deboer, L. B., Tart, C. D., Presnell, K. E., Powers, M. B., Baldwin, A. S., & Smits, J. A. J. (2012). Physical activity as a moderator of the association between anxiety sensitivity and binge eating. *Eating Behaviors*, *13*(3), 194–201. https://doi.org/10.1016/j.eatbeh.2012.01.009.

Farris, S. G., Davis, M. L., Rosenfield, D., Kauffman, B. Y., Baird, S. O., Powers, M. B., … Zvolensky, M. J. (2016). Exercise self-efficacy moderates the relation between anxiety sensitivity and body mass index and exercise tolerance in treatment-seeking smokers. *Mental Health and Physical Activity*, *10*, 25–32. https://doi.org/10.1016/j.mhpa.2016.05.001.

Farris, S. G., Uebelacker, L. A., Brown, R. A., Price, L. H., Desaulniers, J., & Abrantes, A. M. (2017). Anxiety sensitivity predicts increased perceived exertion during a 1-mile walk test among treatment-seeking smokers. *Journal of Behavioral Medicine*, *40*(6), 886–893. https://doi.org/10.1007/s10865-017-9853-z.

Gallagher, M. W., Payne, L. A., White, K. S., Shear, K. M., Woods, S. W., Gorman, J. M., & Barlow, D. H. (2013). Mechanisms of change in cognitive behavioral therapy for panic disorder: the unique effects of self-efficacy and anxiety sensitivity. *Behaviour Research and Therapy*, *51*(11), 767–777. https://doi.org/10.1016/j.brat.2013.09.001.

Gross, J. J., & Thompson, R. A. (2007). Emotion regulation: Conceptual foundations. In *Handbook of emotion regulation* (pp. 3–24). New York, NY: Guilford Press.

Hearon, B. A., Quatromoni, P. A., Mascoop, J. L., & Otto, M. W. (2014). The role of anxiety sensitivity in daily physical activity and eating behavior. *Eating Behaviors*, *15*(2), 255–258. https://doi.org/10.1016/j.eatbeh.2014.03.007.

Horenstein, A., Potter, C. M., & Heimberg, R. G. (2018). How does anxiety sensitivity increase risks for chronic medical conditions. *Clinical Psychology: Science and Practice*. https://doi.org/10.1111/cpsp.12248 (in press).

John, O. P., & Gross, J. J. (2004). Healthy and unhealthy emotion regulation: Personality processes, individual differences, and life span development. *Journal of Personality*, *72*(6), 1301–1334. https://doi.org/10.1111/j.1467-6494.2004.00298.x.

Lejuez, C. W., Paulson, A., Daughters, S. B., Bornovalova, M. A., & Zvolensky, M. J. (2006). The association between heroin use and anxiety sensitivity among inner-city individuals in residential drug use treatment. *Behaviour Research and Therapy*, *44*(5), 667–677. https://doi.org/10.1016/j.brat.2005.04.006.

Leventhal, A. M., & Zvolensky, M. J. (2015). Anxiety, depression, and cigarette smoking: a transdiagnostic vulnerability framework to understanding emotion-smoking comorbidity. *Psychological Bulletin*, *141*(1), 176–212. https://doi.org/10.1037/bul0000003.

Leyro, T. M., Zvolensky, M. J., & Bernstein, A. (2010). Distress tolerance and psychopathological symptoms and disorders: a review of the empirical literature among adults. *Psychological Bulletin*, *136*(4), 576–600. https://doi.org/10.1037/a0019712.

McHugh, R. K., Daughters, S. B., Lejuez, C. W., Murray, H. W., Hearon, B. A., Gorka, S. M., & Otto, M. W. (2011). Shared variance among self-report and behavioral measures of distress intolerance. *Cognitive Therapy and Research*, *35*(3), 266–275. https://doi.org/10.1007/s10608-010-9295-1.

McHugh, R. K., & Otto, M. W. (2011). Domain-general and domain-specific strategies for the assessment of distress intolerance. *Psychology of Addictive Behaviors: Journal of the Society of Psychologists in Addictive Behaviors*, *25*(4), 745–749. https://doi.org/10.1037/a0025094.

Moshier, S. J., Hearon, B. A., Calkins, A. W., Szuhany, K. L., Utschig, A. C., Smits, J. A. J., & Otto, M. W. (2013). Clarifying the link between distress intolerance and exercise: elevated anxiety sensitivity predicts less vigorous exercise. *Cognitive Therapy and Research*, *37*(3), 476–482. https://doi.org/10.1007/s10608-012-9489-9.

Moshier, S. J., Szuhany, K. L., Hearon, B. A., Smits, J. A. J., & Otto, M. W. (2016). Anxiety sensitivity uniquely predicts exercise behaviors in young adults seeking to increase physical activity. *Behavior Modification*, *40*(1–2), 178–198. https://doi.org/10.1177/0145445515603704.

Naragon-Gainey, K. (2010). Meta-analysis of the relations of anxiety sensitivity to the depressive and anxiety disorders. *Psychological Bulletin*, *136*(1), 128–150. https://doi.org/10.1037/a0018055.

Olatunji, B. O., & Wolitzky-Taylor, K. B. (2009). Anxiety sensitivity and the anxiety disorders: a meta-analytic review and synthesis. *Psychological Bulletin*, *135*(6), 974–999. https://doi.org/10.1037/a0017428.

Otto, M. W., Eastman, A., Lo, S., Hearon, B. A., Bickel, W. K., Zvolensky, M., … Doan, S. N. (2016). Anxiety sensitivity and working memory capacity: risk factors and targets for health behavior promotion. *Clinical Psychology Review*, *49*, 67–78. https://doi.org/10.1016/j.cpr.2016.07.003.

Otto, M. W., & Smits, J. A. J. (2018). Anxiety sensitivity, health behaviors, and the prevention and treatment of medical illness. *Clinical Psychology: Science and Practice Clin. Psychol. Sci. Pract. 25*, e12253.
Otto, M. W., Tolin, D. F., Nations, K. R., Utschig, A. C., Rothbaum, B. O., Hofmann, S. G., & Smits, J. A. J. (2012). Five sessions and counting: considering ultra-brief treatment for panic disorder. *Depression and Anxiety*, *29*(6), 465–470. https://doi.org/10.1002/da.21910.
Peterson, R. A., & Reiss, R. J. (1992). *Anxiety sensitivity index manual* (2nd ed.). Worthington, OH: International Diagnostic Systems.
Reiss, S., Peterson, R. A., Gursky, D. M., & McNally, R. J. (1986). Anxiety sensitivity, anxiety frequency and the prediction of fearfulness. *Behaviour Research and Therapy*, *24*(1), 1–8. https://doi.org/10.1016/0005-7967(86)90143-9.
Schmidt, N. B., Eggleston, A. M., Woolaway-Bickel, K., Fitzpatrick, K. K., Vasey, M. W., & Richey, J. A. (2007). Anxiety sensitivity amelioration training (ASAT): a longitudinal primary prevention program targeting cognitive vulnerability. *Journal of Anxiety Disorders*, *21*(3), 302–319. https://doi.org/10.1016/j.janxdis.2006.06.002.
Schmidt, N. B., Lerew, D. R., & Jackson, R. J. (1997). The role of anxiety sensitivity in the pathogenesis of panic: prospective evaluation of spontaneous panic attacks during acute stress. *Journal of Abnormal Psychology*, *106*(3), 355–364. https://doi.org/10.1037/0021-843X.106.3.355.
Silverman, W. K., Fleisig, W., Rabian, B., & Peterson, R. A. (1991). Childhood anxiety sensitivity index. *Journal of Clinical Child Psychology*, *20*(2), 162–168. https://doi.org/10.1207/s15374424jccp2002_7.
Smits, J. A. J., Berry, A. C., Rosenfield, D., Powers, M. B., Behar, E., & Otto, M. W. (2008). Reducing anxiety sensitivity with exercise. *Depression and Anxiety*, *25*(8), 689–699. https://doi.org/10.1002/da.20411.
Smits, J. A. J., Berry, A. C., Tart, C. D., & Powers, M. B. (2008). The efficacy of cognitive-behavioral interventions for reducing anxiety sensitivity: a meta-analytic review. *Behaviour Research and Therapy*, *46*(9), 1047–1054. https://doi.org/10.1016/j.brat.2008.06.010.
Smits, J. A. J., Powers, M. B., Berry, A. C., & Otto, M. W. (2007). Translating empirically supported strategies into accessible interventions: the potential utility of exercise for the treatment of panic disorder. *Cognitive and Behavioral Practice*, *14*(4), 364–374. https://doi.org/10.1016/j.cbpra.2006.07.005.
Smits, J. A. J., Powers, M. B., Cho, Y., & Telch, M. J. (2004). Mechanism of change in cognitive-behavioral treatment of panic disorder: evidence for the fear of fear mediational hypothesis. *Journal of Consulting and Clinical Psychology*, *72*(4), 646–652. https://doi.org/10.1037/0022-006X.72.4.646.
Smits, J. A. J., Tart, C. D., Presnell, K., Rosenfield, D., & Otto, M. W. (2010). Identifying potential barriers to physical activity adherence: anxiety sensitivity and body mass as predictors of fear during exercise. *Cognitive Behaviour Therapy*, *39*(1), 28–36. https://doi.org/10.1080/16506070902915261.
Smits, J. A. J., Zvolensky, M. J., Davis, M. L., Rosenfield, D., Marcus, B. H., Church, T. S., … Baird, S. O. (2016). The efficacy of vigorous-intensity exercise as an aid to smoking cessation in adults with high anxiety sensitivity: a randomized controlled trial. *Psychosomatic Medicine*, *78*(3), 354–364. https://doi.org/10.1097/PSY.0000000000000264.
Stewart, S. H., & Kushner, M. G. (2001). Introduction to the special issue on "anxiety sensitivity and addictive behaviors." *Addictive Behaviors*, *26*(6), 775–785.
Tanay, G., Lotan, G., & Bernstein, A. (2012). Salutary proximal processes and distal mood and anxiety vulnerability outcomes of mindfulness training: a pilot preventive intervention. *Behavior Therapy*, *43*(3), 492–505. https://doi.org/10.1016/j.beth.2011.06.003.

Taylor, S., Zvolensky, M. J., Cox, B. J., Deacon, B., Heimberg, R. G., Ledley, D. R., … Cardenas, S. J. (2007). Robust dimensions of anxiety sensitivity: development and initial validation of the anxiety sensitivity Index-3. *Psychological Assessment*, *19*(2), 176–188. https://doi.org/10.1037/1040-3590.19.2.176.

Zvolensky, M. J., Bernstein, A., & Vujanovic, A. A. (Eds.), (2011). *Distress tolerance: Theory, research, and clinical applications*. Guilford Press.

Zvolensky, M. J., Garey, L., Allan, N. P., Farris, S. G., Raines, A. M., Smits, J. A. J., … Schmidt, N. B. (2018). Effects of anxiety sensitivity reduction on smoking abstinence: an analysis from a panic prevention program. *Journal of Consulting and Clinical Psychology*, *86*(5), 474–485. https://doi.org/10.1037/ccp0000288.

Zvolensky, M. J., Rosenfield, D., Garey, L., Kauffman, B. Y., Langdon, K. J., Powers, M. B., … Smits, J. A. J. (2018). Does exercise aid smoking cessation through reductions in anxiety sensitivity and dysphoria? *Health Psychology: Official Journal of the Division of Health Psychology, American Psychological Association*, *37*(7), 647–657. https://doi.org/10.1037/hea0000588.

Assessing anxiety sensitivity

2

R. Kathryn McHugh
McLean Hospital & Harvard Medical School, Belmont, MA, United States

Chapter Outline

Introduction

Anxiety sensitivity, the fear of anxiety-related symptoms and sensations, contributes to risk for the onset and maintenance of a wide array of psychiatric disorders and behavioral health conditions (e.g., Mackie, Castellanos-Ryan, & Conrod, 2011; Ocanez, McHugh, & Otto, 2010; Schmidt et al., 2010; Zvolensky, Farris, Leventhal, & Schmidt, 2014). Anxiety sensitivity results in an amplification of anxiety-related symptoms, motivating attempts to escape or avoid those sensations. Although anxiety sensitivity is stable over time (McNally, 2002), it is also malleable and can be modified with intervention (Mavissakalian, Perel, Talbott-Green, & Sloan, 1998; Smits, Berry, Tart, & Powers, 2008), with resultant improvements in clinical symptoms (Smits, Powers, Cho, & Telch, 2004). Accordingly, anxiety sensitivity has utility in clinical settings as a potential target for intervention.

The assessment of anxiety sensitivity, predominantly using self-report measures, has been widely studied, and measures have been well validated in clinical and non-clinical populations. Routine assessment of anxiety sensitivity in clinical settings has several potential applications. First, characterizing the level of anxiety sensitivity can

The Clinician's Guide to Anxiety Sensitivity Treatment and Assessment. https://doi.org/10.1016/B978-0-12-813495-5.00002-4

help to identify those at risk for heightened reactivity to symptoms and stressors (Otto et al., 2016; Schmidt, Lerew, & Jackson, 1997). Second, assessing anxiety sensitivity can identify those who may benefit from anxiety sensitivity-reduction interventions, such as interoceptive exposure (Smits, Berry, Rosenfield, et al., 2008; Smits, Berry, Tart, et al., 2008). Third, given its role as a mechanism of action in the efficacy of treatments, the ongoing assessment of anxiety sensitivity during treatment can provide information on interim progress and whether intervention should be continued or modified (Ino et al., 2017; Short et al., 2017; Zvolensky et al., 2018). Notably, this may be of value not only among those with anxiety disorders, but also among those with other conditions, such as substance use disorders or pain-related conditions (Ocanez et al., 2010; Otto et al., 2016).

This chapter will provide an overview of the assessment of anxiety sensitivity. The chapter will begin with an overview of latent structure and construct validity, followed by a description of measures of anxiety sensitivity, and finally guidance on clinical applications of anxiety sensitivity assessment.

Latent structure and validity

Latent structure of anxiety sensitivity

Much like other cognitive and affective constructs (e.g., distress intolerance, worry), anxiety sensitivity was initially hypothesized to have a dimensional latent structure. In other words, anxiety sensitivity was thought to occur along a continuum rather than consisting of discrete categories (e.g., low and high). This perspective is supported by both psychometric studies of the latent structure of anxiety sensitivity (Asmundson, Weeks, Carleton, Thibodeau, & Fetzner, 2011; Broman-Fulks et al., 2008, 2010) as well as a wide array of studies that have identified the relevance of anxiety sensitivity across the range of functioning (e.g., nonclinical and unselected samples as well as clinical samples). Nonetheless, not all studies provide support for this dimensional latent structure, with some studies supporting evidence for "low" and "high" (Bernstein et al., 2006, 2010), or "low/normative," "moderate" and "high" anxiety sensitivity groups (Allan, Korte, Capron, Raines, & Schmidt, 2014). Although this remains a topic of debate (Asmundson et al., 2011; Broman-Fulks et al., 2010), most studies appear to support the perspective that anxiety sensitivity is a dimensional construct, best conceptualized and measured along a continuum.

Research on the latent structure of anxiety sensitivity has also investigated whether it includes meaningful facets. Anxiety sensitivity was initially conceptualized as a single factor (Reiss, Peterson, Gursky, & McNally, 1986); however, subsequent work suggests that it may be better conceptualized as consisting of several lower-order factors. This multidimensional factor structure has been widely replicated in both adult (Asmundson et al., 2011; Taylor et al., 2007; Zinbarg, Barlow, & Brown, 1997) and child samples (Essau, Sasagawa, & Ollendick, 2010; Laurent, Schmidt, Catanzaro, Joiner, & Kelley, 1998). However, studies do not generally agree on the number of lower-order factors, with some identifying two factors (Laurent et al., 1998;

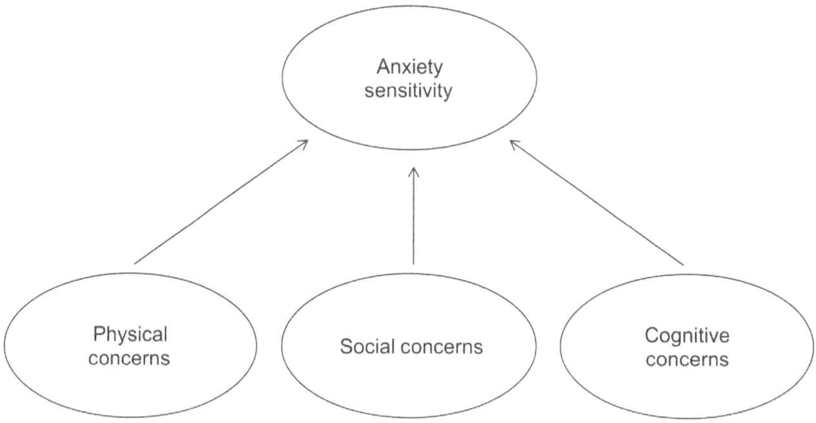

Fig. 1 Hypothesized latent structure of anxiety sensitivity.

Schmidt & Joiner, 2002; Zvolensky et al., 2003), others identifying three (Essau et al., 2010; Farris et al., 2015; Zinbarg et al., 1997), and others identifying four (Hinton, Pich, Safren, Pollack, & McNally, 2006; Taylor & Cox, 1998b). The most consistent finding is that anxiety sensitivity consists of three lower-order factors corresponding to social, physical, and cognitive domains (Asmundson et al., 2011; Calamari, Rector, Woodard, Cohen, & Chik, 2008; Dehon, Weems, Stickle, Costa, & Berman, 2005; Farris et al., 2015; Mohlman & Zinbarg, 2000; Stewart, Taylor, & Baker, 1997; Taylor et al., 2007; Vujanovic, Arrindell, Bernstein, Norton, & Zvolensky, 2007; Walsh, Stewart, McLaughlin, & Comeau, 2004; Zinbarg et al., 1997). Although not all studies have tested hierarchical models (i.e., one in which a higher-order single factor subsumes three lower-order factors; Fig. 1), tests that have included a hierarchical component generally support this model (Calamari et al., 2008; Dehon et al., 2005; Mohlman & Zinbarg, 2000; Rifkin, Beard, Hsu, Garner, & Bjorgvinsson, 2015; Vujanovic et al., 2007; Zinbarg et al., 1997). Accordingly, anxiety sensitivity self-report measures can be used to generate both a total score and scores reflecting these three lower-order domains.

Concurrent and criterion validity

Support for the concurrent and criterion validity of anxiety sensitivity is vast. Anxiety sensitivity is elevated among those with anxiety (Reiss et al., 1986; Rifkin et al., 2015; Taylor, Koch, & McNally, 1992), obsessive-compulsive, (Deacon & Abramowitz, 2006) and traumatic stress disorders (Bardeen, Tull, Stevens, & Gratz, 2015; Taylor et al., 1992) relative to those without. Anxiety sensitivity is also correlated with anxiety symptom severity in both unselected (Keough, Riccardi, Timpano, Mitchell, & Schmidt, 2010) and clinical samples (Deacon & Abramowitz, 2006). Those with higher anxiety sensitivity have heightened responding to distress, such as pain (Zvolensky, Goodie, McNeil, Sperry, & Sorrell, 2001), carbon dioxide inhalation (i.e., panic provocation; McNally & Eke, 1996; Richey, Schmidt, Hofmann, & Timpano, 2010), and psychosocial and traumatic stressors (McHugh, Gratz, & Tull, 2017; Shostak & Peterson, 1990).

Anxiety sensitivity also has been validated with respect to physiological and neurological markers of heightened reactivity to threat-related and other affective stimuli. For example, anxiety sensitivity has been associated with heightened fear-potentiated startle (McMillan, Asmundson, Zvolensky, & Carleton, 2012) and skin conductance response to carbon dioxide challenge (Gregor & Zvolensky, 2008). Neuroimaging studies have indicated that anxiety sensitivity is associated with activation and volumetric differences in limbic structures central to emotional processing, such as the amygdala and the insula (Killgore et al., 2011; Rosso et al., 2010; Stein, Simmons, Feinstein, & Paulus, 2007). Consistent with the perspective that anxiety sensitivity reflects an interpretation of anxiety symptoms and sensations as dangerous or threatening, a recent study identified a role for prefrontal regions that are associated with the appraisal of stimuli (e.g., the anterior cingulate) in anxiety sensitivity (Harrison et al., 2015).

Discriminant validity

One key issue in the assessment of anxiety sensitivity is the degree to which it may overlap with other related constructs. Studies have clearly distinguished anxiety sensitivity from variables reflecting affective states, such as trait anxiety (Reiss et al., 1986) and negative affect (Zinbarg & Barlow, 1996). However, the distinction between anxiety sensitivity and other affect amplification variables, most notably distress intolerance, is less clear.

Distress intolerance refers to the perceived inability to handle or manage distressing states, and is a construct with broad coverage in both theoretical models of mental health and with empirical backing for its relevance across a wide array of symptoms and disorders (Leyro, Zvolensky, & Bernstein, 2010). Distress intolerance, much like anxiety sensitivity, reflects a discomfort with unpleasant states and a desire to escape or avoid these states. Several studies have examined similarities between anxiety sensitivity and distress intolerance. One study found support for a single latent factor that includes both anxiety sensitivity and distress intolerance (McHugh & Otto, 2012b), whereas others suggested that these are distinct latent constructs, subsumed by a single higher-order factor (Bernstein, Zvolensky, Vujanovic, & Moos, 2009), or that anxiety sensitivity is a facet of distress intolerance (Mitchell, Riccardi, Keough, Timpano, & Schmidt, 2013). This difference across studies may be attributable to different analytic approaches, and thus the boundary between anxiety sensitivity and distress intolerance remains unclear. Nonetheless, these variables appear to share at least some overlap.

Understanding of the similarities and differences between these two constructs is also limited by continued debate about the optimal measurement of distress intolerance (McHugh et al., 2011). Distress intolerance has been defined as an inability to persist in the context of distressing states, which may include emotional or somatic states. However, intolerance appears to vary based on the type, or domain, of distress.

For example, intolerance of emotional states (e.g., frustration) is not strongly associated with intolerance of physical states (e.g., pain; McHugh et al., 2011; McHugh & Otto, 2011). Whereas intolerance of distress in general may serve as a risk factor for an array of maladaptive behaviors and both internalizing and externalizing disorders (Cummings et al., 2013), intolerance of specific domains of distress may yield specific patterns of symptoms. For example, intolerance of symptoms of nicotine withdrawal is strongly linked to poor smoking cessation outcome (Sirota et al., 2010), and intolerance of frustration is specifically linked to opioid use disorder (McHugh & Otto, 2012a). Accordingly, anxiety sensitivity—much like other sensitivity/tolerance-related constructs—may offer a specific linkage to anxiety-related responses that can be targeted with treatment. Interestingly, in a study of behavioral and self-report measures of distress intolerance, anxiety sensitivity was robustly associated with behavioral indices of intolerance of pain, respiratory discomfort, and frustration, suggesting that anxiety about distress may be a key feature of distress intolerance (McHugh & Otto, 2011).

Methods for assessing anxiety sensitivity

Anxiety sensitivity has predominantly been assessed using self-report measures. Below, a detailed description of self-report measures is presented, along with a brief overview of behavioral and cognitive measures of anxiety sensitivity.

Self-report measures of anxiety sensitivity

The Anxiety Sensitivity Index (ASI; Reiss et al., 1986) was the first well-validated measure of anxiety sensitivity and has been the gold-standard measure of this domain for a number of years. The ASI has been revised for children (Child Anxiety Sensitivity Index; Muris, 2002; Silverman et al., 1991) and updated several times for adults. Modifications include the ASI-Revised (Taylor & Cox, 1998b), the Anxiety Sensitivity Profile (Taylor & Cox, 1998a), and the ASI-3 (Taylor et al., 2007). Other self-report measures of related constructs including the Body Sensations Questionnaire (measuring the degree of fear in response to arousal-related sensations, such as feeling short of breath) and the Agoraphobic Cognitions Questionnaire (measuring catastrophic cognition about anxiety and panic-related sensations) have also been validated (Chambless, Caputo, Bright, & Gallagher, 1984), but focus more specifically on panic disorder. The two anxiety sensitivity measures with the strongest validation data in adults (ASI, ASI-3) and the most commonly used measure in children (CASI) are presented below in more detail. Each of these measures has strong psychometric support and can be used with confidence in clinical settings.

Anxiety Sensitivity Index (Reiss et al., 1986)

The original 16-item ASI consists of a series of statements related to beliefs about anxiety-related symptoms (e.g., *It scares me when I feel faint*), which respondents rate according to their level of agreement (ranging from *very little* to *very much*). The total score is calculated as a sum of all items, with a possible range from 0 to 64. Normative data for the ASI suggest average total scores from 14 to 20 in nonclinical and student samples (e.g., Peterson & Reiss, 1992; Stewart, Taylor, & Baker, 1997), with higher average scores for samples of adults with anxiety disorders (e.g., 24–26; Reiss et al., 1986), and particularly high scores for adults with panic disorder (e.g., 30–46; Peterson & Reiss, 1992; Reiss et al., 1986). The ASI has extensive evidence for its psychometric properties, including internal consistency reliability, test-retest reliability, criterion validity (e.g., elevations in groups with anxiety disorders), and both convergent and discriminant validity (Dehon et al., 2005; Reiss et al., 1986; Rodriguez et al., 2004; Vujanovic et al., 2007). The ASI has been translated and validated in languages such as Spanish (Novy, Stanley, Averill, & Daza, 2001; Sandin, Chorot, & McNally, 1996, 2001) and Croatian (Jurin, Jokic-Begic, & Korajlija, 2012), among others (McNally, 2002). A criticism of the ASI is that it does not adequately capture the three domains of cognitive, physical, and social concerns. A comparison of the ASI and ASI-3 suggested that the ASI-3 may offer psychometric advantages over the ASI (Taylor et al., 2007). Nonetheless, the original ASI has been extensively validated and is a strong measure for use in clinical settings.

Anxiety Sensitivity Index-3 (Taylor et al., 2007)

Although extensive validation data are available for the ASI, the 18-item ASI-3 has a number of advantages, particularly with respect to the stability of the latent factor

Table 1 Anxiety Sensitivity Index-3 normative data

	Sample size	Mean (SD)
Nonclinical or unselected		
Nonclinical (Taylor et al., 2007)	4720	12.8 (10.6)
Students (Wheaton et al., 2012)	315	13.8 (25.2)
Clinical		
Panic disorder (Taylor et al., 2007)	120	32.6 (14.3)
Panic disorder (Wheaton et al., 2012)	109	32.7 (15.2)
Panic disorder (Rifkin et al., 2015)	17	28.3 (12.8)
PTSD (Rifkin et al., 2015)	13	22.4 (10.7)
Social anxiety disorder (Taylor et al., 2007)	38	31.4 (11.9)
Social anxiety disorder (Wheaton et al., 2012)	73	30.4 (13.1)
Social anxiety disorder (Rifkin et al., 2015)	38	25.1 (12.8)
Obsessive-compulsive disorder (Taylor et al., 2007)	102	26.3 (16.8)
Obsessive-compulsive disorder (Wheaton et al., 2012)	198	27.6 (17.3)
Generalized anxiety disorder (Taylor et al., 2007)	30	27.5 (16.5)
Generalized anxiety disorder (Wheaton et al., 2012)	53	29.9 (16.0)
Generalized anxiety disorder (Rifkin et al., 2015)	45	22.4 (10.7)
Specific phobia (Wheaton et al., 2012)	29	25.2 (15.1)
Clinical but no anxiety diagnosis (Rifkin et al., 2015)	129	19.3 (14.3)
Multiple anxiety diagnoses (Rifkin et al., 2015)	140	31.8 (15.7)

Note. Normative values based on small sample sizes should be interpreted with caution.

structure. The ASI-3 is scored similarly to other versions of the measure, with individual items scaled from 0 to 4, with a total score range of 0–72. Normative data are presented in Table 1. Average total scores for nonclinical and student samples are in the range of 12–14, with samples of adults with anxiety disorders averaging scores in the 22–31 range, and panic disorder samples slightly higher, averaging 29–33 (see Table 1). The ASI-3 also has demonstrated strong psychometric properties, including support for concurrent, discriminant, and criterion validity, and retest and internal consistency reliability (Allan, Capron, Raines, & Schmidt, 2014; Rifkin et al., 2015; Taylor et al., 2007), and has shown sensitivity to change in clinical settings (Rifkin et al., 2015). The ASI-3 has been validated in an array of groups, such as nonclinical and unselected (e.g., student) samples (Taylor et al., 2007; Wheaton, Deacon, McGrath, Berman, & Abramowitz, 2012), adults with anxiety disorders (Osman et al., 2010; Wheaton et al., 2012), smokers (Allan, Raines, et al., 2014; Farris et al., 2015), and mixed clinical samples (Rifkin et al., 2015). It also has been validated in several languages, such as Korean (Lim & Kim, 2012), Italian (Ghisi et al., 2016), German (Kemper, Lutz, Bahr, Ruddel, & Hock, 2012), and Spanish (Sandin, Garcia, Chorot, & Germain, 2007).

Childhood Anxiety Sensitivity Index (Silverman et al., 1991)

The CASI is an 18-item self-report measure based on the original ASI and is the most commonly used self-report measure of anxiety sensitivity for children and adolescents. The CASI follows the original content of the ASI with modifications of language to allow for comprehension in younger respondents. For example, the responses were simplified to "*none*," "*some*," or "*a lot*." The CASI is scored using a sum of these items (rated 1–3), with a total score range of 18–54. Limited information is available on normative values for the CASI. Samples of school-aged children and adolescents (unselected for clinical status) have found means in the 26–28 range (Silverman et al., 1991; Walsh, Stewart, McLaughlin, & Comeau, 2004). Clinical samples report only slightly higher scores (e.g., 28–30; Silverman et al., 1991; Weems, Hammond-Laurence, Silverman, & Ginsburg, 1998), with the exception of panic disorder samples (e.g., 36; Elkins, Pincus, & Comer, 2014). The CASI has been validated for youth and adolescents ranging in age from 6 to 17 years and has demonstrated strong psychometric properties, such as concurrent and discriminant validity, internal consistency reliability, and criterion validity (Kearney, Albano, Eisen, Allan, & Barlow, 1997; McLaughlin, Stewart, & Taylor, 2007; Muris, Schmidt, Merckelbach, & Schouten, 2001; Rabian, Embry, & MacIntyre, 1999). The ability of this measure to capture a construct distinct from anxiety in preadolescence has been questioned (Chorpita & Albano, 1996); however, there is evidence that the CASI predicts responding to stressors even in preadolescents (Rabian et al., 1999) and offers additive benefit to measuring anxiety alone across children and adolescents (Weems et al., 1998). Data on the latent factor structure have also yielded mixed results. Studies have reported 2- (Lambert, Cooley, Campbell, Benoit, & Stansbury, 2004), 3- (Essau et al., 2010; Muris et al., 2001), and 4-factor structures of the CASI (Adornetto et al., 2008; Bernstein, Zvolensky, Stewart, & Comeau,

2007; Silverman, Goedhart, Barrett, & Turner, 2003). Several translations have been validated, in languages such as Serbian (Stevanovic, Silverman, Nichols-Lopez, Popovic-Deusic, & Pejovic-Milovancevic, 2013), German (Adornetto et al., 2008; Essau et al., 2010), Dutch (van Widenfelt, Siebelink, Goedhart, & Treffers, 2002), and Spanish (Sandin, Chorot, Santed, & Valiente, 2002). Further research is needed to provide adequate normative data and clarity on the optimal measurement of anxiety sensitivity in children.

Other strategies for measuring anxiety sensitivity

Measures of anxiety sensitivity beyond self-report are relatively limited and generally are conceptualized more as outcomes or proxy measures than measures of anxiety sensitivity itself. Behavioral tasks assessing anxiety in response to somatic symptom induction have been used as measures of anxiety sensitivity. These include breath holding and carbon dioxide (CO_2) inhalation. These tasks—through inducing respiratory discomfort that is often feared among those with high anxiety sensitivity—can provide a proxy for anxiety sensitivity by evaluating the reaction to these tests. Key metrics may include breath holding duration (i.e., tolerance of respiratory discomfort) and self-reported anxiety and physical discomfort following CO_2 inhalation. The latter can be implemented simply using a technique of breathing into a paper bag (McNally & Eke, 1996) or can entail more precise administration of CO_2 via inhalation of air with a particular percentage of CO_2 (e.g., 35%; Richey et al., 2010).

Behavioral assessment of interoceptive sensitivity has long been a feature of treatment for panic disorder. In such paradigms, a range of anxiety-related sensations is induced to identify the key feared sensations for the individual. For example, brief inductions of key sensations—such as dizziness, shortness of breath, and racing heart—are conducted after which respondents rate the symptom intensity and the level of anxiety the symptom generated. For example, brief inductions of dizziness (spinning while standing), increased heart rate (running in place), and respiratory discomfort (breathing through a straw) can provide information on which of these symptoms elicit the most fear and are important to target. Graded exposure can begin with low-distress symptoms and escalate to inductions eliciting greater distress and intensity.

Although measures that attempt to capture cognitive concepts using implicit methods (i.e., methods that assess cognition outside of conscious control) have improved the measurement of a range of constructs, the application of such methods to anxiety sensitivity has been limited. Much of this research focuses on information processing biases that are conceptually linked to anxiety sensitivity, such as attentional and memory biases toward anxiety-related interoceptive sensations. Critically, studies of this sort have generally not conceptualized these cognitive biases to be a measure of anxiety sensitivity, but rather have tested whether anxiety sensitivity is associated with the degree of bias. Studies have identified associations between self-reported anxiety sensitivity and information processing biases, particularly attentional hypervigilance to stimuli indicating physical symptoms or threat (Hunt,

Keogh, & French, 2006, 2007; Keogh, Dillon, Georgiou, & Hunt, 2001), and anxious interpretation of ambiguous stimuli that are interoceptive in nature (Richards, Austin, & Alvarenga, 2001) as well as memory bias toward threatening stimuli (Teachman, 2005). However, some work has failed to detect this association between anxiety sensitivity and attentional hypervigilance to interoceptive stimuli (Lang & Sarmiento, 2004; Teachman, 2005).

Stability across demographic groups

Anxiety sensitivity has been validated across an array of groups and in multiple languages (e.g., Sandin et al., 1996, 2002). In general, studies have supported the validity of anxiety sensitivity across racial and ethnic groups in the United States and internationally (Ghisi et al., 2016; Lim & Kim, 2012; Sandin et al., 2007; Talkovsky & Norton, 2015; Zvolensky et al., 2003). Specifically, anxiety sensitivity is observed in heterogeneous populations with respect to race, ethnicity, and country of origin, and appears to be consistently linked to anxiety symptoms and disorders. One area of inconsistency is with respect to the latent factor structure, with evidence for variation in the number of lower-order anxiety sensitivity factors across groups (Hinton et al., 2006; Hunter, Keough, Timpano, & Schmidt, 2012; Norton, De Coteau, Hope, & Anderson, 2004). However, it is of note that most of these studies did not directly compare groups within the same study (i.e., a finding in a single group was compared with the literature) or reflected small sample sizes, limiting the ability to determine whether group differences exist.

Notably, this examination of crosscultural differences typically utilizes anxiety sensitivity measures initially developed in the United States in predominantly White samples (c.f., Hinton et al., 2006). Hinton et al. (2006) in their modification of the ASI for use with Cambodian refugees living in the U.S. incorporated items that captured culture-specific panic-related fears. These included beliefs about the physiology of anxiety that are distinct from Western, White samples, such as the believe that anxiety is reflective of a disruption in the flow of "wind" (or air within the body) that can be felt as tension leading to consequences such as shortness of breath, fainting, or even suffocation or cardiac arrest (Hinton & Otto, 2006). The addition of items to the original ASI to evaluate these symptoms allows for consideration of these culture-specific manifestations while maintaining the core anxiety sensitivity construct (Hinton et al., 2006).

In general, the factor structure of anxiety sensitivity appears to be consistent (i.e., invariant) across genders in both children (Walsh et al., 2004) and adults (Stewart et al., 1997); although one study found evidence for gender invariance (Keogh, 2004). Moreover, anxiety sensitivity appears to be a valid construct across an array of ages, including children, adolescents, and young adults (Dehon et al., 2005; Muris, 2002; Silverman, Fleisig, Rabian, & Peterson, 1991), adults (Reiss et al., 1986; Rifkin et al., 2015; Taylor et al., 2007), and older adults (Mohlman & Zinbarg, 2000). Thus, anxiety sensitivity appears to be a variable that can be measured validly in both men and women across development.

Tips for assessing anxiety sensitivity in clinical practice

The ASI can be obtained from IDS Publishing, which owns the copyright to the original ASI and the CASI (www.anxietysensitivityindex.com). Recommendations for the assessment of anxiety sensitivity in clinical settings are described here.

How to interpret anxiety sensitivity scores?

Although scores should be interpreted within the context of other information, such as data from clinical interviews and behavioral observation, normative data provide markers for characterizing the severity of anxiety sensitivity in an individual.

Table 1 presents published normative data on the ASI-3 to aid in the interpretation of measure scores at the individual patient level. Recommended cut-offs for the identification of "elevated" anxiety sensitivity are 25 for the original ASI (Peterson & Plehn, 1999) and 23 for the ASI-3 (Allan, Korte, et al., 2014; Allan, Raines, et al., 2014). Due to relatively small sample sizes and lack of large-scale data in nonclinical child samples, normative data on the CASI are limited.

What is the target population?

Several populations may particularly benefit from assessment of anxiety sensitivity. Assessment of anxiety sensitivity may be of benefit across the range of anxiety, obsessive-compulsive, and traumatic stress disorders to identify those who may benefit from targeted intervention to reduce anxiety sensitivity. However, the measurement of anxiety sensitivity is also applicable in a number of other conditions, in which amplified reaction to distress and maladaptive avoidance and escape behaviors are present.

As described in subsequent chapters (Zvolensky is chapter 6), the assessment of anxiety sensitivity in people with substance use disorders may aid in the identification of those likely to have difficulty with acute and protracted substance withdrawal, as well as those who may be likely to use or relapse in the context of negative affect, withdrawal, or other distressing symptoms. Although anxiety sensitivity has been widely studied with respect to nicotine/cigarette use (Zvolensky, Farris, Guillot, & Leventhal, 2014; Zvolensky, Farris, Leventhal, et al., 2014), it also appears to be a pertinent risk factor in opioid (Hearon et al., 2011; McHugh, Votaw, et al., 2017; McHugh et al., 2016), alcohol (Allan, Albanese, Norr, Zvolensky, & Schmidt, 2015; McCaul, Hutton, Stephens, Xu, & Wand, 2017), and marijuana use (Bonn-Miller, Zvolensky, Marshall, & Bernstein, 2007; Buckner, Zvolensky, et al., 2011). Critically, anxiety sensitivity is also pertinent for drugs of abuse that do not relieve anxiety or may exacerbate it, such as stimulants (Buckner, Proctor, Reynolds, Kopetz, & Lejuez, 2011; Lejuez et al., 2008; Naifeh, Tull, & Gratz, 2012). Anxiety sensitivity also plays a role in chronic and acute pain (Asmundson is chapter 5), and is particularly associated with negative interpretation (i.e., anxious appraisal) of pain (Ocanez et al., 2010).

Another potentially important application of anxiety sensitivity measurement is with respect to medication adherence and discontinuation. Higher anxiety sensitivity has been associated with poorer medication adherence (e.g., blood pressure medication; Alcantara et al., 2014), and thus among those with elevated anxiety sensitivity careful monitoring of medication adherence may be indicated. Moreover, anxiety sensitivity is an important treatment target for benzodiazepine taper, consistent with findings that link anxiety sensitivity to more severe withdrawal from nicotine and cannabis (Bonn-Miller et al., 2007; Zvolensky, Farris, Guillot, et al., 2014). Those with higher anxiety sensitivity may be more reticent to discontinue benzodiazepines, even when indicated (Cook, Biyanova, Thompson, & Coyne, 2007). Treatments targeting anxiety sensitivity improve the success of benzodiazepine taper (Otto, McHugh, Simon, et al., 2010; Otto et al., 1993; Spiegel, Bruce, Gregg, & Nuzzarello, 1994) and the degree of anxiety sensitivity reduction appears to be the mechanism for these improved outcomes (Bruce, Spiegel, Gregg, & Nuzzarello, 1995).

This is certainly not an exhaustive list of potential target populations. The broad applicability and malleability of anxiety sensitivity highlight this as among the key psychological constructs to evaluate in routine care in psychiatric and behavioral health settings.

When and how to measure anxiety sensitivity?

In psychiatric and behavioral health settings, assessment of anxiety sensitivity at intake can be useful in identifying whether this variable should be targeted as part of treatment. In addition to other clinical data, anxiety sensitivity scores indicative of a clinical level (see Table 1) should trigger consideration of incorporating intervention for anxiety sensitivity reduction. Such intervention may include psychoeducation on anxiety sensitivity, cognitive restructuring targeted to interoceptive sensitivity (e.g., decatastrophizing somatic symptoms), and interoceptive exposure via traditional exposure or exercise (Smits, Berry, Rosenfield, et al., 2008; Smits, Berry, Tart, et al., 2008).

Continued assessment of anxiety sensitivity can also aid in the determination of the efficacy of treatments targeting the reduction of this variable. The test-retest reliability of the ASI is strong, yet it is also sensitive to changes in treatment (Rifkin et al., 2015); thus, this can be measured over time as a marker of treatment progress. In a meta-analysis of cognitive-behavioral therapy effects on anxiety sensitivity, results indicated a large reduction in anxiety sensitivity, with a mean reduction of 10.9 points on the ASI, or more than a 1/3rd reduction in ASI score on average (Smits, Berry, Rosenfield, et al., 2008; Smits, Berry, Tart, et al., 2008). Of note, this reduction is largely specific to treatments that actively target anxiety sensitivity, with a large difference between cognitive-behavioral therapy and control conditions (i.e., an average change score of 10.9 vs. 1.1). Thus, successful reduction of anxiety sensitivity likely requires intervention specifically targeted to reducing fearful responding to anxiety symptoms and sensations, and will likely not substantively change with more general treatment interventions. In addition to the use of self-report measures, behavioral provocation can also be a useful tool for informing targeted interoceptive exposures.

What to do if it isn't working?

If anxiety sensitivity is not changing over the course of treatment, several steps should be considered. First, as with any treatment nonresponse, reconsidering diagnostic accuracy and case conceptualization is an important initial step. Second, evaluation of safety behaviors (including subtle or cognitive safety behaviors) should be conducted to determine whether unrecognized behaviors are preventing successful fear extinction during exposure exercises. Third, consider medication status and adherence as something that may hamper the ability to successfully activate the target sensations in exposure exercises. Critically, medications that are commonly prescribed for anxiety may dampen activation of arousal, or otherwise interfere with exposure via interference with extinction learning (Otto, McHugh, & Kantak, 2010). Similarly, investigation of use of substances of abuse is indicated to determine whether substance use is either interfering with the success of exposure (i.e., due to its negative impact on extinction learning; Gu et al., 2008; Holmes et al., 2012; Tian et al., 2008) or whether states of intoxication and acute or protracted withdrawal are causing symptom exacerbations.

Conclusions

Anxiety sensitivity is among the most broadly applicable psychological constructs for clinical populations. Its widespread relevance and its ability to be successfully reduced using both pharmacologic (Mavissakalian et al., 1998) and behavioral interventions (Smits, Berry, Tart, et al., 2008) highlight the importance of its measurement in clinical settings. The broad array of conditions in which anxiety sensitivity may play a critical role highlights the importance of assessing anxiety sensitivity as a part of routine care.

Assessment in clinical practice is often hampered by time constraints. Accordingly, measures must be selected judiciously and with a focus on those that are likely to yield meaningful benefits for guiding treatment and monitoring progress. Self-report measures of anxiety sensitivity are optimal for such settings because (1) they are brief, (2) they are very well validated, and (3) they provide interpretable scores. Both the ASI and ASI-3 have strong psychometric support, and either could be used with confidence; the ASI-3 has demonstrated some additive benefits and can be considered a gold standard based on the current evidence base. For child and adolescent groups, the CASI is an excellent measure for use in age groups 6–17 years old, although guiding normative data are limited.

Assessment should always be conducted with consideration of the context, such as other psychosocial and medical considerations, culture, and gender. The measurement of anxiety sensitivity can provide a key data point in combination with other clinical data to guide decision making and treatment.

References

Adornetto, C., Hensdiek, M., Meyer, A., In-Albon, T., Federer, M., & Schneider, S. (2008). The factor structure of the Childhood Anxiety Sensitivity Index in German children. *Journal of Behavior Therapy and Experimental Psychiatry*, *39*(4), 404–416. https://doi.org/10.1016/j.jbtep.2008.01.001.

Alcantara, C., Edmondson, D., Moise, N., Oyola, D., Hiti, D., & Kronish, I. M. (2014). Anxiety sensitivity and medication nonadherence in patients with uncontrolled hypertension. *Journal of Psychosomatic Research*, *77*(4), 283–286. https://doi.org/10.1016/j.jpsychores.2014.07.009.

Allan, N. P., Albanese, B. J., Norr, A. M., Zvolensky, M. J., & Schmidt, N. B. (2015). Effects of anxiety sensitivity on alcohol problems: evaluating chained mediation through generalized anxiety, depression and drinking motives. *Addiction*, *110*(2), 260–268. https://doi.org/10.1111/add.12739.

Allan, N. P., Capron, D. W., Raines, A. M., & Schmidt, N. B. (2014). Unique relations among anxiety sensitivity factors and anxiety, depression, and suicidal ideation. *Journal of Anxiety Disorders*, *28*(2), 266–275. https://doi.org/10.1016/j.janxdis.2013.12.004.

Allan, N. P., Korte, K. J., Capron, D. W., Raines, A. M., & Schmidt, N. B. (2014). Factor mixture modeling of anxiety sensitivity: a three-class structure. *Psychological Assessment*, *26* (4), 1184–1195. https://doi.org/10.1037/a0037436.

Allan, N. P., Raines, A. M., Capron, D. W., Norr, A. M., Zvolensky, M. J., & Schmidt, N. B. (2014). Identification of anxiety sensitivity classes and clinical cut-scores in a sample of adult smokers: results from a factor mixture model. *Journal of Anxiety Disorders*, *28*(7), 696–703. https://doi.org/10.1016/j.janxdis.2014.07.006.

Asmundson, G. J., Weeks, J. W., Carleton, R. N., Thibodeau, M. A., & Fetzner, M. G. (2011). Revisiting the latent structure of the anxiety sensitivity construct: more evidence of dimensionality. *Journal of Anxiety Disorders*, *25*(1), 138–147. https://doi.org/10.1016/j.janxdis.2010.08.013.

Bardeen, J. R., Tull, M. T., Stevens, E. N., & Gratz, K. L. (2015). Further investigation of the association between anxiety sensitivity and posttraumatic stress disorder: examining the influence of emotional avoidance. *Journal of Contextual Behavioral Science*, *4*(3), 163–169. https://doi.org/10.1016/j.jcbs.2015.05.002.

Bernstein, A., Stickle, T. R., Zvolensky, M. J., Taylor, S., Abramowitz, J., & Stewart, S. (2010). Dimensional, categorical, or dimensional-categories: testing the latent structure of anxiety sensitivity among adults using factor-mixture modeling. *Behavior Therapy*, *41*(4), 515–529. https://doi.org/10.1016/j.beth.2010.02.003.

Bernstein, A., Zvolensky, M. J., Kotov, R., Arrindell, W. A., Taylor, S., Sandin, B., … Schmidt, N. B. (2006). Taxonicity of anxiety sensitivity: a multi-national analysis. *Journal of Anxiety Disorders*, *20*(1), 1–22. https://doi.org/10.1016/j.janxdis. 2004.11.006.

Bernstein, A., Zvolensky, M. J., Stewart, S., & Comeau, N. (2007). Taxometric and factor analytic models of anxiety sensitivity among youth: exploring the latent structure of anxiety psychopathology vulnerability. *Behavior Therapy*, *38*(3), 269–283. https://doi.org/10.1016/j.beth.2006.08.005.

Bernstein, A., Zvolensky, M. J., Vujanovic, A. A., & Moos, R. (2009). Integrating anxiety sensitivity, distress tolerance, and discomfort intolerance: a hierarchical model of affect sensitivity and tolerance. *Behavior Therapy*, *40*(3), 291–301. https://doi.org/10.1016/j.beth.2008.08.001.

Bonn-Miller, M. O., Zvolensky, M. J., Marshall, E. C., & Bernstein, A. (2007). Incremental validity of anxiety sensitivity in relation to marijuana withdrawal symptoms. *Addictive Behaviors*, *32*(9), 1843–1851. https://doi.org/10.1016/j.addbeh.2006.12.016.

Broman-Fulks, J. J., Deacon, B. J., Olatunji, B. O., Bondy, C. L., Abramowitz, J. S., & Tolin, D. F. (2010). Categorical or dimensional: a reanalysis of the anxiety sensitivity construct. *Behavior Therapy*, *41*(2), 154–171. https://doi.org/10.1016/j.beth.2009.02.005.

Broman-Fulks, J. J., Green, B. A., Olatunji, B. O., Berman, M. E., Arnau, R. C., Deacon, B. J., & Sawchuk, C. N. (2008). The latent structure of anxiety sensitivity—revisited. *Assessment*, *15*(2), 188–203. https://doi.org/10.1177/1073191107311284.

Bruce, T. J., Spiegel, D. A., Gregg, S. F., & Nuzzarello, A. (1995). Predictors of alprazolam discontinuation with and without cognitive behavior therapy in panic disorder. *The American Journal of Psychiatry*, *152*(8), 1156–1160. https://doi.org/10.1176/ajp.152.8.1156.

Buckner, J. D., Proctor, S. L., Reynolds, E. K., Kopetz, C., & Lejuez, C. W. (2011). Cocaine dependence and anxiety sensitivity among patients presenting for residential drug use treatment. *Journal of Cognitive Psychotherapy*, *25*(1), 22–30.

Buckner, J. D., Zvolensky, M. J., Smits, J. A., Norton, P. J., Crosby, R. D., Wonderlich, S. A., & Schmidt, N. B. (2011). Anxiety sensitivity and marijuana use: an analysis from ecological momentary assessment. *Depression and Anxiety*, *28*(5), 420–426. https://doi.org/10.1002/da.20816.

Calamari, J. E., Rector, N. A., Woodard, J. L., Cohen, R. J., & Chik, H. M. (2008). Anxiety sensitivity and obsessive—compulsive disorder. *Assessment*, *15*(3), 351–363. https://doi.org/10.1177/1073191107312611.

Chambless, D. L., Caputo, G. C., Bright, P., & Gallagher, R. (1984). Assessment of fear of fear in agoraphobics: the body sensations questionnaire and the agoraphobic cognitions questionnaire. *Journal of Consulting and Clinical Psychology*, *52*(6), 1090–1097.

Chorpita, B. F., & Albano, A. M. (1996). Child Anxiety Sensitivity Index: considerations for children. *Journal of Clinical Child Psychology*, *25*(1), 77 [Article].

Cook, J. M., Biyanova, T., Thompson, R., & Coyne, J. C. (2007). Older primary care patients' willingness to consider discontinuation of chronic benzodiazepines. *General Hospital Psychiatry*, *29*(5), 396–401. https://doi.org/10.1016/j.genhosppsych.2007.07.001.

Cummings, J. R., Bornovalova, M. A., Ojanen, T., Hunt, E., MacPherson, L., & Lejuez, C. (2013). Time doesn't change everything: the longitudinal course of distress tolerance and its relationship with externalizing and internalizing symptoms during early adolescence. *Journal of Abnormal Child Psychology*, *41*(5), 735–748. https://doi.org/10.1007/s10802-012-9704-x.

Deacon, B., & Abramowitz, J. (2006). Anxiety sensitivity and its dimensions across the anxiety disorders. *Journal of Anxiety Disorders*, *20*(7), 837–857. https://doi.org/10.1016/j.janxdis.2006.01.003.

Dehon, C., Weems, C. F., Stickle, T. R., Costa, N. M., & Berman, S. L. (2005). A cross-sectional evaluation of the factorial invariance of anxiety sensitivity in adolescents and young adults. *Behaviour Research and Therapy*, *43*(6), 799–810. https://doi.org/10.1016/j.brat.2004.06.008.

Elkins, R. M., Pincus, D. B., & Comer, J. S. (2014). A psychometric evaluation of the panic disorder severity scale for children and adolescents. *Psychological Assessment*, *26*, 609–618. https://doi.org/10.1037/a0035283.

Essau, C. A., Sasagawa, S., & Ollendick, T. H. (2010). The facets of anxiety sensitivity in adolescents. *Journal of Anxiety Disorders*, *24*(1), 23–29. https://doi.org/10.1016/j.janxdis.2009.08.001.

Farris, S. G., DiBello, A. M., Allan, N. P., Hogan, J., Schmidt, N. B., & Zvolensky, M. J. (2015). Evaluation of the Anxiety Sensitivity Index-3 among treatment-seeking smokers. *Psychological Assessment*, *27*(3), 1123–1128. https://doi.org/10.1037/pas0000112.

Ghisi, M., Bottesi, G., Altoe, G., Razzetti, E., Melli, G., & Sica, C. (2016). Factor structure and psychometric properties of the Anxiety Sensitivity Index-3 in an Italian community sample. *Frontiers in Psychology*. *7*, 160. https://doi.org/10.3389/fpsyg.2016.00160.

Gregor, K. L., & Zvolensky, M. J. (2008). Anxiety sensitivity and perceived control over anxiety-related events: evaluating the singular and interactive effects in the prediction of anxious and fearful responding to bodily sensations. *Behaviour Research and Therapy*, *46*(9), 1017–1025. https://doi.org/10.1016/j.brat.2008.06.003.

Gu, C., Li, P., Hu, B., Ouyang, X., Fu, J., Gao, J., … Hu, X. (2008). Chronic morphine selectively impairs cued fear extinction in rats: implications for anxiety disorders associated with opiate use. *Neuropsychopharmacology*, *33*(3), 666–673. https://doi.org/10.1038/sj.npp.1301441.

Harrison, B. J., Fullana, M. A., Soriano-Mas, C., Via, E., Pujol, J., Martinez-Zalacain, I., … Cardoner, N. (2015). A neural mediator of human anxiety sensitivity. *Human Brain Mapping*, *36*(10), 3950–3958. https://doi.org/10.1002/hbm.22889.

Hearon, B. A., Calkins, A. W., Halperin, D. M., McHugh, R. K., Murray, H. W., & Otto, M. W. (2011). Anxiety sensitivity and illicit sedative use among opiate-dependent women and men. *The American Journal of Drug and Alcohol Abuse*, *37*(1), 43–47. https://doi.org/10.3109/00952990.2010.535581.

Hinton, D. E., & Otto, M. W. (2006). Symptom presentation and symptom meaning among traumatized Cambodian refugees: relevance to a somatically focused cognitive-behavior therapy. *Cognitive and Behavioral Practice*, *13*, 249–260. https://doi.org/10.1016/j.cbpra.2006.04.006.

Hinton, D. E., Pich, V., Safren, S. A., Pollack, M. H., & McNally, R. J. (2006). Anxiety sensitivity among Cambodian refugees with panic disorder: a factor analytic investigation. *Journal of Anxiety Disorders*, *20*(3), 281–295. https://doi.org/10.1016/j.janxdis.2005.02.006.

Holmes, A., Fitzgerald, P. J., MacPherson, K. P., DeBrouse, L., Colacicco, G., Flynn, S. M., … Camp, M. (2012). Chronic alcohol remodels prefrontal neurons and disrupts NMDAR-mediated fear extinction encoding. *Nature Neuroscience*, *15*(10), 1359–1361. https://doi.org/10.1038/nn.3204.

Hunt, C., Keogh, E., & French, C. C. (2006). Anxiety sensitivity: the role of conscious awareness and selective attentional bias to physical threat. *Emotion*, *6*(3), 418–428. https://doi.org/10.1037/1528-3542.6.3.418.

Hunt, C., Keogh, E., & French, C. C. (2007). Anxiety sensitivity, conscious awareness and selective attentional biases in children. *Behaviour Research and Therapy*, *45*(3), 497–509. https://doi.org/10.1016/j.brat.2006.04.001.

Hunter, L. R., Keough, M. E., Timpano, K. R., & Schmidt, N. B. (2012). Ethnoracial differences in anxiety sensitivity: examining the validity of competing Anxiety Sensitivity Index subscales. *Journal of Anxiety Disorders*, *26*(4), 511–516. https://doi.org/10.1016/j.janxdis.2012.02.004.

Ino, K., Ogawa, S., Kondo, M., Imai, R., Ii, T., Furukawa, T. A., & Akechi, T. (2017). Anxiety sensitivity as a predictor of broad dimensions of psychopathology after cognitive behavioral therapy for panic disorder. *Neuropsychiatric Disease and Treatment*, *13*, 1835–1840. https://doi.org/10.2147/NDT.S121360.

Jurin, T., Jokic-Begic, N., & Korajlija, A. L. (2012). Factor structure and psychometric properties of the Anxiety Sensitivity Index in a sample of Croatian adults. *Assessment*, *19*(1), 31–41. https://doi.org/10.1177/1073191111402459.

Kearney, C. A., Albano, A. M., Eisen, A. R., Allan, W. D., & Barlow, D. H. (1997). The phenomenology of panic disorder in youngsters: an empirical study of a clinical sample. *Journal of Anxiety Disorders*, *11*(1), 49–62.

Kemper, C. J., Lutz, J., Bahr, T., Ruddel, H., & Hock, M. (2012). Construct validity of the Anxiety Sensitivity Index-3 in clinical samples. *Assessment*, *19*(1), 89–100. https://doi.org/10.1177/1073191111429389.

Keogh, E. (2004). Investigating invariance in the factorial structure of the Anxiety Sensitivity Index across adult men and women. *Journal of Personality Assessment*, *83*(2), 153–160. https://doi.org/10.1207/s15327752jpa8302_09.

Keogh, E., Dillon, C., Georgiou, G., & Hunt, C. (2001). Selective attentional biases for physical threat in physical anxiety sensitivity. *Journal of Anxiety Disorders*, *15*(4), 299–315.

Keough, M. E., Riccardi, C. J., Timpano, K. R., Mitchell, M. A., & Schmidt, N. B. (2010). Anxiety symptomatology: the association with distress tolerance and anxiety sensitivity. *Behavior Therapy*, *41*(4), 567–574. https://doi.org/10.1016/j.beth.2010.04.002.

Killgore, W. D., Britton, J. C., Price, L. M., Gold, A. L., Deckersbach, T., & Rauch, S. L. (2011). Neural correlates of anxiety sensitivity during masked presentation of affective faces. *Depression and Anxiety*, *28*(3), 243–249. https://doi.org/10.1002/da.20788.

Lambert, S. F., Cooley, M. R., Campbell, K. D., Benoit, M. Z., & Stansbury, R. (2004). Assessing anxiety sensitivity in inner-city African American children: psychometric properties of the childhood Anxiety Sensitivity Index. *Journal of Clinical Child and Adolescent Psychology*, *33*(2), 248–259. https://doi.org/10.1207/s15374424jccp3302_5.

Lang, A. J., & Sarmiento, J. (2004). Relationship of attentional bias to anxiety sensitivity and panic. *Depression and Anxiety*, *20*(4), 190–194. https://doi.org/10.1002/da.20030.

Laurent, J., Schmidt, N. B., Catanzaro, S. J., Joiner, T. E., Jr., & Kelley, A. M. (1998). Factor structure of a measure of anxiety sensitivity in children. *Journal of Anxiety Disorders*, *12*(4), 307–331.

Lejuez, C. W., Zvolensky, M. J., Daughters, S. B., Bornovalova, M. A., Paulson, A., Tull, M. T., … Otto, M. W. (2008). Anxiety sensitivity: a unique predictor of dropout among inner-city heroin and crack/cocaine users in residential substance use treatment. *Behaviour Research and Therapy*, *46*(7), 811–818. https://doi.org/10.1016/j.brat.2008.03.010.

Leyro, T. M., Zvolensky, M. J., & Bernstein, A. (2010). Distress tolerance and psychopathological symptoms and disorders: a review of the empirical literature among adults. *Psychological Bulletin*, *136*(4), 576–600. https://doi.org/10.1037/a0019712.

Lim, Y. J., & Kim, J. H. (2012). Korean Anxiety Sensitivity Index-3: its factor structure, reliability, and validity in non-clinical samples. *Psychiatry Investigation*, *9*(1), 45–53. https://doi.org/10.4306/pi.2012.9.1.45.

Mackie, C. J., Castellanos-Ryan, N., & Conrod, P. J. (2011). Personality moderates the longitudinal relationship between psychological symptoms and alcohol use in adolescents. *Alcoholism, Clinical and Experimental Research*, *35*(4), 703–716. https://doi.org/10.1111/j.1530-0277.2010.01388.x.

Mavissakalian, M. R., Perel, J. M., Talbott-Green, M., & Sloan, C. (1998). Gauging the effectiveness of extended imipramine treatment for panic disorder with agoraphobia. *Biological Psychiatry*, *43*(11), 848–854.

McCaul, M. E., Hutton, H. E., Stephens, M. A., Xu, X., & Wand, G. S. (2017). Anxiety, anxiety sensitivity, and perceived stress as predictors of recent drinking, alcohol craving, and social stress response in heavy drinkers. *Alcoholism, Clinical and Experimental Research*, *41*(4), 836–845. https://doi.org/10.1111/acer.13350.

McHugh, R. K., Daughters, S. B., Lejuez, C. W., Murray, H. W., Hearon, B. A., Gorka, S. M., & Otto, M. W. (2011). Shared variance among self-report and behavioral measures of distress intolerance. *Cognitive Therapy and Research*, *35*(3), 266–275.

McHugh, R. K., Gratz, K. L., & Tull, M. T. (2017). The role of anxiety sensitivity in reactivity to trauma cues in treatment-seeking adults with substance use disorders. *Comprehensive Psychiatry*, *78*, 107–114. https://doi.org/10.1016/j.comppsych.2017.07.011.

McHugh, R. K., & Otto, M. W. (2011). Domain-general and domain-specific strategies for the assessment of distress intolerance. *Psychology of Addictive Behaviors*, *25*(4), 745–749. https://doi.org/10.1037/a0025094.

McHugh, R. K., & Otto, M. W. (2012a). Profiles of distress intolerance in a substance-dependent sample. *The American Journal of Drug and Alcohol Abuse*, *38*(2), 161–165. https://doi.org/10.3109/00952990.2011.643990.

McHugh, R. K., & Otto, M. W. (2012b). Refining the measurement of distress intolerance. *Behavior Therapy*, *43*(3), 641–651. https://doi.org/10.1016/j.beth.2011.12.001.

McHugh, R. K., Votaw, V. R., Bogunovic, O., Karakula, S. L., Griffin, M. L., & Weiss, R. D. (2017). Anxiety sensitivity and nonmedical benzodiazepine use among adults with opioid use disorder. *Addictive Behaviors*, *65*, 283–288. https://doi.org/10.1016/j.addbeh.2016.08.020.

McHugh, R. K., Weiss, R. D., Cornelius, M., Martel, M. O., Jamison, R. N., & Edwards, R. R. (2016). Distress intolerance and prescription opioid misuse among patients with chronic pain. *The Journal of Pain*, *17*(7), 806–814. https://doi.org/10.1016/j.jpain.2016.03.004.

McLaughlin, E. N., Stewart, S. H., & Taylor, S. (2007). Childhood Anxiety Sensitivity Index factors predict unique variance in DSM-IV anxiety disorder symptoms. *Cognitive Behaviour Therapy*, *36*(4), 210–219. https://doi.org/10.1080/16506070701499988. [Article].

McMillan, K. A., Asmundson, G. J., Zvolensky, M. J., & Carleton, R. N. (2012). Startle response and anxiety sensitivity: subcortical indices of physiologic arousal and fear responding. *Emotion*, *12*(6), 1264–1272. https://doi.org/10.1037/a0029108.

McNally, R. J. (2002). Anxiety sensitivity and panic disorder. *Biological Psychiatry*, *52*(10), 938–946.

McNally, R. J., & Eke, M. (1996). Anxiety sensitivity, suffocation fear, and breath-holding duration as predictors of response to carbon dioxide challenge. *Journal of Abnormal Psychology*, *105*(1), 146–149.

Mitchell, M. A., Riccardi, C. J., Keough, M. E., Timpano, K. R., & Schmidt, N. B. (2013). Understanding the associations among anxiety sensitivity, distress tolerance, and discomfort intolerance: a comparison of three models. *Journal of Anxiety Disorders*, *27*(1), 147–154. https://doi.org/10.1016/j.janxdis.2012.12.003.

Mohlman, J., & Zinbarg, R. E. (2000). The structure and correlates of anxiety sensitivity in older adults. *Psychological Assessment*, *12*(4), 440–446.

Muris, P. (2002). An expanded Childhood Anxiety Sensitivity Index: its factor structure, reliability, and validity in a non-clinical adolescent sample. *Behaviour Research and Therapy*, *40*(3), 299–311.

Muris, P., Schmidt, H., Merckelbach, H., & Schouten, E. (2001). Anxiety sensitivity in adolescents: factor structure and relationships to trait anxiety and symptoms of anxiety disorders and depression. *Behaviour Research and Therapy*, *39*(1), 89–100.

Naifeh, J. A., Tull, M. T., & Gratz, K. L. (2012). Anxiety sensitivity, emotional avoidance, and PTSD symptom severity among crack/cocaine dependent patients in residential treatment. *Cognitive Therapy and Research*, *36*(3), 247–257. https://doi.org/10.1007/s10608-010-9337-8.

Norton, P. J., De Coteau, T. J., Hope, D. A., & Anderson, J. (2004). The factor structure of the Anxiety Sensitivity Index among Northern Plains Native Americans. *Behaviour Research and Therapy*, *42*(2), 241–247. https://doi.org/10.1016/j.brat.2003.10.002.

Novy, D. M., Stanley, M. A., Averill, P., & Daza, P. (2001). Psychometric comparability of English- and Spanish-language measures of anxiety and related affective symptoms. *Psychological Assessment*, *13*(3), 347–355.

Ocanez, K. L., McHugh, R. K., & Otto, M. W. (2010). A meta-analytic review of the association between anxiety sensitivity and pain. *Depression and Anxiety*, *27*(8), 760–767. https://doi.org/10.1002/da.20681.

Osman, A., Gutierrez, P. M., Smith, K., Fang, Q., Lozano, G., & Devine, A. (2010). The Anxiety Sensitivity Index-3: analyses of dimensions, reliability estimates, and correlates in non-clinical samples. *Journal of Personality Assessment*, *92*(1), 45–52. https://doi.org/10.1080/00223890903379332.

Otto, M. W., Eastman, A., Lo, S., Hearon, B. A., Bickel, W. K., Zvolensky, M., … Doan, S. N. (2016). Anxiety sensitivity and working memory capacity: risk factors and targets for health behavior promotion. *Clinical Psychology Review*, *49*, 67–78. https://doi.org/10.1016/j.cpr.2016.07.003.

Otto, M. W., McHugh, R. K., & Kantak, K. M. (2010). Combined pharmacotherapy and cognitive-behavioral therapy for anxiety disorders: medication effects, glucocorticoids, and attenuated treatment outcomes. *Clinical Psychologist (New York)*, *17*(2), 91–103. https://doi.org/10.1111/j.1468-2850.2010.01198.x.

Otto, M. W., McHugh, R. K., Simon, N. M., Farach, F. J., Worthington, J. J., & Pollack, M. H. (2010). Efficacy of CBT for benzodiazepine discontinuation in patients with panic disorder: further evaluation. *Behaviour Research and Therapy*, *48*(8), 720–727. https://doi.org/10.1016/j.brat.2010.04.002.

Otto, M. W., Pollack, M. H., Sachs, G. S., Reiter, S. R., Meltzer-Brody, S., & Rosenbaum, J. F. (1993). Discontinuation of benzodiazepine treatment: efficacy of cognitive-behavioral therapy for patients with panic disorder. *The American Journal of Psychiatry*, *150*(10), 1485–1490. https://doi.org/10.1176/ajp.150.10.1485.

Peterson, R. A., & Plehn, K. (1999). Measuring anxiety sensitivity. In S. Taylor (Ed.), *Anxiety sensitivity: Theory, research and treatment of the fear of anxiety*. New York: Routledge.

Peterson, R. A., & Reiss, S. (1992). *Anxiety Sensitivity Index manual* (2nd ed.). Worthington, OH: International Diagnostic Systems.

Rabian, B., Embry, L., & MacIntyre, D. (1999). Behavioral validation of the Childhood Anxiety Sensitivity Index in children. *Journal of Clinical Child Psychology*, *28*(1), 105–112. https://doi.org/10.1207/s15374424jccp2801_9.

Reiss, S., Peterson, R. A., Gursky, D. M., & McNally, R. J. (1986). Anxiety sensitivity, anxiety frequency and the predictions of fearfulness. *Behaviour Research and Therapy*, *24*(1), 1–8. https://doi.org/10.1016/0005-7967(86)90143-9.

Richards, J. S., Austin, D. W., & Alvarenga, M. E. (2001). Interpretation of ambiguous interoceptive stimuli in panic disorder and nonclinical panic. *Cognitive Therapy and Research*, *25*(3), 235–246.

Richey, J. A., Schmidt, N. B., Hofmann, S. G., & Timpano, K. R. (2010). Temporal and structural dynamics of anxiety sensitivity in predicting fearful responding to a 35% CO_2 challenge. *Journal of Anxiety Disorders*, *24*(4), 423–432. https://doi.org/10.1016/j.janxdis.2010.02.007.

Rifkin, L. S., Beard, C., Hsu, K. J., Garner, L., & Bjorgvinsson, T. (2015). Psychometric properties of the Anxiety Sensitivity Index-3 in an acute and heterogeneous treatment sample. *Journal of Anxiety Disorders*, *36*, 99–102. https://doi.org/10.1016/j.janxdis.2015.09.010.

Rodriguez, B. F., Bruce, S. E., Pagano, M. E., Spencer, M. A., & Keller, M. B. (2004). Factor structure and stability of the Anxiety Sensitivity Index in a longitudinal study of anxiety disorder patients. *Behaviour Research and Therapy*, *42*(1), 79–91.

Rosso, I. M., Makris, N., Britton, J. C., Price, L. M., Gold, A. L., Zai, D., … Rauch, S. L. (2010). Anxiety sensitivity correlates with two indices of right anterior insula structure in specific animal phobia. *Depression and Anxiety*, *27*(12), 1104–1110. https://doi.org/10.1002/da.20765.

Sandin, B., Chorot, P., & McNally, R. J. (1996). Validation of the Spanish version of the Anxiety Sensitivity Index in a clinical sample. *Behaviour Research and Therapy*, *34*(3), 283–290.

Sandin, B., Chorot, P., & McNally, R. J. (2001). Anxiety Sensitivity Index: normative data and its differentiation from trait anxiety. *Behaviour Research and Therapy*, *39*(2), 213–219.

Sandin, B., Chorot, P., Santed, M. A., & Valiente, R. M. (2002). Análisis factorial confirmatorio del Índice de Sensibilidad a la Ansiedad para Niños [A confirmatory factor analysis of the Childhood Anxiety Sensitivity Index]. *Psicothema*, *14*(2), 333–339.

Sandin, B., Garcia, R. M. V., Chorot, P., & Germain, M. A. S. (2007). ASI-3: nueva escala para la evaluación de la sensibilidad a la ansiedad [ASI-3: a new scale for the assessment of anxiety sensitivity]. *Spanish Journal of Clinical Psychology*, *12*(2), 91–104.

Schmidt, N. B., & Joiner, T. E. (2002). Structure of the Anxiety Sensitivity Index psychometrics and factor structure in a community sample. *Journal of Anxiety Disorders*, *16*(1), 33–49.

Schmidt, N. B., Keough, M. E., Mitchell, M. A., Reynolds, E. K., Macpherson, L., Zvolensky, M. J., & Lejuez, C. W. (2010). Anxiety sensitivity: prospective prediction of anxiety among early adolescents. *Journal of Anxiety Disorders*, *24*(5), 503–508. https://doi.org/10.1016/j.janxdis.2010.03.007.

Schmidt, N. B., Lerew, D. R., & Jackson, R. J. (1997). The role of anxiety sensitivity in the pathogenesis of panic: prospective evaluation of spontaneous panic attacks during acute stress. *Journal of Abnormal Psychology*, *106*(3), 355–364.

Short, N. A., Boffa, J. W., King, S., Albanese, B. J., Allan, N. P., & Schmidt, N. B. (2017). A randomized clinical trial examining the effects of an anxiety sensitivity intervention on insomnia symptoms: replication and extension. *Behaviour Research and Therapy*, *99*, 108–116. https://doi.org/10.1016/j.brat.2017.09.013.

Shostak, B. B., & Peterson, R. A. (1990). Effects of anxiety sensitivity on emotional response to a stress task. *Behaviour Research and Therapy*, *28*(6), 513–521.

Silverman, W. K., Fleisig, W., Rabian, B., & Peterson, R. A. (1991). Childhood Anxiety Sensitivity Index. *Journal of Clinical Child Psychology*, *20*, 162–168.

Silverman, W. K., Goedhart, A. W., Barrett, P., & Turner, C. (2003). The facets of anxiety sensitivity represented in the Childhood Anxiety Sensitivity Index: confirmatory analyses of factor models from past studies. *Journal of Abnormal Psychology*, *112*(3), 364–374.

Sirota, A. D., Rohsenow, D. J., Mackinnon, S. V., Martin, R. A., Eaton, C. A., Kaplan, G. B., … Swift, R. M. (2010). Intolerance for smoking abstinence questionnaire: psychometric properties and relationship to tobacco dependence and abstinence. *Addictive Behaviors*, *35*(7), 686–693. https://doi.org/10.1016/j.addbeh.2010.02.014.

Smits, J. A., Berry, A. C., Rosenfield, D., Powers, M. B., Behar, E., & Otto, M. W. (2008). Reducing anxiety sensitivity with exercise. *Depression and Anxiety*, *25*(8), 689–699. https://doi.org/10.1002/da.20411.

Smits, J. A., Berry, A. C., Tart, C. D., & Powers, M. B. (2008). The efficacy of cognitive-behavioral interventions for reducing anxiety sensitivity: a meta-analytic review. *Behaviour Research and Therapy*, *46*(9), 1047–1054. https://doi.org/10.1016/j.brat.2008.06.010.

Smits, J. A., Powers, M. B., Cho, Y., & Telch, M. J. (2004). Mechanism of change in cognitive-behavioral treatment of panic disorder: evidence for the fear of fear mediational hypothesis. *Journal of Consulting and Clinical Psychology*, *72*(4), 646–652. https://doi.org/10.1037/0022-006x.72.4.646.

Spiegel, D. A., Bruce, T. J., Gregg, S. F., & Nuzzarello, A. (1994). Does cognitive behavior therapy assist slow-taper alprazolam discontinuation in panic disorder? *The American Journal of Psychiatry*, *151*(6), 876–881. https://doi.org/10.1176/ajp.151.6.876.

Stein, M. B., Simmons, A. N., Feinstein, J. S., & Paulus, M. P. (2007). Increased amygdala and insula activation during emotion processing in anxiety-prone subjects. *The American Journal of Psychiatry*, *164*(2), 318–327. https://doi.org/10.1176/ajp.2007.164.2.318.

Stevanovic, D. S., Silverman, W. K., Nichols-Lopez, K. A., Popovic-Deusic, S. D., & Pejovic-Milovancevic, M. M. (2013). Facets of the childhood Anxiety Sensitivity Index among Serbian youth. *Cognitive Behaviour Therapy*, *42*(4), 342–346. https://doi.org/10.1080/16506073.2013.773060.

Stewart, S. H., Taylor, S., & Baker, J. M. (1997). Gender differences in dimensions of anxiety sensitivity. *Journal of Anxiety Disorders*, *11*(2), 179–200.

Talkovsky, A. M., & Norton, P. J. (2015). Anxiety sensitivity across four ethnoracial groups in an undergraduate sample. *Cognitive Behaviour Therapy*, *44*(1), 33–43. https://doi.org/10.1080/16506073.2014.953568.

Taylor, S., & Cox, B. J. (1998a). Anxiety sensitivity: multiple dimensions and hierarchic structure. *Behaviour Research and Therapy*, *36*(1), 37–51.

Taylor, S., & Cox, B. J. (1998b). An expanded Anxiety Sensitivity Index: evidence for a hierarchic structure in a clinical sample. *Journal of Anxiety Disorders*, *12*(5), 463–483.

Taylor, S., Koch, W. J., & McNally, R. J. (1992). How does anxiety sensitivity vary across anxiety disorders. *Journal of Anxiety Disorders*, *6*(3), 249–259. https://doi.org/10.1016/ 0887-6185(92)90037-8.

Taylor, S., Zvolensky, M. J., Cox, B. J., Deacon, B., Heimberg, R. G., Ledley, D. R., … Cardenas, S. J. (2007). Robust dimensions of anxiety sensitivity: development and initial validation of the Anxiety Sensitivity Index-3. *Psychological Assessment*, *19*(2), 176–188. https://doi.org/10.1037/1040-3590.19.2.176.

Teachman, B. A. (2005). Information processing and anxiety sensitivity: cognitive vulnerability to panic reflected in interpretation and memory biases. *Cognitive Therapy and Research*, *29*(4), 479–499.

Tian, S., Gao, J., Han, L., Fu, J., Li, C., & Li, Z. (2008). Prior chronic nicotine impairs cued fear extinction but enhances contextual fear conditioning in rats. *Neuroscience*, *153*(4), 935–943. https://doi.org/10.1016/j.neuroscience.2008.03.005.

van Widenfelt, B. M., Siebelink, B. M., Goedhart, A. W., & Treffers, P. D. (2002). The Dutch Childhood Anxiety Sensitivity Index: psychometric properties and factor structure. *Journal of Clinical Child and Adolescent Psychology*, *31*(1), 90–100. https://doi.org/10.1207/s15374424jccp3101_11.

Vujanovic, A. A., Arrindell, W. A., Bernstein, A., Norton, P. J., & Zvolensky, M. J. (2007). Sixteen-item Anxiety Sensitivity Index: confirmatory factor analytic evidence, internal consistency, and construct validity in a young adult sample from the Netherlands. *Assessment*, *14*(2), 129–143. https://doi.org/10.1177/1073191106295053.

Walsh, T. M., Stewart, S. H., McLaughlin, E., & Comeau, N. (2004). Gender differences in Childhood Anxiety Sensitivity Index (CASI) dimensions. *Journal of Anxiety Disorders*, *18*(5), 695–706. https://doi.org/10.1016/s0887-6185(03)00043-4.

Weems, C. F., Hammond-Laurence, K., Silverman, W. K., & Ginsburg, G. S. (1998). Testing the utility of the anxiety sensitivity construct in children and adolescents referred for anxiety disorders. *Journal of Clinical Child Psychology*, *27*(1), 69–77. https://doi.org/10.1207/s15374424jccp2701_8.

Wheaton, M. G., Deacon, B. J., McGrath, P. B., Berman, N. C., & Abramowitz, J. S. (2012). Dimensions of anxiety sensitivity in the anxiety disorders: evaluation of the ASI-3. *Journal of Anxiety Disorders*, *26*(3), 401–408. https://doi.org/10.1016/j.janxdis.2012.01.002.

Zinbarg, R. E., & Barlow, D. H. (1996). Structure of anxiety and the anxiety disorders: a hierarchical model. *Journal of Abnormal Psychology*, *105*(2), 181–193.

Zinbarg, R. E., Barlow, D. H., & Brown, T. A. (1997). Hierarchical structure and general factor saturation of the Anxiety Sensitivity Index: evidence and implications. *Psychological Assessment*, *9*(3), 277–284. https://doi.org/10.1037/1040-3590.9.3.277.

Zvolensky, M. J., Arrindell, W. A., Taylor, S., Bouvard, M., Cox, B. J., Stewart, S. H., … Eifert, G. H. (2003). Anxiety sensitivity in six countries. *Behaviour Research and Therapy*, *41*(7), 841–859.

Zvolensky, M. J., Farris, S. G., Guillot, C. R., & Leventhal, A. M. (2014). Anxiety sensitivity as an amplifier of subjective and behavioral tobacco abstinence effects. *Drug and Alcohol Dependence*, *142*, 224–230. https://doi.org/10.1016/j.drugalcdep.2014.06.023.

Zvolensky, M. J., Farris, S. G., Leventhal, A. M., & Schmidt, N. B. (2014). Anxiety sensitivity mediates relations between emotional disorders and smoking. *Psychology of Addictive Behaviors*, *28*(3), 912–920. https://doi.org/10.1037/a0037450.

Zvolensky, M. J., Goodie, J. L., McNeil, D. W., Sperry, J. A., & Sorrell, J. T. (2001). Anxiety sensitivity in the prediction of pain-related fear and anxiety in a heterogeneous chronic pain population. *Behaviour Research and Therapy*, *39*(6), 683–696.

Zvolensky, M. J., Rosenfield, D., Garey, L., Kauffman, B. Y., Langdon, K. J., Powers, M. B., Otto, M. W., Davis, M. L., Marcus, B. H., Church, T. S., Frierson, G. M., Hopkins, L. B., Paulus, D. J., Baird, S. O., & Smits, J. A. J. (2018). Does exercise aid smoking cessation through reductions in anxiety sensitivity and dysphoria? *Health Psychology*, *37*(7), 647–657.

Further reading

Olatunji, B. O., & Fan, Q. (2015). Anxiety sensitivity and post-traumatic stress reactions: evidence for intrusions and physiological arousal as mediating and moderating mechanisms. *Journal of Anxiety Disorders*, *34*, 76–85. https://doi.org/10.1016/j.janxdis.2015.06.002.

Integrating patients' anxiety sensitivity profile into one's case formulation and treatment planning

3

Michael J. Telch
The University of Texas at Austin, Austin, TX, United States

Chapter Outline

Introduction and chapter overview

The overarching aim of this chapter is to provide clinicians strategies for incorporating clients' anxiety sensitivity profile to enhance one's case formulation and treatment planning for individual's presenting with various anxiety-related complaints. I will do my best to stay focused on anxiety sensitivity as it pertains to case formulation

The Clinician's Guide to Anxiety Sensitivity Treatment and Assessment. https://doi.org/10.1016/B978-0-12-813495-5.00003-6

and treatment planning and not stray too far on other important topics related to anxiety sensitivity. Other chapters in this volume will provide essential material on the conceptualization, assessment, and modification of anxiety sensitivity.

For the purposes of this chapter, anxiety sensitivity will be conceptualized as a multifactor dispositional (trait-like) tendency to respond with an exaggerated threat response to various somatic, cognitive, and emotional cues associated with stress, anxiety, or panic. An important underlying assumption of this conceptualization is that patients presenting with anxiety disorders often display one or more specific anxiety sensitivity profiles. Consequently, optimal case formulation and treatment tailoring are best achieved when clinicians go beyond simple unitary conceptions of anxiety sensitivity as a fear of anxiety. Although such a broad conceptualization is not incorrect, it lacks the specificity to construct potent pinpointed interventions for correcting the specific fears that patients display in connection with the experience of stress, anxiety, and panic. My hope is that this chapter will help clinicians address two fundamental questions—"what are the specific perceived threats that my patient attaches to the experience of stress, anxiety, or panic" and "how might I intervene to lessen my patients' specific fears of stress, anxiety and panic"

The chapter will begin by providing a brief overview of case formulation from a clinical science perspective with particular emphasis on the distinction between two classes of causal factors of illness—*etiological* versus *maintaining/exacerbating*. The distinction is not trivial because the relative importance placed on the assessment of these two classes of causes has important implications for case formulation and treatment planning. Next, I offer a conceptual framework for understanding anxiety sensitivity in the bigger picture of dispositional vulnerabilities/sensitivities and how they interact with internal and external contexts in the expression of anxiety pathology. Finally, most of the chapter is devoted to describing with case examples commonly observed anxiety sensitivity profiles, along with assessment and intervention strategies for each.

Case formulation from a science-practitioner perspective

Working definition

Case formulation has been construed as the clinician's conceptual framework for understanding and correcting the patient's problems (Ingram, 2012). Case formulation from a science-based perspective is an ongoing iterative process consisting of the following three primary activities: (a) data collection; (b) hypothesis generation; and (c) hypothesis testing. A second important assumption of science-based case formulation is that these three activities reciprocally influence each other. For example, early clinical hypotheses about the patient's core problems are likely to undergo modifications as a function of the incoming data from various sources (e.g., clinical interview, patient-rating scales, behavioral observation, and information from significant others). Similarly, as certain clinical hypotheses undergo testing, many may be jettisoned and replaced with new ones. In turn, the testing of these new hypotheses may require the introduction of new assessment measures and the discarding of others.

Table 1 Typical questions governing relevant hypothesis testing for case formulation

Question	Functional domain
What is the nature and severity of the patient's anxiety problems?	Assessment of presenting problems/symptoms
Does the patient pose an immediate threat to self or others?	Assessment of lethality
What factors may have contributed to the development/ onset of the patient's anxiety problems?	Assessment of factors contributing to onset
What factors may be currently maintaining the patient's problems; of these, which seem to be most influential?	Assessment of maintaining factors
What strategies can be used to attenuate the effects of the current maintaining factors?	Selection and sequencing of intervention strategies
Are these strategies resulting in symptom reduction and enhanced quality of life?	Assessment of treatment efficacy

Obviously, the strategies for testing clinical hypotheses involve more than the collection and interpretation of the data. Just as experimental manipulation of putative causal factors is a powerful tool for scientific discovery, the introduction of various treatment elements in therapy and their corresponding effects on the patient's symptoms, function as a powerful tool for evaluating one's clinical case formulation.

Up to now we have been discussing clinical hypotheses and their testing more generally. Not surprisingly, effective case formulation requires some degree of specificity for achieving its overarching objective of developing an accurate conceptual framework for understanding and correcting the patient's problems. Clinical hypotheses can be construed as *tentative answers* to relevant questions related to the nature, severity, causes, possible therapeutic interventions, and their efficacy (Table 1).

A third and crucial feature of science-based case formulation is the integration of prior research findings in guiding the generation of tentative hypotheses about diagnoses, current maintaining factors, selection of assessment strategies and measures, and selection of intervention strategies.

Causal risk factors for illness and psychological dysfunction

Like with all physical or mental illnesses, epidemiologists studying the *causes* of disease have made major progress in identifying *risk factors* that contribute to the development of a countless number of physical and mental illnesses. With the exception of certain infectious diseases, which have only one specific cause, most physical and mental disorders have multiple contributing causes. For example, we now know that cigarette smoking, elevated LDL cholesterol, high blood pressure, obesity, and family history each independently contribute to an increased risk for developing heart disease. Similarly, our group has recently shown that soldiers deployed to Iraq were more likely to develop PTSD symptoms and depression in response to war-zone stressors if they possessed one or two short alleles of the serotonin transporter gene

(Telch et al., 2015), yet even among short allele carriers, most did not go on to develop PTSD or depression. The take-home message is that risk factors only increase one's risk for illness, they do not guarantee it.

Etiological vs. maintaining causes of anxiety pathology

There is an important distinction between causal risk factors that contribute to the initial development and onset of a disorder or disease versus factors that contribute to *maintaining* the disease or disorder in question. This latter group of causes is sometimes referred to as *causal maintaining factors* (Kraemer, Kazdin, Offord, et al., 1997) because they operate to maintain or even worsen the illness or disorder in question.

Let's take an example to illustrate the distinction between an *etiological cause* and a *maintaining cause*. Experiencing a helicopter crash while serving in Iraq might serve as an important *etiological* factor in the development of PTSD. In contrast, we also now know that the soldier's actions subsequent to the crash (e.g., avoiding flying, conversations, or newscasts about flying), as well as certain beliefs (e.g., flying is not a safe activity), are likely to operate as important factors in *maintaining* the soldier's fear of flying and PTSD symptoms.

Of course, it is possible for a given risk variable to function as a causal risk factor in both capacities (etiology and maintenance). For example, there is ample evidence that heightened anxiety sensitivity increases risk for the *development* of panic disorder (Schmidt, Schmidt, Lerew, & Jackson, 1997), as well as other forms of anxiety pathology (Schmidt, Schmidt, Zvolensky, & Maner, 2006); but also functions as an important causal maintenance factor in panic disorder (Smits, Powers, Cho, & Telch, 2004).

From a case formulation perspective, the identification of both etiological and maintaining causes provides the clinician with the most in-depth picture for understanding the onset and maintenance of the patient's current difficulties. However, from a treatment perspective, identification of current maintaining causes is paramount for the simple reason that many etiological risk factors are not modifiable (e.g., short allele carrier of the HTTLPR, or environmental exposure to a traumatic natural disaster). Consequently, our treatments are most likely to be successful if we are able to identify and attenuate/eliminate the current maintaining causes contributing to the patient's dysfunction. Getting back to our example of the soldier who developed PTSD following their helicopter crash, we obviously cannot go back in time and prevent the original crash (an etiological cause) but we can intervene in working with the patient to overcome selected modifiable maintaining causes such as his exaggerated emotional reactivity to the memory of the crash, self-defeating coping behaviors such as avoidance and other unnecessary safety behaviors, and his exaggerated perceptions of threat connected to his own anxiety reactions (i.e., heightened anxiety sensitivity).

A two-factor interactive model of maintaining causes of anxiety pathology

Based on clinical observation and controlled experimental research, Telch et al. (2010) and Telch, Harrington, Smits, and Powers (2011) have proposed a conceptual framework for conceptualizing *current maintaining causes* of anxiety pathology. This framework has potentially heuristic value in assisting clinicians in developing case formulations and idiographic treatment tailoring for the patient. The context-sensitivity vulnerability theory proposes two distinct classes of current maintaining causes of anxiety pathology—*contextual factors* and *sensitivity factors*. Here, context is defined as any internal or external stimulus that influences one's *perception of threat*. Internal context cues involve sensory input from within the person. Examples include somatic reactions (chest tightness), specific thoughts (I'm going to lose control), emotions (anger), images (picturing a shark while swimming), or specific memories (child choking at the dinner table). External contextual cues involve sensory input coming from *outside* the patient and may include certain objects, situations, people, etc. Contextual cues may elicit threat reactions or serve as signals for safety.

In our model, sensitivities are conceptualized as modifiable dispositional traits that influence threat perception and emotional responding (see Tellegen, 1991). As noted by Lilienfeld, Turner, and Jacob (1993) in their hierarchical model of anxiety sensitivity, dispositional traits can be conceptualized across a bandwidth continuum ranging from traits that influence emotional responding across a wide range of contexts (e.g., negative emotionality, neuroticism, distress tolerance, experiential avoidance, trait anxiety), to medium-band sensitivities such as anxiety sensitivity, intolerance for uncertainty, need for control, perfectionism, to more narrow-band sensitivities such as disgust sensitivity, respiratory sensitivity, and cardiac sensitivity. Although some may quibble about the specific ordering of these sensitivities on the continuum, the important point here is that there is now compelling evidence that dispositional sensitivities such as anxiety sensitivity serve to potentiate one's emotional responding to certain contexts. We refer to this assertion as the *sensitivity potentiation hypothesis* (Telch et al., 2010). Fundamental to this hypothesis is the assumption that dispositional traits interact with contexts/situations to influence behavior. The view that dispositional traits influence emotional and behavioral responding to some situations and not others dates back to the pioneering work of personality theorists such as Alport (1937) and Tellegen (1991).

Our theory further posits that the level of anxious responding to potential threat-relevant internal or external cues/contexts depends on the *conceptual match* between the dispositional sensitivity profile of the person and the threat-relevant context. This latter prediction has been termed the *context-sensitivity matching hypothesis* (Telch et al., 2010) and helps to reconcile the commonly observed within-patient variation in emotional responding across different situations/contexts. Evidence supporting this assertion comes from an experiment in our laboratory in which college students completed measures of anxiety sensitivity, respiratory sensitivity, and cardiac sensitivity and then underwent an established panic provocation challenge—a single inhalation of 35% CO_2/65% O_2 gas. Immediately prior to completing the CO_2 challenge, half of the subjects witnessed a staff member wheel in a cardiac defibrillator into the room, whereas the other half did not. Consistent with the context-sensitivity matching hypothesis, the presence of the defibrillator significantly increased subjects' likelihood of panic to the CO_2 challenge, but only among those subjects scoring high on cardiac sensitivity (Telch et al., 2010).

How do certain sensitivities potentiate exaggerated threat responding to certain contexts? We have argued that certain dispositional sensitivities such as anxiety sensitivity may increase the likelihood that certain contexts (internal or external) will be perceived as threatening (*threat appraisal hypothesis*). In another CO_2 challenge study (Telch et al., 2011), participants were randomly assigned to receive instructions that the gas would make them quite aroused (expected arousal) or instructions that the gas would make them quite relaxed (unexpected arousal). Consistent with the threat appraisal hypothesis, high anxiety sensitivity participants who perceived their CO_2-induced arousal as *unexpected* (i.e., threat enhancing context) displayed markedly higher fear responding than high anxiety sensitivity those who perceived their CO_2-induced arousal as expected (i.e., threat attenuation context). As predicted, those low in anxiety sensitivity showed low fear responding regardless of the instructional set they received.

What are the implications of this theory for case formulation and treatment planning? One fairly obvious implication is the importance of a thorough assessment of patients' *anxiety sensitivity profile* rather than relying on a single global index of anxiety sensitivity. My use of the word *profile* reflects our clinical experience and research findings (Telch, Brouillard, Telch, Agras, & Taylor, 1989), suggesting that there are several profiles of anxiety sensitivity that vary across patients and serve as important modifiable maintaining factors in contributing to a diverse range of anxiety-related clinical presentations. Failure to assess the patient's idiographic anxiety sensitivity profile is a missed opportunity to identify and potentially modify these narrow-band sensitivities that maintain the patient's anxiety pathology.

Anxiety sensitivity profiles

In this next section, we review several of the most common anxiety sensitivity profiles. For each, we present a brief description with a case example, along with specific strategies for assessing its presence and severity.

Cardiac sensitivity

Clinical presentation

The cardiac concerns profile, as the name implies, is commonly observed in patients with panic disorder, agoraphobia, health illness disorder (health anxiety), and generalized anxiety disorder. Patients with this profile perceive normal cardiac reactions in response to stress, anxiety, or panic as signaling potential heart problems. Even for this specific anxiety sensitivity profile, there is some degree of variability in its clinical presentation. For instance, some individuals display exaggerated fear responding to physical changes in either heart rate acceleration (heart racing) or stroke volume increases (heart pounding). Others show fear activation in response to cues of chest tightness, pressure, or pain in the pectoral region often brought about by stress-induced hyperventilation, stressors, or both. Not surprisingly, patients with this profile display extreme hypervigilance to cardiac cues as well as enhanced interoceptive awareness of changes in their heartbeat (Dunn et al., 2010).

Patients with this anxiety sensitivity profile typically cope with their cardiac fear by engaging in cardiac-fear related avoidance and other false safety behaviors (FSBs), which we define as *unnecessary actions taken to prevent, escape from, or reduce the severity of a perceived threat* (Telch & Lancaster, 2012). Common avoidance FSBs for this profile include coffee, energy drinks, certain cold remedies, stressful encounters, and strenuous exercise. Other commonly observed false safety behaviors associated with this anxiety sensitivity profile include checking one's pulse or blood pressure, researching articles on the Internet or newspaper about heart attacks, or heart-related medical procedures, excessive visits to the doctor or emergency room, and seeking reassurance from family members or friends. Less often, patients may show avoidance of being alone or places in which medical assistance may be unavailable. Given the extensive research findings suggesting that these unnecessary protective actions may function as an important maintaining factor in anxiety pathology (see Telch & Lancaster, 2012; Telch & Zaizar, in press), a thorough assessment of the patient's avoidance patterns and safety behaviors should be routinely conducted and included in the clinician's case formulation and treatment planning for each patient.

Case example

Bill is a 40-year-old executive working for a major software company in Central Texas. Anticipating that he would have to pull an all-nighter to complete a final report for an important client, Bill consumed three energy drinks over a span of 3 h. All of a sudden, Bill noticed his heart pounding and racing and felt like he couldn't catch his breath. He called 911 in a state of panic believing that he might be having a heart attack. When the paramedics arrived at his house, Bill was sitting on his couch weeping. After questioning Bill and performing a standard EKG, they informed Bill that he had experienced a panic attack and that there was no need to take him to the hospital. Although reassured initially, over the next several weeks Bill began to experience significant apprehension over the possibility that the paramedics had missed something especially since Bill was experiencing tightness in his chest as well as rapid heartbeat. Although Bill exercised regularly, he began to avoid the gym because he feared that the exertion may be too much for his heart to take. Likewise, he cut out his morning cup of coffee and even started to avoid chocolate for fear that the caffeine might not be good for his heart. Despite these efforts, he noticed his anxiety escalating to the point where he was having trouble concentrating at work and was distracted from both his wife and children.

It is also worth noting that during the intake interview Bill disclosed that his older brother Dan, died of a heart attack at age 52.

Bill's case is fairly typical of patient's displaying the cardiac fear anxiety sensitivity profile. Normal physical reactions of increased cardiac output (increased heart rate and increased stroke volume) brought about by stress, anxiety, ingestion of stimulants, or certain over-the-counter cold remedies are misconstrued as signaling a potential heart problem.

Bill's case also illustrates the close connection between the underlying bogus threat (heart problem) and the kinds of false safety behaviors Bill adopted in an attempt to cope with this misperceived threat. Although these safety behaviors had nothing to do with his initial panic reaction, they played a significant causal maintaining role in fueling his anxiety and phobic behavior following the event. Note too that Bill's use of false safety behaviors (FSBs) started with checking his pulse and blood pressure but soon expanded to include avoidance of previously routine activities such as exercise, drinking coffee, consuming chocolate, and avoidance of stressful encounters at work. These FSBs expanded further to carrying aspirin in his shirt pocket, and his mental analysis (checking) of what the paramedics told him after his panic attack.

Assessment strategies

Clinical interview

Specific probes during the clinical interview can be quite helpful in identifying cardiac sensitivity. These include queries such as, "Do you notice that you sometimes feel uneasy when you notice your heart beating fast, or feel tightness in your chest?" "Do you avoid certain activities for fear that they might trigger a cardiac problem?" "Do you sometimes have thoughts that something might be wrong with your heart?" "Do you frequently check your pulse, or blood pressure?"

Patients who answer affirmatively should be queried as to whether they have been diagnosed with a cardiac-related problem by a physician. For patients presenting with actual cardiac-related problems, cardiac sensitivity is an adaptive reaction and should not be construed as "pathological." Of course, the behavioral challenge assessments described here should *not* be administered for those patients with actual cardiac problems, or with elderly patients.

Patient-rating scales

Specific patient-rating scales for the initial assessment and monitoring of this profile include the (a) Cardiac Questionnaire (Eifert et al., 2000); (b) items 3, 7, 8, and 12 of the Anxiety Sensitivity Scale (ASI-3; Taylor & Cox, 1998); (c) Texas Safety Maneuver Questionnaire-R (Kamphuis & Telch, 1998); and (d) the cardiac sensitivity subscale of the Texas Multifactor Anxiety Sensitivity Scale (see Appendix).

Behavioral challenge assessment strategies

Behavioral challenge assessments can be useful in the identification and ongoing assessment of patients' cardiac sensitivity. Two specific challenges are described here: (a) assessing patients' emotional distress while having them perform a physical exercise that accelerates cardiac output (e.g., running in place, stair climbing); and (b) assessing patients' emotional distress while ingesting a stimulant beverage. Neither of the challenges described here should be used with elderly patients or patients with a history of cardiovascular, respiratory, or orthopedic disorders unless approved by the patient's treating physician.

1. *Exercise challenge*: The patient is informed that you would like to assess his/her subjective and behavioral reactions while performing an aerobic exercise. Depending on availability, the patient may by fitted with a heart-rate wrist monitor. We have found that briskly walking up and down one flight of stairs repeatedly is a fast and convenient method for inducing increased cardiac output, although running in place can be substituted when stairs are not available. Prior to starting the challenge, the patient is asked to rate on a 0–100 scale their anticipated fear and anticipated threat connected to performing the exercise. While performing the challenge, the patient is instructed to focus on the physical sensations and emotions elicited during the exercise and to report to the therapist if he/she starts to feel dizzy or lightheaded. The clinician should carefully observe the patient's respiration after each flight

and *terminate the challenge*[1] when the patient is displaying clear signs of being winded. The number of flights to achieve a moderate degree of windedness varies greatly as a function of fitness level, age, and weight. With the exception of the highly aerobically fit person, this challenge is usually terminated after 5 up-and-down flights have been completed. Immediately upon terminating the challenge, the patient is asked to rate on a 0–100 their peak fear and anticipated threat at any time while performing the challenge. To enhance compliance, clinicians should make it clear to the patient that they can stop the exercise at any time. For those who refuse the challenge, the patient should be queried as to their anticipated threat and anticipated level of fear on a 0–100 scale *if* they were to perform the challenge.

2. *Stimulant ingestion challenge*: This challenge involves informing the patient that you would like to assess his/her emotional reactions in response to ingesting a beverage[2] containing a stimulating herb that is likely to produce a moderate increase in their heart-rate. The patient is then asked to rate on a 0–100 scale his/her anticipated fear and anticipated threat just prior to the ingestion of the beverage. For patients who agree to take part in the challenge, four repeated assessments of peak fear and anticipated threat are collected at 5-min intervals starting at 20 min post ingestion. For those who refuse the challenge, the patient should be queried as to their anticipated threat and anticipated level of fear *if* he/she were to perform the challenge.

Respiratory sensitivity

Clinical presentation

Patients presenting with the respiratory sensitivity anxiety sensitivity profile tend to perceive the normal respiratory changes during states of stress as signaling the threat of suffocation. This profile is most commonly observed among patients with panic disorder, claustrophobia, and to a lesser extent illness anxiety disorder (health anxiety). Hyperventilation is very often part of the clinical picture and may often play a key role in the development of certain forms of anxiety pathology (Ley, 1985). Although increased respiration is a normal response to stress, approximately 10% of the general population display a chronic pattern of overbreathing (Thomas, McKinley, Freeman, Foy, & Price, 2005). This overbreathing results in a chain reaction in which pCO_2 levels decrease resulting in elevated pH levels (respiratory alkalosis), which in turn lead to feelings of lightheadedness[3] and breathlessness (air hunger). Paradoxically, feelings of air hunger prompt the person to breathe deeper, which further maintains the state of respiratory alkalosis.

Not surprisingly, patients with respiratory sensitivity display hypervigilance to their breathing, which further increases the perception of breathlessness, thus leading

[1] We have found that some patients with cardiac sensitivity anxiety sensitivity profile may be able to drink coffee without anxiety, but become quite distressed when an unfamiliar beverage is introduced with the same amount of caffeine.

[2] Note that some people display overbreathing patterns without displaying elevated emotional reactivity to the feelings.

[3] Many people will mislabel lightheadedness as feeling "dizzy."

to compensatory overbreathing. They also may show avoidance of activities such as snorkeling or scuba diving, wearing nose clips while swimming, or avoidance of enclosed spaces such as crowded elevators, crowded subways, and undergoing certain medical procedures such as magnetic resonance imaging (MRI). Other safety behaviors include carrying inhalers, excessive visits to physicians or emergency rooms, and excessive reassurance seeking.

Case example

Ray is a 71-year-old retired gastroenterologist happily married for 50 years with no prior history of mental health treatment. He presented with repeated panic attacks, extreme feelings of lightheadedness, debilitating worry and hypervigilance related to his breathing, and phobic avoidance related to being left alone. The onset of Ray's panic attacks began about 8 months prior while having outpatient cataract surgery. He was very lightly sedated during the surgery and requested that his hands not be restrained during the procedure. As his ophthalmologist brought the apparatus close to his face, he began to feel panicky and felt a strong urge to get up and run away, but he didn't. He told the doctor of his burgeoning feeling of panic and requested an assistant to hold his hand and talk to him to "calm him down". Following the operation, the surgeon indicated that there was a mild complication from the procedure on his second eye, but that it should resolve within several weeks. Over the next week, Ray could not stop worrying about the surgery and began experiencing more panic attacks. During these attacks he would experience intense lightheadedness, tightness in his chest, and thoughts that his nasal passages were closing and that he was not getting sufficient air, but reported that he knew this was irrational. Within days, he became hyperfocused on his breathing and the sensations of lightheadedness and pressure in his chest. He also reported difficulty sleeping, marked irritability, and constant pacing, which he reported made him feel slightly better. Over the ensuing months, he began to curtail what was a very active lifestyle, began turning down invitations to socialize with friends, and developed phobic avoidance of being left alone at home or any situation or activity that might "stress him out."

During his first session, Ray also mentioned that he had a longstanding fear of enclosed places dating back to a childhood trauma. At age 5, Ray lacerated his upper cheek during an accident while playing. His parents took him to a pediatrician to sew up the wound. Ray recalled very vividly how the doctor had him stand up very straight, "like a soldier," with his arms stiffly by his side. He then wrapped his body up tightly in a sheet "like a mummy" where he remembers struggling trying to free his arms but to no avail. Next, the doctor laid him down and sutured the wound. Although he felt no physical pain during the suturing, he was wide awake through all of it, grievously crying throughout. He recalled feeling extremely angry both at being completely restrained and being "tricked." When it was finally over and he was taken off the table, he kicked the doctor in the shin as hard as he could. Ray recalled that following this experience he was uncomfortable in all tight spaces including snorkeling or even holding his breath underwater, but that his claustrophobia did not interfere at all with his life.

Assessment strategies

Clinical interview

Astute observation of the patient's breathing patterns, especially during the start of the interview may reveal signs of overbreathing. Specific signs of hyperventilation include intermittent gasping for air, breath holding, or excessive yawning. Note that some people display overbreathing patterns without displaying elevated emotional reactivity to the feelings. Specific probes during the clinical interview can be quite helpful in identifying respiratory sensitivity. These include queries such as, "Do you notice that you sometimes feel that is hard to catch your breath? Do you sometimes find yourself feeling lightheaded or dizzy? Do you sometimes find yourself focused on your breathing or whether you are getting sufficient air? Do you avoid or feel uncomfortable being in enclosed spaces like crowded elevators or subways?" For patients showing respiratory sensitivity, it is important for the clinician to rule out an actual respiratory medical problem such as asthma or COPD. Patients should be queried as to whether they have been diagnosed with asthma, COPD, or another respiratory disorder. For patients presenting with a diagnosed respiratory disorder, respiratory sensitivity is an adaptive reaction and should not be construed as pathological.

Patient-rating scales

Specific patient-rating scales useful in the initial detection and ongoing assessment of respiratory sensitivity include: (a) Claustrophobia Questionnaire (Rachman & Taylor, 1993); (b) Claustrophobia Concerns Questionnaire (Valentiner, Telch, Petruzzi, & Bolte, 1996); and (c) respiratory sensitivity subscale of the Texas Multifactor Anxiety Sensitivity Scale (see Appendix).

Behavioral challenge assessment strategies

There are several useful behavioral challenge strategies that help identify those with heightened respiratory sensitivity. These include:

1. *Straw breathing challenge*: This behavioral challenge involves having the patient pinch their nose shut while breathing through a small coffee straw for 2 min while the clinician times how long (in seconds) the patient is able to perform the task. The clinician should first model the procedure for the patient or have the patient watch a video demonstration of a person performing the challenge. Upon completing the challenge, the patient is asked to provide ratings of their physical and emotional distress on a 0–100 scale. Typically we find that patients who score high on other measures of respiratory sensitivity terminate the task within the first 60 s.
2. *Hyperventilation challenge*: This behavioral challenge has the patient take full vital capacity breaths at a rate of 60 breaths/min for 60 s. At the end of the 60 s, the patient is asked to rate on a 0–100 scale their level of pure physical reactions (most typically lightheadedness, tingling in the extremities, and chest discomfort). Next, the patient is asked to rate on the same 0–100 scale their peak fear (i.e., highest level of fear experienced at any point during the challenge). To minimize throat discomfort during the procedure, we have also found it helpful to instruct patients to exhale by blowing out as if one is blowing out candles on a birthday cake. To increase compliance, it is important that the clinician models the procedure for the patient or have the patient watch a video demonstration of a person performing the challenge. Patients high in respiratory sensitivity may sometimes terminate the challenge early as they start to experience the physical reactions elicited by the overbreathing procedure. Note that that reports of moderate-to-high levels of fear during the procedure may be due to other perceived threats unrelated to suffocation—the most common of which is the fear of fainting. Interview probes such as "did you start to have any concerns or threatening thoughts during the challenge?" can be quite helpful in disentangling the primary threat(s) evoked by the challenge.

Loss of control sensitivity

Clinical presentation

Although perceived control over potentially threatening happenings plays an important role in mitigating stress and anxiety (Averill, 1973; Telch, Silverman, & Schmidt, 1996), some display an excessive need for control that can be indexed by the level of discomfort one experiences under conditions when control is low or absent (Averill, 1973). Unlike this general need for control, the distinctive feature of the loss of control (LOC) anxiety sensitivity profile is that the individual perceives loss of control as a specific consequence of anxiety or panic. Thus, it is both possible and common to be low in overall need for control but still display heightened LOC anxiety sensitivity. Note too that even within this anxiety sensitivity profile, there are several common variations that can be distinguished based on one or more of the following response control systems. They include: (a) fear of losing behavioral control (e.g., jumping from a balcony, driving one's car into ongoing traffic); (b) fear of losing control of physiological functioning (e.g., bladder control, bowel control, erectile control); and (c) fear of losing control of mental/perceptual functioning (e.g., fear of becoming psychotic, amnestic, manic). Although the loss of control anxiety sensitivity profile is common in panic disorder and agoraphobia, it may also serve as a key maintaining factor in other anxiety presentations such as obsessive-compulsive disorder, specific phobia, health anxiety, and social anxiety disorder.

Case example

Emma is a 33-year-old single woman working as an accountant. At age 24 while experiencing significant work-related stress and significant conflict in her romantic relationship, she experienced an out-of-the-blue panic attack while driving to work. During her panic reaction, she became acutely lightheaded and felt this horrifying feeling of unreality come over her. She recalled having the thought that she was losing her mind and that she might lose control of her vehicle and injure or kill herself or others. She pulled over to the side of the road, put on her flashers, and called her partner. While waiting for her partner to arrive, she called her work and informed them that she was not coming in today. Within minutes, her partner arrived and brought her home. For the rest of the day, Emma became obsessed with the idea that she was going crazy and would lose all control of her senses. That night she got very little sleep and continued to ruminate about her experience in the car the day before. That next morning, she announced to her partner that she didn't think she could drive to work safely. Her partner accommodated her request to be driven to work. At that point things got much worse, not only with respect to having more panic attacks, but she became totally unable to leave the house alone for fear that she would panic and lose control of her behavioral and mental faculties. By the time she was referred to us, she had already undergone several rounds of psychotherapy and pharmacotherapy, all of which were unsuccessful.

This case nicely illustrates the "loss of control" anxiety sensitivity profile as a causal factor in the onset and maintenance of this patient's symptoms of panic and agoraphobia. Note the conceptual linkage between the patient's specific threat profile (i.e., fear of losing behavioral and mental control during a panic attack) and the patient's specific pattern of avoidance (being alone, activities in which loss of behavioral control might cause harm or death to self or others) and other false safety behaviors (relying on her partner to drive her to work).

Assessment strategies

Clinical interview

It has been our experience that relative to the other anxiety sensitivity profiles, patients presenting with the loss of control anxiety sensitivity profile may be more likely to come to their first appointment accompanied by a spouse, parent, or friend and request that the accompanying person remain present during the interview. Even among patients who come to their appointment alone, they may still display heightened distress especially when queried about potential threats related to loss of control. Several specific probes during the clinical interview can be useful in identifying the presence of the loss of control anxiety sensitivity profile. These include, "When you get highly anxious or panicky, do you ever worry that the fear will cause you to lose control of your ability to drive safely or cause you to do something that you really don't want to do such as harm yourself or harm other people?" "Do you ever worry that the fear will cause you to lose control of your senses and that you will start to hear voices or see things that aren't really there?" "Do you ever worry that the fear will cause you to lose your ability to control a bodily function such as your bladder or your bowels?"

Patient-rating scales

Specific patient-rating scales useful in the initial detection and ongoing assessment of loss of control sensitivity include items 2, 5, 10, 14, and 16 of the ASI-3 (Taylor et al., 2007), Items 1, 3, 6, 7, and 15 of Scale 2 of the Panic Appraisal Inventory (Telch et al., 1989), and the Loss of Control Sensitivity subscale of the Texas Multifactor Anxiety Sensitivity Scale (see Appendix).

Behavioral challenge assessment strategies

Several behavioral challenge strategies for identifying patients displaying heightened loss of control anxiety sensitivity appear here. Note that the common central feature inherent in these strategies is to set up in collaboration with the patient a situation in which the patient *temporarily relinquishes control.* Prior to starting the challenge, the clinician asks the patient to provide (a) their anticipated fear as well as (b) their anticipated threatening outcome. During the actual challenge, ratings of *actual* fear and threat ratings are assessed.

1. *Blindfold challenge—being a passenger in the car*: Because visual scanning is a common defensive action for threat detection, patients with loss of control anxiety concerns sometimes perceive being blindfolded as threatening—especially in some contexts like being a passenger in a car. The patient is provided the rationale that by allowing oneself to be blindfolded while being a passenger, one is relinquishing control, which for some may activate anxiety. Ratings of anticipated fear and anticipated threat are collected based on the expectation of a 5-min car ride. The challenge should be terminated early for those reporting low levels of fear and threat while riding.
2. *Placebo challenge*: This challenge involves informing the patient that you would like them to ingest a harmless short-acting pill that is likely to temporarily activate moderate-to-high levels of anxiety within several minutes. The patient is further instructed and agrees that once

the pill is ingested, the therapist will *not* answer any questions about the pill or its effects. Ratings of anticipated fear and anticipated threat are obtained just prior to placebo ingestion. Additional ratings are collected at 1-min intervals for 5 min. For those who refuse the challenge, the patient should be queried as to their anticipated threat and anticipated level of fear *if* they were to perform the challenge.

Social sensitivity

Clinical presentation

The central feature of the anxiety sensitivity social threat profile is perceiving that experiencing panic, anxiety, or sometimes even high stress will lead to negative judgments from others. This belief is often fueled by a two-pronged inferential error in which the patient (a) overestimates the likelihood that others will notice their anxiety/panic, and/or (b) overestimates the likelihood that once detected, one's anxiety will lead others to judge them as weird, weak, mentally ill, or defective in some way. Patient's displaying this profile still show some variability in its clinical presentation. For instance, some are extremely concerned that others will notice some physical reaction like sweating, blushing, or trembling; whereas others worry that people will judge them negatively because of some change in the way they act while anxious, e.g., appearing quiet, distracted, or spacey. Not surprisingly, this anxiety sensitivity profile is commonly seen in patients with social anxiety disorder. However, it is often present in a subset of cases of panic disorder or agoraphobia. In social situations, patients with this profile often display avoidance of social situations, and a self-defeating safety behavior pattern consisting of excessive self-monitoring and rehearsal, which has been labeled *impression management* (Hirsch, Meynen, & Clark, 2004). Paradoxically, this impression management safety behavior profile has been shown to actually elicit negative social evaluations from others (Plasencia, Alden, & Taylor, 2011).

Case example

Matt is a happily married 33-year-old socially skilled professional working for a large computer company in central Texas. At the time of intake, Matt presented with panic attacks, severe anticipatory anxiety[4] centered around others "noticing his anxiety," and marked situational anxiety and panic, when having to converse with work colleagues—particularly at lunch. When probed as to what he perceived would happen if one or more work colleagues noticed his anxiety, he quickly replied "they would think I'm weird and reject me." Matt also developed an interesting set of impression management safety behaviors to cope with his fear of others noticing his anxiety. Being socially skilled, Matt would tell jokes or funny stories as a way of controlling others' impressions of him. During gaps, Matt would become extremely self-focused, at which time he would check his anxiety level and mentally plan what he could say next to keep others from noticing his anxiety. Inspection of Matt's responses on the Assessment of Social Concerns scale that Matt completed as part of his intake assessment, revealed a marked concern of sweating in front of others, which was confirmed by the patient during the clinical interview. This specific fear became an important variable in the case formulation and treatment, because it served as a proxy cue for activating his fear that others would notice his anxiety and ultimately reject him.

Interestingly, Matt also reported a strong feeling of shame in connection with his anxiety and panic episodes. Possible early learning experiences may have contributed to this specific clinical feature as well as the patient's overall heightened social threat sensitivity. During the intake interview, Matt described his childhood as "stressful." Matt's parents divorced when he was just 4 and he and his younger brother lived with his mother who was described as an "emotional nightmare." He described his mother's anger as being like a time bomb and reported feeling like he was always walking on eggs shells in his attempt to please her and not provoke her anger. Although often unprovoked, Matt soon learned that his mother's rage could be triggered when he himself displayed negative emotions—particularly fear. He recalled a specific memory in first grade in which he got lost while trying to walk to his new school, found his way home sobbing in fear only to have his mother scold him for being afraid.

This case nicely illustrates the "social concerns" anxiety sensitivity profile as a likely causal factor in the onset and maintenance of this patient's anxiety and avoidance symptoms. Particularly noteworthy is the specificity of the patient's social concerns, namely, appearing anxious in front of others. Matt's case is in sharp contrast to patients with generalized social phobia whose social evaluative concerns extend well beyond simply the threat of displaying anxiety/panic in front of others. Note the connection between the patient's specific anxiety sensitivity threat profile (i.e., fear of others noticing his anxiety) and the patient's specific pattern of self-defeating impression management safety behaviors (i.e., self-monitoring of his anxiety, and mental rehearsing conversations in advance).

[4] Educational handouts are available from the author.

Assessment strategies

Clinical interview

Observation of the patient's behavior during the interview can often be quite telling. We have found that people with social concerns about becoming anxious may apologize to the interviewer for being anxious. Some may also display an avoidance of eye contact with the interviewer. Specific probes during the clinical interview can be quite helpful in identifying the anxiety sensitivity social threat profile. These include queries such as, "When you're in social situations, do you worry that others will notice your anxiety? What might happen if you become anxious while having lunch with co-workers? Do you often focus on how you're coming across to others or notice yourself rehearsing what you might say during conversations with people? When you're feeling stressed or anxious in front of people, do you make an effort to hide it?"

During the interview, it is useful to assess whether the *primary* focus of threat in social situations is becoming anxious. Probes such as, "If you could be guaranteed that you would not become anxious when conversing with others, are there other concerns or worries you have about how others view you?" Note that the presence of other threat foci of negative evaluation independent of anxiety is common (e.g., appearing weird, boring, or stupid) and is important in the case formulation and selection of treatment targets.

Patient-rating scales

Specific patient-rating scales useful in the initial detection and ongoing assessment and monitoring of social threat sensitivity include the Brief Fear of Negative Evaluation Scale (BFNE; Leary, 1983), the Assessment of Social Concerns (ASC;

Telch et al., 2004), the social threat scale of the Panic Appraisal Inventory (Telch et al., 1989), the Social Behavior Questionnaire (SBQ; Clark et al., 1995), and the Social Threat Sensitivity subscale of the Texas Multifactor Anxiety Sensitivity Scale (see Appendix).

Behavioral challenges

There are several useful behavioral challenge strategies that help identify those with heightened social sensitivity. These include:

1. *Video-recorded impromptu speech*: This challenge consists of having the patient complete a recorded speech in front of the therapist on a specific topic selected by the patient. The topic should be one in which the patient has some familiarity of the subject matter. Examples of topics include: (a) Describe your personal views regarding the pros and cons of laws requiring the mandatory wearing of seat belts; (b) Describe one of your most embarrassing memories and the thoughts and feelings about it; and (c) Describe something about yourself that you are most proud of. Procedurally, the challenge is completed in the following sequential steps: (1) Presentation of the rationale for the speech challenge; (2) Selection of the specific topic; (3) Two-minute anticipatory preparation period; (4) Patient is asked to provide ratings (0–100) of anticipated fear and anticipated performance; (5) Delivering the speech; (6) Patient and therapist complete assessment ratings of *peak distress and overall performance* on a 0–100 scale; (7) Patient and therapist watch the recording together; (8) Patient rerates his/her distress and performance level; and (9) Open-ended discussion of the experience. Often the data review from this challenge provides a wealth of information that may help the clinician gain greater insight into the behavioral, physical, and cognitive appraisal reactions of the patient.
2. *Video-recorded role play with the therapist*: As the name implies, this challenge has the patient and therapist role play a social interaction that the patient reports as anxiety provoking. Common examples include job interview, first date meeting over coffee, confronting a friend about something they did that upset you. In all examples, the patients should play the role of themselves during the role play. Procedurally the challenge should follow the steps described here for the impromptu speech.
3. *In vivo assessment of fear and performance while conversing with others in an actual fear-provoking situation*: In this challenge, the therapist and patient enter a situation that has previously been determined as fear proving based on the patient's self-report. Typically, the patient and therapist will enter the establishment (coffee shop, boutique, etc.) separately and pretend that they do not know each other, while the patient approaches one of the sales or service staff and strikes up a brief conversation. Prior to entering the establishment, the patient will be asked to provide a rating of anticipated distress and performance on a 0–100 scale. Upon completing the interaction, the patient and therapist meet outside and the patient provides the therapist with his or her postchallenge ratings of emotional distress and performance.

Implications for treatment

As alluded to earlier, one important function of a thorough case formulation is to assist in the *selection* and *sequencing* of treatment strategies tailored to the patient's specific profile of external and internal maintaining factors. Careful assessment of each patient's anxiety sensitivity profile constitutes a central but not *sufficient* element for effective case formulation and treatment planning. This final section aims to provide specific recommendations for tailoring treatment based on the specific anxiety sensitivity profiles presented earlier.

Tailoring psychoeducation and cognitive restructuring to patients' anxiety sensitivity profile

We believe it is important to tailor the psychoeducation and cognitive restructuring based on the patient's anxiety sensitivity threat profile. For instance, patients' displaying cardiac concerns are often quite misinformed about the nature and causes of heart attacks and erroneously believe that the normal increases in cardiac output during stress, anxiety, or panic is harmful to the heart or may be indicative of an existing heart problem. Consequently, our psychoeducation handouts[5] and didactic review of the educational material place greater emphasis on (a) normal reactions of the heart to stress, anxiety, and panic; (b) adaptive function of these reactions (i.e., help supply increased oxygen to the muscles); (c) nature and causes (risk factors) of heart attacks; and (d) objective warning signs of a *real* heart problem. Likewise, our subsequent cognitive work with the patient focuses on identifying and challenging of specific faulty assumptions linking anxiety or panic to cardiac-related concerns.

Similarly, patients displaying the respiratory anxiety sensitivity threat profile receive more extensive psychoeducation emphasizing (a) normal respiratory reactions to stress, anxiety, and panic; (b) the adaptive function of these reactions (i.e., help supply increased oxygen to cope with threat); (c) nature and causes of hyperventilation; (d) nature and causes of fainting and suffocation; and (e) methods for controlling overbreathing. Follow-up cognitive work with the patient focuses on identifying and correcting specific erroneous assumptions relating anxiety or panic to suffocation or fainting.

In contrast, those exhibiting the loss of control anxiety sensitivity profile receive knowledge elements specific to their fear of losing control. These include: (a) normal physical, mental, and behavioral reactions associated with stress, anxiety, and panic; (b) the adaptive functions of these reactions; and (c) distinction between "*thoughts*" of losing control versus the *actual loss of control*. Follow-up cognitive work targets the identification and modification of specific threat forecasts related to loss of control concerns related to mental, behavioral, or physiological functioning.

For patients presenting with the social threat anxiety sensitivity profile, the psychoeducation includes knowledge elements focusing on (a) debunking certain myths such as "everyone can notice my anxiety," "people will judge me negatively if I'm sweating," "it would be horrible if someone notices that I am anxious"; and (b) education on the paradoxical anxiety-promoting effects of avoidance and other self-defeating impression management strategies (e.g., mentally rehearsing

[5]Psychometric data are not yet available.

conversation with others). Additional cognitive work for this anxiety sensitivity profile focuses primarily on correcting the exaggerated conditional belief that anxiety or panic will lead to social rejection from others.

Tailoring of exposure and safety behavior fading

The specific behavioral challenges described earlier in this chapter for each of the anxiety sensitivity sensitivities can be used to conduct repeated therapeutic exposure trials both in session and for home practice. The overarching strategy is to have the patient engage in an activity (e.g., repeated stair climbing for a patient with the cardiac anxiety sensitivity profile) that activates the perceived threat (e.g., fear of heart attack), while the therapist provides guided threat reappraisal in vivo to enhance threat disconfirmation and safety learning. This exposure augmentation technique consists of three distinct procedural elements. First, prior to exposure to the feared context, the therapist assists the patient in identifying specific anticipated threats related to the exposure task (e.g., "I might lose control and make a scene"). For the threats identified, the patient is asked to rate on a 0 to 100 scale (a) the likelihood that the threat will occur, and (b) the severity of each threat should it occur. Next, during the full duration of the exposure trial, the patient is encouraged to focus on the threat(s) identified earlier and to look for evidence supporting or refuting the specific threat forecast. Upon completing the exposure trial, the therapist and patient review the evidence pertaining to the patient's original threat appraisals. These steps are repeated for each of the subsequent exposure trials. This specific guided threat reappraisal procedure has been shown to improve therapeutic outcome relative to exposure therapy alone in two independent trials (Kamphuis & Telch, 2000; Sloan & Telch, 2002).

It has been our experience that patients do not achieve complete normalization of their specific anxiety sensitivity profile unless they also eliminate their safety behaviors such as checking pulse or blood pressure, excessive medical work-ups, and other forms of reassurance seeking. Thus, we work closely with the patient to construct an action plan for the graduated fading of these false safety behaviors (see Telch & Lancaster, 2012).

Table 2 provides examples of treatment strategies for each of the four anxiety sensitivity profiles.

Treating patients with multiple anxiety sensitivity profiles

For conceptual clarity and ease of presentation, we have presented these four anxiety sensitivity profiles singularly. The clinical reality is that patients often present with two or more of these anxiety sensitivity profile combinations. This reality poses an additional challenge for case formulation because the clinician must formulate hypotheses relative to three fundamental questions: (a) What is the nature of the relationships between the multiple anxiety sensitivity profiles? (b) What is the relative strength of each anxiety sensitivity profile in contributing to the patient's symptoms? and (c) Are certain anxiety sensitivity profiles more easily modified than others? For the first two questions, the answers are likely to vary markedly as a function

Table 2 Examples of exposure and safety behavior fading strategies by anxiety sensitivity profile

Anxiety sensitivity profile	Exposure strategies	SB fading targets
Cardiac sensitivity	Stair climbing; running in place; ingesting stimulants; intentionally placing oneself in a stressful situation.	Checking pulse or BP; reading about heart attacks; avoiding strenuous exercise; avoiding stress; use of beta blockers or tranquilizers.
Respiratory sensitivity	Breathing through a straw; voluntary hyperventilation; wearing nose clips while swimming; holding one's breath underwater.	Avoiding enclosed spaces; avoiding snorkeling; carrying inhalers; checking your breathing.
Loss of control sensitivity	Ingestion of stimulating herbs; standing the longest line of a department store; performing errands outside of the house without your cell phone.	Avoiding driving in the left-hand lane; avoiding traveling in other people's vehicles; checking for the presence of bathrooms and exits: checking one's thoughts; searching for stories about mental illness online
Social threat sensitivity	Impromptu speeches; feigning panic in public; intentionally volunteering a wrong answer in class.	Avoiding parties/social gatherings; reliance on alcohol or tranquilizers prior to social engagements; rehearsing conversations in advance; avoiding voicing your opinion in a group.

of the individual patient and will likely become clearer as treatment progresses and additional data are gathered over time. However, with respect to the question of which of the anxiety sensitivity profiles are most treatment responsive, my experience has been that although all four anxiety sensitivity profiles are modifiable, patients presenting with the cardiac or respiratory anxiety sensitivity profiles improve significantly more quickly than those presenting with either the social or loss of control profiles.

Are patients displaying multiple anxiety sensitivity profiles more challenging to treat? Probably so. Baseline total anxiety sensitivity scores have been recently shown to predict a less favorable response to CBT treatments for OCD (Blakey, Abramowitz, Reuman, Leonard, & Riemann, 2017). And, because scoring high on the ASI means greater elevations on multiple factors, one can infer that scoring high on multiple ASI factors is associated with a poorer outcome.

Beyond anxiety sensitivity

From its early beginnings (Reiss & McNally, 1985), the anxiety sensitivity construct has proved to be an important etiological factor in the development of anxiety pathology (Cobb, Lancaster, Meyer, Lee, & Telch, 2017; Schmidt et al., 2006) as well as an important mediator of therapeutic change (Smits et al., 2004). However, there is now growing support that other dispositional sensitivities conceptually distinct from anxiety sensitivity may also play a role in the onset and maintenance of certain forms of anxiety pathology and like anxiety sensitivity may be amenable to modification. Several of the more promising include *experiential avoidance* (Hayes et al., 1996), *thought-action fusion* (Shafran et al., 1996), *intolerance of uncertainty* (Ladouceur et al., 1997), and *cognitive fusion* (Gillanders et al., 2014). Although space limitations preclude describing these, the interested reader should consult the references provided above and give them serious consideration for inclusion as potentially valuable tools for the clinical assessment and case formulation of those with anxiety-related disorders.

Appendix: Texas Multifactor Anxiety Sensitivity Scale (TMASS)

Note: The TMASS is a theoretically derived instrument that is currently undergoing psychometric testing. Accordingly, items may be altered, added, or deleted in order to maximize measure performance.

Instructions: Listed here are various concerns that people sometimes have about anxiety and its effects. Read each statement carefully and then select the response that best reflects how much you agree with each statement.

TMASS scoring and interpretation

Scoring: Each item on the TMASS is rated on a 5-point scale (0 = not at all; 1 = a little; 2 = somewhat; 3 = moderate; and 4 = very much). The score for each of the five TMASS profiles (cardiac, respiratory, loss of control, social, and incapacitation) is calculated by averaging the score for each of the 4 items for each profile. Items for each profile are listed here.

Item breakdown of specific TMASS profiles

Cardiac profile = Items 1, 4, 10, 18

Respiratory profile = Items 11, 14, 16, 20

Loss of control profile = 6, 8, 13, 15

Social profile = 2, 5, 12, 19

Incapacitation profile = 3, 7, 9, 17

Score interpretation: Mean Scores between 1 and 2 for any of the five anxiety sensitivity Profile suggest mild sensitivity; Mean Scores between 2 and 3 suggest moderate sensitivity; and Mean Scores greater than 3 suggest severe sensitivity.

A profile specificity/pervasiveness index can be calculated using the following formula: (Mean TMASS Score (across all items)/Mean Score for the highest scoring Anxiety Sensitivity Profile) × 100. This index can range from 20% (Extreme Specificity) to 100% (Extreme Pervasiveness).

TMASS

Instructions: Listed below are various concerns that people sometimes have about anxiety its effects. Read each statement carefully and then select the response that best reflects how much you agree with each statement.

	Not at all	A little	Somewhat	Moderately	Very much
1. My anxiety may ultimately lead to a heart attack.	○	○	○	○	○
2. People will perceive me as weak because of my anxiety.	○	○	○	○	○
3. My anxiety may result in complete work disability.	○	○	○	○	○
4. My heart cannot handle the stress of so much anxiety.	○	○	○	○	○
5. My anxiety will lead me to embarrass myself in front of others.	○	○	○	○	○
6. Anxiety may eventually cause me to lose touch with reality.	○	○	○	○	○
7. Anxiety may cause me to lose my capacity to take care of myself.	○	○	○	○	○
8. My anxiety may reach a point where I will lose control of my senses and hurt myself or someone else.	○	○	○	○	○
9. My anxiety will makes it impossible for me to have a happy romantic relationship.	○	○	○	○	○
10. My anxiety may cause long-term damage to my heart.	○	○	○	○	○
11. My anxiety may get so bad that I won't be able to breathe.	○	○	○	○	○
12. Others will think I'm weird because of my anxiety.	○	○	○	○	○
13. My anxiety may cause me to eventually go insane.	○	○	○	○	○
14. When I become anxious, I sometimes worry that I may not be getting enough air.	○	○	○	○	○
15. Anxiety may cause me to lose control of my bladder or bowels.	○	○	○	○	○
16. Anxiety may cause my lungs to shut down.	○	○	○	○	○
17. My anxiety may ultimately result in my having to be institutionalized.	○	○	○	○	○
18. If I don't get my anxiety under control, my heart may give out.	○	○	○	○	○
19. My anxiety will lead others to lose respect for me.	○	○	○	○	○
20. My anxiety may become so intense that I might suffocate.	○	○	○	○	○

References

Alport, G. W. (1937). *Personality: A psychological interpretation*. New York: Holt.

Averill, J. R. (1973). Personal control over aversive stimuli and its relationship to stress. *Psychological Bulletin*, *80*(4), 286–303.

Blakey, S. M., Abramowitz, J. S., Reuman, L., Leonard, R. C., & Riemann, B. C. (2017). Anxiety sensitivity as a predictor of outcome in the treatment of obsessive-compulsive disorder. *Journal of Behavior Therapy and Experimental Psychiatry*, *57*, 113–117. https://doi.org/10.1016/j.jbtep.2017.05.003.

Clark, D. M., Butler, G., Fennell, M., Hackmann, A., McManus, F., & Wells, A. (1995). Social behaviour questionnaire. In *Oxford University*. Oxford: England (Unpublished manuscript).

Cobb, A. R., Lancaster, C. L., Meyer, E. C., Lee, H.-J., & Telch, M. J. (2017). Pre-deployment trait anxiety, anxiety sensitivity and experiential avoidance predict war-zone stress-evoked psychopathology. *Journal of Contextual Behavioral Science*, *6*(3), 276–287. https://doi.org/10.1016/j.jcbs.2017.05.002.

Dunn, B. D., Stefanovitch, I., Evans, D., Oliver, C., Hawkins, A., & Dalgleish, T. (2010). Can you feel the beat? Interoceptive awareness is an interactive function of anxiety- and depression-specific symptom dimensions. *Behaviour Research and Therapy*, *48*(11), 1133–1138. https://doi.org/10.1016/j.brat.2010.07.006.

Eifert, G. H., Thompson, R. N., Zvolensky, M. J., Edwards, K., Frazer, N. L., Haddad, J. W., & Davig, J. (2000). The cardiac anxiety questionnaire: development and preliminary validity. *Behaviour Research and Therapy*, *38*(10), 1039–1053.

Gillanders, D. T., Bolderston, H., Bond, F. W., Dempster, M., Flaxman, P. E., Campbell, L., et al. (2014). The development and initial validation of the Cognitive Fusion Questionnaire. *Behavior Therapy*, 45, 83–101. https://doi.org/10.1016/j.beth.2013.09.001.

Hayes, S. C., Wilson, K. G., Gifford, E. V., Follette, V. M., & Strosahl, K. (1996). Experiential avoidance and behavioral disorders: a functional dimensional approach to diagnosis and treatment. *Journal of Consulting and Clinical Psychology*, *64*(6), 1152–1168. https://doi.org/10.1037/0022-006X.64.6.1152.

Hirsch, C. R., Meynen, T., & Clark, D. M. (2004). Negative self-imagery in social anxiety contaminates social interactions. *Memory, Special Issue: Mental Imagery and Memory in Psychopathology*, *12*, 496–506.

Ingram, B. L. (2012). *Clinical case formulations: Matching the integrative treatment plan to the client* (2nd ed.). Hoboken, NJ: John Wiley & Sons.

Kamphuis, J. H., & Telch, M. J. (1998). Assessment of strategies to manage or avoid perceived threats among panic disorder patients: the Texas Safety Maneuver Scale (TSMS). *Clinical Psychology and Psychotherapy*, *5*, 177–186.

Kamphuis, J. H., & Telch, M. J. (2000). Effects of distraction and guided threat reappraisal on fear reduction during exposure-based treatments for specific fears. *Behaviour Research and Therapy*, *38*(12), 1163–1181.

Kraemer, H. C., Kazdin, A. E., Offord, D. R., et al. (1997). Coming to terms with the terms of risk. *Archives of General Psychiatry*, *54*(4), 337–343.

Ladouceur, R., Talbot, F., & Dugas, M. J. (1997). Behavioral expressions of intolerance of uncertainty in worry. Experimental findings. *Behavior Modification*, *21*(3), 355–371. https://doi.org/10.1177/01454455970213006.

Leary, M. R. (1983). A brief version of the fear of negative evaluation scale. *Personality and Social Psychology Bulletin*, *9*(3), 371–375. https://doi.org/10.1177/0146167283093007.

Ley, R. (1985). Agoraphobia, the panic attack and the hyperventilation syndrome. *Behaviour Research and Therapy*, *23*(1), 79–81.

Lilienfeld, S. O., Turner, S. M., & Jacob, R. G. (1993). Anxiety sensitivity: an examination of theoretical and methodological issues. *Advances in Behaviour Research and Therapy*, *15* (2), 147–183. https://doi.org/10.1016/0146-6402(93)90019-X.

Plasencia, M. L., Alden, L. E., & Taylor, C. T. (2011). Differential effects of safety behaviour subtypes in social anxiety disorder. *Behaviour Research and Therapy*, *49*(10), 665–675. https://doi.org/10.1016/j.brat.2011.07.005.

Rachman, S., & Taylor, S. (1993). Analyses of claustrophobia. *Journal of Anxiety Disorders*, *7* (4), 281–291. https://doi.org/10.1016/0887-6185(93)90025-G.

Reiss, S., & McNally, R. J. (1985). Expectancy model of fear. In S. Reiss & R. R. Bootzin (Eds.), *Theoretical issues in behavior therapy*. New York: Academic Press.

Schmidt, N. B., Schmidt, N. B., Lerew, D. R., & Jackson, R. J. (1997). The role of anxiety sensitivity in the pathogenesis of panic: prospective evaluation of spontaneous panic attacks during acute stress. *Journal of Abnormal Psychology*, *106*(3), 355–364.

Schmidt, N. B., Schmidt, N. B., Zvolensky, M. J., & Maner, J. K. (2006). Anxiety sensitivity: prospective prediction of panic attacks and Axis I pathology. *Journal of Psychiatric Research*, *40*(8), 691–699. http:/doi.org/10.1016/j.jpsychires.2006.07.009.

Shafran, R., Thordarson, D. S., & Rachman, S. (1996). Thought-action fusion in obsessive compulsive disorder. *Journal of Anxiety Disorders*, *10*(5), 379–391. https://doi.org/10.1016/0887-6185(96)00018-7.

Sloan, T., & Telch, M. J. (2002). The effects of safety-seeking behavior and guided threat reappraisal on fear reduction during exposure: an experimental investigation. *Behaviour Research and Therapy*, *40*(3), 235–251.

Smits, J. A. J., Powers, M. B., Cho, Y., & Telch, M. J. (2004). Mechanism of change in cognitive-behavioral treatment of panic disorder: evidence for the fear of fear mediational hypothesis. *Journal of Consulting and Clinical Psychology*, *72*(4), 646–652. https://doi.org/10.1037/0022-006X.72.4.646.

Taylor, S., & Cox, B. J. (1998). An expanded Anxiety Sensitivity Index: evidence for a hierarchic structure in a clinical sample. *Journal of Anxiety Disorders*, *12*, 463–484. https://doi.org/10.1016/S0887-6185(98)00028-0.

Taylor, S., Zvolensky, M. J., Cox, B. J., Deacon, B., Heimberg, R. G., Ledley, D. R., Abramowitz, J. S., et al. (2007). Robust dimensions of anxiety sensitivity: Development and initial validation of the Anxiety Sensitivity Index-3. *Psychological Assessment*, *19* (2), 176–188. https:/doi.org/10.1037/1040-3590.19.2.176.

Telch, M. J., Beevers, C. G., Rosenfield, D., Lee, H.-J., Reijntjes, A., Ferrell, R. E., & Hariri, A. R. (2015). 5-HTTLPR genotype potentiates the effects of war zone stressors on the emergence of PTSD, depressive and anxiety symptoms in soldiers deployed to Iraq. *World Psychiatry*, *14*(2), 198–206. http:/doi.org/10.1002/wps.20215.

Telch, M. J., Brouillard, M., Telch, C. F., Agras, W. S., & Taylor, C. B. (1989). Role of cognitive appraisal in panic-related avoidance. *Behaviour Research and Therapy*, *27*(4), 373–383.

Telch, M. J., Harrington, P. J., Smits, J. A. J., & Powers, M. B. (2011). Unexpected arousal, anxiety sensitivity, and their interaction on CO_2-induced panic: further evidence for the context-sensitivity vulnerability model. *Journal of Anxiety Disorders*, *25*(5), 645–653. https://doi.org/10.1016/j.janxdis.2011.02.005.

Telch, M. J., & Lancaster, C. L. (2012). Is there room for safety behaviors in exposure therapy for anxiety disorders? In P. Neudeck & H. U. Wittchen (Eds.), *Exposure therapy: Rethinking the model- Refining the method* (pp. 313–334). New York, NY: Springer.

Telch, M. J., Lucas, R. A., Smits, J. A., et al. (2004). Appraisal of social concerns: A cognitive assessment instrument for social phobia. *Depression and Anxiety*, *19*, 217–224.

Telch, M. J., Silverman, A., & Schmidt, N. B. (1996). Effects of anxiety sensitivity and perceived control on emotional responding to caffeine challenge. *Journal of Anxiety Disorders*, *10*(1), 21–35. https://doi.org/10.1016/0887-6185(95)00032-1.

Telch, M. J., Smits, J. A. J., Brown, M., Dement, M., Powers, M. B., Lee, H., & Pai, A. (2010). Effects of threat context and cardiac sensitivity on fear responding to a 35% CO_2 challenge: a test of the context-sensitivity panic vulnerability model. *Journal of Behavior Therapy and Experimental Psychiatry*, *41*(4), 365–372. https://doi.org/10.1016/j.jbtep.2010.03.008.

Telch, M. J., & Zaizar, E. D. (in press). Safety behaviors. In J. S. Abramowitz & S. M. Blakey (Eds.), *Clinical handbook of fear and anxiety: Psychological processes and treatment mechanisms*. Washington DC: American Psychological Association Press.

Tellegen, A. (1991). Personality traits: issues of definition, evidence, and assessment. In D. Cicchetti & W. M. Grove (Eds.), *Thinking clearly about psychology: Essays in honor of Paul E. Meehl*. Minneapolis: University of Minnesota Press.

Thomas, M., McKinley, R. K., Freeman, E., Foy, C., & Price, D. (2005). The prevalence of dysfunctional breathing in adults in the community with and without asthma. *Primary Care Respiratory Journal*, *14*(2), 78–82. https://doi.org/10.1016/j.pcrj.2004.10.007.

Valentiner, D. P., Telch, M. J., Petruzzi, D. C., & Bolte, M. C. (1996). Cognitive mechanisms in claustrophobia: an examination of Reiss and McNally's expectancy model and Bandura's self-efficacy theory. *Cognitive Therapy and Research*, *20*(6), 593–612. https://doi.org/10.1007/BF02227963.

Treating anxiety sensitivity in adults with anxiety and related disorders

4

Steven Taylor
University of British Columbia, Vancouver, BC, Canada

Chapter Outline

Introduction

Empirical and conceptual foundations

Anxiety sensitivity is the fear of arousal-related bodily sensations, arising from beliefs about the meaning of the sensations (Reiss, 1999). People with high levels of anxiety sensitivity tend to believe that arousal-related bodily sensations are dangerous. They

The Clinician's Guide to Anxiety Sensitivity Treatment and Assessment. https://doi.org/10.1016/B978-0-12-813495-5.00004-8

tend to harbor beliefs such as "If my heart beats rapidly, it means that I might be having a heart attack," or "If my hands tremble, people will reject me," or "If I feel lightheaded, it means that I might have a brain tumor." People with low levels of anxiety sensitivity tend to believe that arousal-related sensations such as palpitations, trembling, or lightheadedness are harmless and inconsequential.

Anxiety sensitivity is conceptualized as an amplification factor that exacerbates anxiety, panic, and other forms of distress (Reiss, Peterson, Gursky, & McNally, 1986). To illustrate, by becoming anxious about arousal-related bodily sensations, the sensations themselves become amplified and anxiety escalates. Accumulating evidence indicates that anxiety sensitivity is a predisposing factor for many different types of psychopathology. Research shows that anxiety sensitivity is most strongly related to panic disorder and posttraumatic stress disorder, but also tends to be elevated in other anxiety and related disorders (Naragon-Gainey, 2010; Olatunji & Wolitzky-Taylor, 2009; Schmidt et al., 2010; Schmidt, Lerew, & Jackson, 1997, 1999).

Anxiety sensitivity, as assessed by contemporary instruments such as the Anxiety Sensitivity Index-3 (ASI-3; Reiss, Peterson, Taylor, Schmidt, & Weems, 2008; Taylor et al., 2007), tends to be stable (trait-like) in the absence of treatment (Farris et al., 2015; Mantar, Yemez, & Alkin, 2010; Sandin, Valiente, Chorot, & Santed, 2007; Taylor et al., 2007; Wang et al., 2014). However, the severity of a person's anxiety sensitivity can be reduced by various interventions. Thus, anxiety sensitivity is a modifiable risk factor for anxiety-related psychopathology. It is of transdiagnostic relevance in that elevated scores on anxiety sensitivity or its factors is associated with a range of psychiatric disorders. Normative data (means, SDs) on the ASI-3 are presented in Table 1.

Behavioral-genetic (twin) studies show that individual differences in anxiety sensitivity are the result of a combination of genetic and environmental factors (Brown et al., 2012; Taylor, Jang, Stewart, & Stein, 2008). The genetic factors are additive in nature rather than being dominance effects. That is, it appears likely that numerous

Table 1 Means (and SDs) on the Anxiety Sensitivity Index-3 subscales and total score

Sample	*N*	Physical concerns	Cognitive concerns	Social concerns	Total score
Normal controls	4720	4 (4)	3 (4)	6 (5)	13 (11)
Panic disorder	120	11 (7)	9 (6)	12 (6)	33 (14)
Obsessive-compulsive disorder	102	8 (6)	8 (6)	10 (7)	26 (17)
Social anxiety disorder	38	6 (5)	8 (6)	17 (5)	31 (12)
Generalized anxiety disorder	30	8 (5)	9 (7)	11 (7)	28 (17)

Source: Reprinted from Taylor, S., Zvolensky, M. J., Cox, B. J., Deacon, B., Heimberg, R. G., Ledley, D. R., ... Cardenas, S. J. (2007). Robust dimensions of anxiety sensitivity: development and initial validation of the Anxiety Sensitivity Index-3. *Psychological Assessment, 19*, 176–188, with permission from American Psychological Association.

genes, each with small effects, incrementally add to the person's risk for having high anxiety sensitivity. The actual genes (polymorphisms) involved in anxiety sensitivity are currently unknown. Such genes likely play a role in the brain structures involved in the processing of threat, such as the anterior cingulate cortex, medial prefrontal cortex, and insula. Neuroimaging research suggests that a person's level of anxiety sensitivity is positively correlated with the degree of activation of these structures when a person is present with threat-related stimuli (Holtz, Pane-Farre, Wendt, Lotze, & Hamm, 2012; Poletti et al., 2015).

With regard to the environmental factors involved in anxiety sensitivity, learning experiences may play a role, especially those experiences that cause a person to believe that arousal-related sensations are dangerous (Knapp, Frala, Blumenthal, Badour, & Leen-Feldner, 2013; Stewart et al., 2001; Watt, Stewart, & Cox, 1998).

Rationale for targeting anxiety sensitivity in treatment

If anxiety sensitivity is a vulnerability factor for various forms of psychopathology, particularly anxiety disorders and related clinical conditions, then the risk of developing these disorders can be reduced by identifying people with high anxiety sensitivity and then encouraging them to complete an anxiety sensitivity reduction program (see Chapter 1).

For people presenting to tertiary care clinics for treatment of anxiety or related disorders, anxiety sensitivity-reduction interventions might be an important part of their treatment. Anxiety sensitivity reduction might not be sufficient for the person's presenting problems, but might play an important role. For example, in the treatment of panic disorder with agoraphobia, anxiety sensitivity-reduction exercises could be implemented (e.g., interoceptive exposure), combined with a series of exposure exercises to reduce agoraphobic avoidance (Taylor, 2000).

Several different types of transdiagnostic vulnerability factors have been identified, of which anxiety sensitivity is one (Boswell et al., 2013; Norton & Paulus, 2017). Others include perfectionism (Limburg, Watson, Hagger, & Egan, 2016), intolerance of distress (Wolitzky-Taylor et al., 2016), and intolerance of uncertainty (Jensen, Cohen, Mennin, Fresco, & Heimberg, 2016). These factors can interact with one another (e.g., Allan, Macatee, Norr, & Schmidt, 2014). For patients in which there is evidence of multiple transdiagnostic vulnerability factors, an intervention for reducing anxiety sensitivity might be one of several interventions that are implemented.

Historical perspective

Historically, anxiety sensitivity-related treatment development and evaluation has proceeded in three overlapping phases. In the first phase, cognitive-behavior therapy (CBT) was developed for specific disorders, such as CBT for panic disorder (Beck, 1988; Beck & Emery, 1985; Clark, 1989). Anxiety sensitivity reduction exercises—consisting of psychoeducation, cognitive restructuring, and interoceptive exposure, and situation exposure—were included as part of the CBT package for panic disorder.

It later became apparent that there were psychological vulnerability factors and interventions that were common to many different kinds of emotional disorders. This led to the development and evaluation of transdiagnostic forms of CBT (Barlow et al., 2011;

Mansell, Carey, & Tai, 2013; Norton, 2012). As discussed earlier in this chapter, anxiety sensitivity is considered to be a transdiagnostic vulnerability factor. Accordingly, interventions for reducing anxiety sensitivity were included in transdiagnostic CBT (Boswell et al., 2013). A number of transdiagnostic treatment protocols have been developed in which the same protocol is used to treat patients with any of a range of anxiety disorders and comorbid clinical conditions. The rationale is that many different disorders are influenced by transdiagnostic etiological factors (e.g., anxiety sensitivity) and that the interventions used to treat these factors (e.g., interoceptive exposure) can therefore be beneficial for a range of clinical conditions, including comorbid cases. The most widely studied transdiagnostic treatment is the unified protocol developed by Barlow and colleagues (Barlow et al., 2011), which was developed to treat anxiety disorders and unipolar mood disorders, although it can also be applied to other clinical conditions such as somatoform disorders. The protocol, administered individually or in groups, includes interoceptive exposure (up to 4 sessions) as one of the components of this 18-session protocol. The unified protocol, particularly its interoceptive exposure component, leads to a reduction in anxiety sensitivity (Boswell et al., 2013). For a range of anxiety disorders, a growing number of treatment studies support the efficacy of this protocol (e.g., Bullis et al., 2015; Ellard, Fairholme, Boisseau, Farchione, & Barlow, 2010; Farchione et al., 2012; Reinholt et al., 2017). Little is known about the importance of interoceptive exposure as compared to other components in the unified protocol. Theoretically, interceptive exposure is most likely to be beneficial for those patients who have elevated anxiety sensitivity. Accordingly, interoceptive exposure should be relevant to many, but not all, patients with emotional disorders.

The third phase involved the development of brief (e.g., 1 session) interventions that specifically targeted anxiety sensitivity. These were developed for people who had high levels of anxiety sensitivity but did not necessarily have a mental disorder. The goal of these programs was preventative; that is, to reduce the risk of high anxiety sensitivity people developing disorders in the future.

Meta-analytic research shows that CBT in its various forms, as compared to control conditions, reduces anxiety sensitivity, both in treatment-seeking samples (e.g., samples of patients seeking treatment for anxiety disorders) and in prevention studies of at-risk samples (e.g., samples of people with high anxiety sensitivity and therefore at risk for developing future psychopathology) (Smits, Berry, Tart, & Powers, 2008).

The focus of this chapter is on the treatment of adults presenting for treatment of anxiety and related disorders in which anxiety sensitivity interventions are relevant. A discussion of anxiety sensitivity interventions for the purpose of disorder prevention appears in this chapter and the assessment of anxiety sensitivity is discussed in Chapter 2.

Interventions for panic disorder

Psychoeducation

Patient education, also known as psychoeducation, is the first step toward correcting misconceptions and filling information gaps that the patient has about the nature and treatment of anxiety sensitivity and panic disorder. This corrective information can be

Table 2 Psychoeducational handout

What is anxiety sensitivity?
Anxiety sensitivity is the fear of arousal-related bodily sensations. *What are arousal-related sensations?* These sensations occur when your body is stressed, exerted by physical exercise, or stimulated by substances such as coffee. The sensations include rapid heartbeat, sweating, dizziness, and trembling. The sensations are *harmless* although some people are frightened of the sensations. *Why are some people frightened of these sensations?* A person's beliefs about the sensations influence whether or not they are afraid of the sensations. Here are some examples. Jim has *high anxiety sensitivity*. He believes that harmless arousal-related sensations are dangerous. One morning, Jim drank a lot of coffee before going to work. As a result of having so much coffee his heart began to race. That is, Jim was experiencing arousal-related bodily sensations. Jim began to worry about his racing heart. He worried that "If my heart races too fast then I might have a heart attack and die." This made Jim really frightened. As a result, his heart race even faster, to the point that he had a panic attack. Karen has *low anxiety sensitivity*. She believes that arousal-related sensations are harmless. One lunchtime Karen drank a lot of coffee before heading back to work. As a result of all the coffee, Karen's heart began to race. She thought to herself, "Hmm, my heart is racing. I guess I've had too much coffee. No big deal." These examples show how a person's belief's about their bodily sensations can influence how they feel. Jim was frightened about his racing heart and thought that he might be having a heart attack. As a result of becoming increasingly frightened, his heart raced even faster, to the point that he panicked. Karen, in comparison, was not concerned about her racing heart. She did not become anxious and so her heart rate did not increase. *Why is anxiety sensitivity important?* High anxiety sensitivity can amplify or worsen anxiety symptoms and can cause panic attacks. Panic attacks are harmless but nevertheless very uncomfortable anxiety reactions. Most people with panic disorder have high levels of anxiety sensitivity. *Is your anxiety sensitivity high or low?* Your therapist can help you answer that question by talking with you and by asking you to complete some psychological tests. If you have high anxiety sensitivity, ask your therapist about the various scientifically proven options for reducing your anxiety sensitivity.

presented during the first few sessions, along with patient handouts and other materials for the patient to read between therapy sessions. The information can be revisited as needed throughout treatment. Table 2 presents a short patient handout that explains and illustrates the concept of anxiety sensitivity. The handout is intentionally brief and written in simple terms, so that it can be understood by people from a range of educational backgrounds. The therapist should check the patient's understanding of such handouts and expand and clarify on the material as necessary.

Cognitive restructuring

Cognitive restructuring of arousal-related beliefs is based on the general principles of cognitive therapy (e.g., Beck, 1988; Beck & Emery, 1985; Clark & Beck, 2010). Cognitive restructuring, which builds on psychoeducation, entails several methods applied in the context of a collaborative relationship between patient and therapist. Several different types of cognitive restructuring can be implemented. Examples are as follows.

Empirical disputes. These are exercises in which the patient and therapist review the available evidence for and against the patient's catastrophic beliefs. Evidence is collected from the patient's own past experiences and from other sources. For each catastrophic belief, the therapist and patient develop an innocuous, plausible, and accurate alternative belief statement (Salkovskis & Clark, 1991). The evidence for and against each belief is then listed. There are several questions that patients can ask themselves to facilitate this process:

- What evidence do I have for this belief?
- Are my beliefs based on facts?
- Is there another explanation or alternative way of looking at things?

The example in Table 3 illustrates the evidence for and against a catastrophic belief and its noncatastrophic alternative. Once a list like this is generated, the patient and therapist review the evidence to decide which belief is best supported.

Challenging beliefs by reviewing the sensations. To develop realistic interpretations of feared sensations, the patient and therapist can review the differences between the symptoms of potentially hazardous events versus the symptoms of harmless events. The patient's personal experience can be used to make this distinction. Ms. D. had a history of recurrent panic attacks in which dizziness was the sensation she feared the most. She catastrophically misinterpreted dizziness as a sign that she was about to faint, which (she believed) would cause her to fall, hit her head, and die. A noncatastrophic alternative belief was that the dizziness was due to stress-induced acute hyperventilation, which would not lead to fainting. To discriminate between the symptoms of hyperventilation versus fainting, Ms. D. was asked to recall an episode in which she had fainted, and then to compare this experience to the way she felt when she was dizzy and panicking. The two differed primarily in that a feeling of sleepiness occurred just before she fainted, but never occurred when she was dizzy and panicking. A further distinction was that palpitations occurred when she was dizzy and panicking, but not on the occasion when she actually fainted. This information helped Ms. D. develop more accurate beliefs about her dizziness (e.g., "If my heart is pounding and I'm not feeling sleepy, then I'm not going to faint"). This intervention was supplemented by corrective information. The therapist informed her that fainting is associated with a drop in blood pressure, whereas panic is associated with an increase in blood pressure. Thus, if her dizziness occurred while she was anxious or panicky, her blood pressure would be increased, not decreased (Clark, 1989).

Challenging the components of catastrophic beliefs. Catastrophic beliefs can be challenged by breaking them down into components, such as overestimations of the *probability* and overestimations of the *cost* (badness) of unpleasant events. The components are then challenged separately. Whenever Mr. C. felt dizzy in a department store, he overestimated the probability of collapsing. He also overestimated how bad it would be if he did collapse. Mr. C. believed that if he did collapse, then (a) he

Table 3 Cognitive restructuring exercise: evidence for and against a catastrophic belief and its noncatastrophic alternative

	Evidence for belief	Evidence against belief
Catastrophic belief: My bouts of chest pain indicate that there is something seriously wrong with my heart	• Heart disease runs in families; my father died of a heart attack and therefore I could have something wrong with my heart. • The pain is in my chest and arms, which is what happens when people have heart attacks.	• I've had extensive medical evaluations. All the tests indicate that my heart is healthy. • If the pain is due to heart disease, then it should get worse when I exert myself. Yet, my pain tends to go away when I exercise. • Pain location is not a reliable indicator of its cause. All sorts of things can cause pain in the chest and arms, including muscle spasms.
Noncatastrophic alternative belief: My chest pain is due to harmless, stress-related tension in my chest muscles	• The pain tends to get worse after I've been feeling stressed out. • The pain eases off when I'm focusing on things I enjoy, such as when I'm watching a good movie. • The pain gets worse when I worry about my heart. Worry causes muscle tension, not heart attacks.	• Sometimes the pain occurs even when I'm not feeling stressed. (But the pain could be a carryover effect from a prior stressful episode.)

would definitely injure himself, and (b) everyone would think he collapsed because he had some serious disease and would avoid him thereafter.

There are several strategies for challenging these overestimations (e.g., Craske, Meadows, & Barlow, 1994; Taylor, 2000). The therapist can guide the patient to examine questions such as these:

- Am I overestimating how likely ____ would be? Has it happened in the past?
- Realistically, how bad would it be if ____ occurred? Am I overestimating how bad things would be?

- Am I overestimating how long ____ would last? Can I cope with a few minutes of ____ in my day? (These questions are particularly helpful for patients who fail to realize that intense arousal sensations or panic attacks are short-lived events.)
- Am I exaggerating how uncomfortable ____ would be? Have I been able to tolerate discomfort in the past? (These questions are useful when patients catastrophize about the unpleasantness of body sensations or panic attacks.)

Another useful strategy for challenging overestimations is to evaluate whether the patient's belief in the probability of a feared event is consistent with his or her past experience (Craske et al., 1994). For example, a patient might believe that the odds of having a heart attack if she experienced palpitations were 1 in 100. Yet, if the patient is asked to estimate the number of times that she has experienced derealization, she might come to realize that she has had thousands of episodes of palpitations, all without harmful consequences.

Cognitive interventions typically entail some form of homework. Patients might complete a workbook summarizing the session's material, or make notes from an audiotape of the session. Other written assignments are also commonly completed as homework, where, for example, the patient might write out a disputation of a catastrophic belief and consider the evidence for a noncatastrophic alternative. Cognitive interventions are most commonly used in conjunction with behavioral exercises such as interoceptive exposure. The combination of the two increases the odds that treatment will reduce anxiety sensitivity-related catastrophic beliefs. For details of the potential ordering and integration of these interventions, see Taylor (2000).

Interoceptive exposure

Interoceptive exposure exercises are designed to induce arousal-related body sensations. The goals of interoceptive exposure are to: (a) produce potent tests of catastrophic beliefs, (b) help patients discover the likely noncatastrophic causes of their feared sensations, and (c) test whether patients' coping strategies (e.g., safety behaviors) ameliorate or exacerbate their problems.

The exercises are performed in the therapist's office and then as homework assignments. The patient plays an active role in choosing what exposure exercises to attempt and when to attempt them. These exercises are set up as "no lose" assignments; something important is learned regardless of the outcome. The exercises also can be used as behavioral experiments, in which they are performed over several trials until corrective learning takes place. The choice of exercise depends on which sensations they evoke. Exercises that induce a given sensation (e.g., dizziness) are used to test beliefs about that sensation (e.g., "Dizziness leads to physical collapse").

Table 4 provides a summary of interoceptive exposure exercises commonly used in treatment, and examples of beliefs they can test. Table 5 provides a list of potential contraindications. If there is any doubt about the safety of a given intervention for a given patient, then either the exercise should not be used or the patient's treating physician should be consulted. The exercises are usually practiced repeatedly in the therapy session and as homework. A patient might perform, for example, three trials of

Table 4 Interoceptive exposure exercises

Examples of exercises	Examples of catastrophic beliefs that can be tested[a]
Shake head rapidly from side to side, or roll head in circles (30 s)	"Dizziness leads to insanity"
Place head between knees for 30 s and then lift head quickly up to a normal (upright) position	"When I feel lightheaded it means I could be having a stroke"
Spin around while standing up with arms stretched out (1 min)	"I will throw up if I let myself feel nauseous"
Hold breath (30 s)	"Chest tightness means I'm having a heart attack"
Hyperventilate (1 min)	"If I start to feel unsteady it means I will physically collapse"
Breathe through a narrow straw without breathing through nose (2 min)	"Choking sensations are dangerous"
Stare continuously at a ceiling fluorescent light (1 min)	"If my surroundings start to look weird it means I'm going mad"
Stare continuously at reflection in mirror (2 min)	"If I let myself feel spacey I could permanently lose touch with reality"
Stare continuously at spot on wall or at one's hand (3 min)	"Feeling unreal is a sign that I'm having a stroke"
Stare for 3 min at a visual grid that induces visual illusions (e.g., https:/en.wikipedia.org/wiki/Grid_illusion)	"Staring at visual illusions or other unsettling images could tip me over the edge into permanent insanity.
Tense all muscles in body while sitting in a chair (1 min)	"People will laugh at me if I start to tremble"
Jog on the spot or run up stairs (1 min)	"I will have a heart attack if my heart starts pounding"
Face a heater, hair dryer, or hand dryer: heater blowing hot air at the face (5 min)	"People will ridicule me if they see I'm having hot flushes"
Tongue depressor: place tongue depressor at back of throat (30 s)	"If my stomach gets upset I'll vomit uncontrollably"
Drink hot coffee (2–3 cups)	"I could go crazy if I get too jittery"
To induce throat tightness, one can ask the patient to start to swallow and then hold the throat in the "midswallow" position for 5–10 s.	"If my throat feels tight it means I'm about to choke to death"
To induce chest pain, ask the patient to interlock their fingers and place hands behind the head while stretching the elbows backwards. The patient then takes a deep breath and then tries to chest breath at a rate of 1 breath/s for 1 min.	"Chest pain means I'm having a heart attack"

[a]These exercises are also used to test noncatastrophic alternative explanations of the sensations; e.g., "Palpitations are simply due to my lack of physical fitness."

Source: Reprinted from Taylor, S. (2000). *Understanding and treating panic disorder: Cognitive-behavioural approaches*. New York: Wiley, with permission from Wiley and Sons.

Table 5 Potential contraindications for using interoceptive exposure exercises

Exercise	Potential contraindication
Shake or roll head	Cervical pain or disease (e.g., whiplash injury), history of falling due to dizziness or balance disorder.[a]
Place head between knees and stand up	Postural hypotension, lower-back pain, history of falling due to dizziness or balance disorder.[a]
Spin around	Pregnancy, history of falling due to dizziness or balance disorder.[a]
Hold breath	Chronic obstructive lung disease.
Hyperventilate	Chronic obstructive lung disease, severe asthma, cardiac conditions, epilepsy, renal disease, pregnancy.
Breath through a narrow straw	Chronic obstructive pulmonary disease.
Stare at fluorescent light	History of seizures caused by staring at flickering lights.
Stare at reflection in mirror	No apparent contraindications.
Stare at spot on wall or at one's hand	No apparent contraindications.
Stare at a visual grid that induces visual illusions	History of seizures or migraine headaches (these can be triggered by the grids)
Tense all muscles	Pain disorders. If pain is localized, patients could tense all but the afflicted region.
Jog on the spot or run up stairs	Cardiac conditions, severe asthma, lower-back pain, pregnancy.
Heater blowing hot air at face	No apparent contraindications.
Tongue depressor at back of throat	Prominent gag reflex (stimulation of which will induce vomiting).
Drink hot coffee	History of severe insomnia.
Hold throat in "midswallow"	Prominent gag reflex.
Hands behind head while stretching elbows backwards	Chronic obstructive pulmonary disease, severe asthma, cardiac conditions, epilepsy, pregnancy, pain disorders. If pain is localized, patients could tense all but the afflicted region.

[a]Some forms of vertigo habituate to these exercises.
Source: Reprinted from Taylor, S. (2000). *Understanding and treating panic disorder: Cognitive-behavioural approaches*. New York: Wiley, with permission from Wiley and Sons.

two of these exercises in a 60-min treatment session (six trials in all), and then practice the six trials four times in the following week.

Most of the exercises in Table 4 are self-explanatory, although the procedure for conducting the hyperventilation exercise requires some comment. It is among the most commonly used exercises because it induces a host of arousal-related sensations. Patients are asked to pant deeply and vigorously through the mouth and nose at a rate of 1–2 breaths/s. Predominantly upper-chest movement is necessary to maintain a high rate of respiration. This can be demonstrated by the therapist. In later trials, the effects of the hyperventilation can be enhanced by having the patient overbreathe while standing up with their eyes closed. The standing position introduces new sensations (e.g., body sway), which can be useful in testing catastrophic beliefs (e.g., "Unsteadiness leads to physical collapse").

Homework exposure exercises are presented to patients as important elements of treatment. Homework should be reviewed in each session and any difficulties should be addressed. Homework assignments should be clearly explained beforehand so that the patient and therapist can determine afterwards whether or not the tasks were completed. Patients should be reinforced (and encouraged to self-reinforce) for their efforts. Patients are advised to practice the exercises regularly, regardless of how they feel. They should attempt the exercises even on "bad days," when they might feel particularly anxious or panicky. Indeed, exercises can be most fruitful when conducted on those days (e.g., "Even when I was feeling really anxious, I still didn't go crazy when I hyperventilated").

Adherence can be improved by asking patients to record each exercise on a homework rating form. On the form the patient notes the day the exercise was attempted, its duration, peak anxiety (0 – 100), and the predictions derived from the catastrophic belief and its noncatastrophic alternative. The patient can also note on the form what they learned from each exercise.

Naturalistic interoceptive exercises

Naturalistic interoceptive exposure refers to exposure to daily tasks or activities that have been avoided or endured with dread because of the associated sensations (Craske & Barlow, 1993). The following is a list of examples (from Taylor, 2000) that can be set as homework assignments.

- Wear several layers of clothes on a warm day (to induce hot flushes, sweating, and palpitations).
- Wear a tight collar or necktie (to induce choking sensations).
- Watch arousing videos at home (e.g., thrillers or horror films).
- Take a hot shower with the windows and doors closed and the ventilation fan turned off (dyspnea, choking and smothering sensations, chest tightness).
- Drink 2–3 cups of strong, hot coffee at home (trembling, palpitations, hot flushes, sweating).
- Perform activities that intensify sensations *during* naturally occurring panic attacks (e.g., deliberately hyperventilate, focus on one's body, run up a flight of stairs). By increasing the intensity of panic sensations, the activities provide strong tests of beliefs about the consequences of arousal-related sensations.
- Participate in an exercise program; e.g., cycling, jogging, exercise classes (aerobics or weight training), dancing classes, swimming classes, or water aerobics. These activities induce a variety of arousal-related sensations, such as palpitations and dyspnea. Water aerobics is useful for patients whose physical condition prevents them from participating in other exercise programs (i.e., conditions such as joint diseases, lower back pain, or severe obesity). Exercise programs not only disconfirm catastrophic beliefs (e.g., "My heart is weak") but also are very useful for testing the noncatastrophic alternative that the feared sensations are due to lack of physical fitness (e.g., "I'm short of breath because I'm out of shape"). If the noncatastrophic alternative is accurate, then the sensations should abate as fitness improves. Evidence shows that even brief exercise programs are able to reduce

anxiety sensitivity (Fetzner & Asmundson, 2015; LeBouthillier & Asmundson, 2015; Medina et al., 2014; Sabourin et al., 2008; Sabourin, Watt, Krigolson, & Stewart, 2016; Smits, Berry, Rosenfield, et al., 2008).

Situational exposure

Situational exposure is the treatment of choice for phobic disorders (e.g., agoraphobia, specific phobia) (Abramowitz, Deacon, & Whiteside, 2011). For people with such disorders, situational exposure has the added benefit that it also reduces anxiety sensitivity (Taylor, 2000). In situational exposure, the patient repeatedly encounters feared external stimuli (objects or places) in order to challenge maladaptive beliefs about these situations, such as beliefs about catastrophic outcomes (e.g., dying, going crazy, losing control). The situations are typically those in which patients believe they would panic (e.g., crossing bridges or tunnels), or situations in which they believe it would be dangerous or embarrassing to panic (e.g., "I would make a fool of myself if I panicked in the grocery store," "I could crash the car if I panicked on the freeway").

The distinction between "situational exposure" and "naturalistic interoceptive exposure" is arbitrary but clinically useful. Both entail some degree of exposure to arousal-related sensations. They differ in the intent of the exercise and, to some degree, in the nature of the experience. Interoceptive exposure is designed to induce intense arousal-related sensations. Situational exposure emphasizes encounters with situations that are feared and avoided, regardless of whether the situations induce intense sensations. The distinction between the two types of exposure is useful to underscore the fact that it important to reduce patient's fear and avoidance of *situations* in which the feared sensations might occur. Extended discussions of how to conduct situational exposure appear elsewhere (Abramowitz et al., 2011; Taylor, 2000).

Eliminating safety signals and safety behaviors

Safety signals are stimuli that the person associates with the absence of feared outcomes. Safety signals include medicine containers, cellular phones, and good luck charms. *Safety behaviors* are things the person does to ward off feared events. Such behaviors include escape, avoidance, and other "coping" behaviors. Safety signals and safety behaviors can prevent catastrophic beliefs from being disconfirmed; e.g., "If I hadn't distracted myself, my anxiety would have escalated to the point that I'd have gone crazy." Safety signals and behaviors are often related to one another; a cellular phone can be a safety signal, and making a call to a significant other can be a safety behavior.

By definition, interoceptive and situational exposure lead the patient to eliminate the more obvious safety behaviors (i.e., frank escape or avoidance) and to eliminate the more prominent safety signals (e.g., presence of a trusted companion). However, this may not eliminate the more subtle safety signals and behaviors. There are a great many of these that could be used in any given situation. A person frightened of showering with the doors and windows closed, for example, might take a cool drink, anxiolytic medication, or cellular phone into the bathroom because these things confer (for him or her) a sense of safety. Safety signals and behaviors are important to eliminate from all kinds of exposure—interoceptive, situational, and their combination.

Applications to other disorders

Anxiety sensitivity-reducing interventions were developed for, and extensively evaluated with, panic disorder. More recently, researchers have begun to investigate how anxiety sensitivity interventions can be based applied to other disorders.

Posttraumatic stress disorder (PTSD)

Given that research indicates that anxiety sensitivity is elevated in PTSD (as described earlier), this suggests that interoceptive exposure may play a useful role in treating PTSD. That is, interoceptive exposure reduces anxiety sensitivity, which in turn was hypothesized to reduce PTSD symptoms, particularly hyperarousal symptoms. Interoceptive exposure was also hypothesized to facilitate trauma-related exposure (for a description of the latter, see (Taylor, 2017). That is, it can be difficult to conduct trauma-related exposure if the person is highly fearful of arousal sensations. Accordingly, by reducing anxiety sensitivity, it becomes easier for the patient to complete a course of trauma-related exposure. Research from our investigations (Wald & Taylor, 2007, 2008, 2010; Wald, Taylor, Chiri, & Sica, 2010) and other studies (reviewed in Taylor, 2017) suggest that interoceptive exposure is useful in the treatment of PTSD. Interoceptive exposure for PTSD proceeds in much the same way as it does for panic disorder. The exception is that for PTSD, interoceptive exposure sometimes triggers trauma-related memories. Examples are as follows (from Wald & Taylor, 2008): In one patient, the breath-holding exercise triggered memories of childhood abuse in which she, as a child, hid in a closet and held her breath, hoping not to be discovered by her drunken, abusive father. Jogging on the spot or running up stairs triggers memories of running away from an abusive parent in another patient. A tongue depressor on the back of the throat triggered memories of being choked during a sexual assault. In such cases, interoceptive exposure would appear to serve a dual purpose; it can reduce anxiety sensitivity and can serve as a form of trauma-related exposure therapy to help reduce the patient's distress about trauma-related memories (for further details, see Taylor, 2017).

Obsessive-compulsive disorder (OCD)

Little is known about the role and utility of anxiety sensitivity-reduction interventions in OCD. Case reports suggest that interoceptive exposure can play a useful role in the cognitive-behavioral treatment of OCD (Blakey & Abramowitz, 2017). For example, interventions targeting the cognitive dyscontrol facet of anxiety sensitivity (harboring beliefs such as "If my mind races, it means I'm losing control and going crazy") may be useful, especially for patients who worry about acting on their unwanted intrusive thoughts. Interoceptive exercises also can be helpful in reducing distress during exposure therapy for OCD (i.e., exposure and response prevention), as in PTSD treatment.

Social anxiety disorder (SAD)

The anxiety sensitivity social-concerns facet can be targeted in the treatment of SAD. Many of the interoceptive exposure tasks in Table 4 (e.g., hyperventilation) elicit publicly observable anxiety reactions, such as facial flushing and sweating, and evoke distress in people with SAD (Collimore & Asmundson, 2014; Dixon, Kemp, Farrell, Blakey, & Deacon, 2015).

Specific phobias

Case reports suggest that emetophobia (fear of vomiting) can be successfully treated by CBT protocols that include interoceptive exposure exercises that induce gastrointestinal discomfort (eating beyond feeling full) and other exercises that evoke gastrointestinal, cardiovascular, and respiratory sensations that triggered a patient's fear of vomiting (e.g., hyperventilating, wearing a heavy sweater so that one felt hot) (Boettcher, Brake, & Barlow, 2016; Hunter & Antony, 2009). Similarly, specific phobias of choking can be treated by using interoceptive exposure tasks that trigger the gag reflex, such as the use of a tongue depressor, rapid swallowing, or hold swallow in mid-action (e.g., Ball & Otto, 1994).

Other clinical problems

Interoceptive exposure exercises can be readily adapted and applied to a range of clinical conditions, with the choice of exposure exercises limited only by the therapist's ingenuity. For example, in a case series of patients presenting for treatment of depersonalization, McKay and Moretz (2008) used 3D glasses to induce depersonalization as an interoceptive exposure exercise. Other interoceptive exercises such as hyperventilation also can produce depersonalization and derealization (see Lickel, Nelson, Lickel, & Deacon, 2008).

Interoceptive exposure exercises can similarly be applied to a host of other anxiety-related problems (e.g., health anxiety and fear of pain) and can be used in smoking cessation programs in which patients have difficulty tolerating the discomfort associated with withdrawal symptoms (Otto, 2008; Walker & Furer, 2008; Zvolensky, Bogiaizian, Salazar, Farris, & Bakhshaie, 2014). Interoceptive exposure can also reduce alcohol consumption in high anxiety sensitivity people who drink in order to cope with anxiety (Olthuis, Watt, Mackinnon, & Stewart, 2015).

Troubleshooting for anxiety sensitivity-reduction interventions

Adherence problems

Adherence problems are the most common difficulties encountered when using interoceptive and situational exposure. Patients may refuse to perform the exercises. Other, more subtle, adherence problems consist of using distraction during the exercise, or limiting the intensity or duration of exposure; for example; a patient might avoid deep, rapid breathing during a hyperventilation exercise, and may stop the task as soon as any sensations are noticed. The best strategy for dealing with adherence problems is to avoid them before they occur. The following can help avoid these difficulties:

- Ensure that patients know why the exercises are important. Periodically check their understanding.
- The interventions should not be too complicated. Understandably, patients might become confused if asked to do many things at once in a given situation. Patients also may get confused if the interventions appear to be at crosspurposes with one another, such as the combination of an interoceptive exercise (e.g., "Take a shower with the doors and windows closed to test whether or not you will suffocate") and a coping exercise (e.g., slow, diaphragmatic breathing). Simpler is often better. During exposure to fear-evoking stimuli, patients could focus on just the sensations and the situation, using cognitive interventions judiciously, such as when they feel compelled to escape (e.g., "Am I making a catastrophic prediction? What evidence do I have?").
- Ensure that the patient understands that the selection of exercises is a collaborative venture, negotiated between patient and therapist. Tasks can be readily modified in such a way that the patient can perform them. If the patient is too frightened to hyperventilate for 1 min, then a shorter duration can be used. Mrs. J. was extremely frightened of performing this exercise. For her, interoceptive exposure was a slow process, starting with exercises that simply consisted of taking two deep breaths and then observing the effects. With time and patience, however, she was eventually able to complete a series of 2-min hyperventilation exercises.
- Perform the exercises yourself so the patient can see they are safe. As a rationale, the therapist might tell the patient, "I wouldn't ask you to do something that I wouldn't do myself, so I'll show you how this exercise is done."
- Adherence can be maintained at an adequate level if the patient is sufficiently motivated to complete the various treatment exercises. To sustain motivation, it can be useful to (a) reinforce (e.g., verbally praise) the patient for their efforts in completing each therapy assignment, and (b) have the patient self-reinforce for these efforts (e.g., praising oneself or using other incentives). Initially, reinforcement from the therapist should occur frequently. As therapy progresses, reinforcement from the therapist can be faded out as patient continues to use self-reinforcement.

If adherence continues to be poor, then it is important to identify the source of the problem. Is the exercise a credible test of the patient's beliefs? If not, then the patient may regard the task as pointless. Is the timing right for using exposure? More time may need to be spent on developing a trusting therapeutic relationship. Also, more time might be needed for cognitive restructuring to address beliefs about the exercises and about the sensations they induce. If the patient is using safety signals or safety behaviors, then a hierarchy can be constructed, where the sources of safety are gradually faded out. For patients on PRN (as needed) medication, it is important to ensure that medication isn't used as a way of dampening the sensations (see Otto & Pollack, 2009).

When exposure induces a panic attack

If a panic attack occurs during an exposure exercise, the patient should attempt to complete as much of the exercise as they can. Afterwards, the therapist and patient should conduct a "postmortem" of the experience, tracing the sequence of events. Links between body sensations, catastrophic cognitions, and emotions are identified, and cognitive restructuring can be used as needed (e.g., "What evidence do you have that you were about to pass out?"). It is also important to identify whether the patient did anything to avoid the feared consequences. Patients who have panic attacks during interoceptive exposure often terminate the exercise as soon as they start to panic, believing the sensations would have catastrophic consequences. Aborted exercises should be discussed with the patient, pointing out that by discontinuing the exercise they failed to learn the true consequences of the sensations.

The patient should attempt the exposure exercise again, preferably soon after the panic attack. If the patient is reluctant to do this, then alternative strategies can be explored, such as performing a shortened version of the exercise. While repeating the exercise, patients should simply observe any sensations arising, without trying to make them less intense. A related, useful strategy is for patients to relax passively while experiencing the sensations (e.g., "Try to relax the muscles in your jaw, face, and neck while observing your heart pounding"). This is referred to this as relaxing with the sensations (Otto, Jones, Craske, & Barlow, 1996).

Treating overvalued beliefs

Integrated cognitive and exposure interventions are particularly useful when patients have overvalued (i.e., strongly held and sustained) beliefs in the dangerousness of arousal-related sensations. Mr. G. had frequent panic attacks that appeared to be triggered by catastrophic misinterpretations of chest pain. He was convinced the pain was due to an undiagnosed heart condition, and that he was "fated" to die of a heart attack, just like his older brother. Reluctantly, Mr. G. permitted his cardiologist to refer him for a course of CBT. Although he had undergone many medical evaluations that all failed to detect any abnormality, Mr. G. continued to believe he had undiagnosed heart disease. Accordingly, he avoided all forms of physical exertion so that his heart would not beat too fast. He also frequently checked his pulse for tachycardia. Mr. G. surreptitiously obtained a supply of nitroglycerin, which he took whenever he thought his heart was beating too fast. This safety behavior prevented him from learning that tachycardia was harmless. Mr. G. was unwilling to drop this safety behavior or engage in any form of interoceptive exposure.

To treat a case like this, it can be fruitful to draw on cognitive-behavioral approaches for treating delusions (Chadwick, Birchwood, & Trower, 1996) and on those used for treating hypochondriasis (Taylor & Asmundson, 2004). The strategies for treating overvalued beliefs in panic disorder are not greatly different from treating other catastrophic beliefs. The main difference is in the way the strategies are introduced and implemented. The following approaches can be used for treating overvalued beliefs:

- For patients who strongly believe they have an undiagnosed medical condition, CBT is presented as a "no-lose" option. Patients are told that if a trial of CBT is effective, then they will have overcome their problems. If CBT is ineffective, then further medical evaluation can be pursued.
- The therapist attempts to identify all the relevant catastrophic beliefs, including ancillary beliefs. As per standard CBT, the strength of each belief is rated on a 0–100 scale (0 = do not believe that ____ is true, to 100 = completely believe it is true).

- Begin by applying cognitive restructuring to beliefs that are least strongly held. These are likely to be most amenable to change. Then proceed up a hierarchy from weak to strongly held beliefs. Mr. G. agreed to initially focus on his belief that "Frequently pulse checking is vital to my health."
- Do not directly confront the beliefs. Direct confrontation can strengthen overvalued beliefs (Brehm, 1962). Instead, ask the patient to simply explore alternative, noncatastrophic possibilities.
- Challenge the evidence for the beliefs, not the beliefs themselves. Instead of challenging Mr. G's belief that he had heart disease, the therapist challenged the notion that chest pain is evidence for this belief; "What sorts of harmless things could be causing your chest pain?" Socratic dialogue can be used throughout; e.g., "Did your cardiologist find evidence of heart disease?" Mr. G. replied "no." The therapist replied, "Why do you think the cardiologist was so sure his tests ruled out heart disease?"
- Look for naturally occurring fluctuations in belief strength. Was there a time in the past week when the patient doubted—even for a moment—the veracity of a given catastrophic belief? Explore and build on these doubts during the therapy session. During one session, Mr. G. remarked that "the last time I had chest pain I noticed that my rib muscles were twitching. This made me think that the pain came from these muscles, not from my heart." This observation led to a review of the evidence for the hypothesis that his pain was stress-related.
- Once the patient has begun to doubt the veracity of a given belief, the therapist can suggest some simple, easily accomplished behavioral experiments. Mr. G. began by walking up a flight of 4 steps to see what effect this had on his chest pain. He noticed that this produced no increase in pain, which was inconsistent with the belief that the pain was due to a cardiac condition. The following week he was willing to walk up 8 steps, which similarly had no effect on this pain. Thus, behavioral experiments were gradually implemented at a pace acceptable to Mr. G.

Summary

This chapter reviewed the theory, research, and practice concerning the treatment of anxiety sensitivity in adults with anxiety and related disorders. We considered major DSM-5 anxiety disorders (e.g., panic disorder, specific phobia, social anxiety disorder) along with the two major anxiety-related disorders (PTSD and OCD). Empirically supported anxiety sensitivity-reduction interventions were described, implemented as standalone treatments, or as part of multicomponent treatment programs. The major interventions for reducing anxiety sensitivity are psychoeducation, cognitive restructuring and various forms of therapeutic exposure, particularly interoceptive exposure.

References

Abramowitz, J. S., Deacon, B., & Whiteside, S. P. (2011). *Exposure therapy for anxiety: Principles and practice*. New York: Guilford.

Allan, N. P., Macatee, R. J., Norr, A. M., & Schmidt, N. B. (2014). Direct and interactive effects of distress tolerance and anxiety sensitivity on generalized anxiety and depression. *Cognitive Therapy and Research*, *38*, 530–540.

Ball, S. G., & Otto, M. W. (1994). Cognitive-behavioral treatment of choking phobia: 3 case studies. *Psychotherapy and Psychosomatics*, *62*, 207–211.

Barlow, D. H., Farchione, T. J., Fairholme, C. P., Ellard, K. K., Boisseau, C. L., Allen, L. B., & May, J. T. (2011). *Unified protocol for transdiagnostic treatment of emotional disorders*. New York: Oxford University Press.

Beck, A. T. (1988). Cognitive approaches to panic disorder: theory and therapy. In S. Rachman & J. D. Maser (Eds.), *Panic: Psychological perspectives* (pp. 91–109). Hillsdale, NJ: Erlbaum.

Beck, A. T., & Emery, G. (1985). *Anxiety disorders and phobias: A cognitive perspective*. New York: Basic Books.

Blakey, S. M., & Abramowitz, J. S. (2017). Interoceptive exposure: an overlooked modality in the cognitive-behavioral treatment of OCD. *Cognitive and Behavioral Practice*. https://doi.org/10.1016/j.cbpra.2017.01.002.

Boettcher, H., Brake, C. A., & Barlow, D. H. (2016). Origins and outlook of interoceptive exposure. *Journal of Behavior Therapy and Experimental Psychiatry*, *53*, 41–51.

Boswell, J. F., Farchione, T. J., Sauer-Zavala, S., Murray, H. W., Fortune, M. R., & Barlow, D. H. (2013). Anxiety sensitivity and interoceptive exposure: a transdiagnostic construct and change strategy. *Behavior Therapy*, *44*, 417–431.

Brehm, J. W. (1962). *A theory of psychological reactance*. New York: Academic.

Brown, H. M., Trzaskowski, M., Zavos, H. M. S., Rijsdijk, F. V., Gregory, A. M., & Eley, T. C. (2012). Phenotypic and genetic structure of anxiety sensitivity in adolescence and early adulthood. *Journal of Anxiety Disorders*, *26*, 680–688.

Bullis, J. R., Sauer-Zavala, S., Bentley, K. H., Thompson-Hollands, J., Carl, J. R., & Barlow, D. H. (2015). The unified protocol for transdiagnostic treatment of emotional disorders: preliminary exploration of effectiveness for group delivery. *Behavior Modification*, *39*, 295–321.

Chadwick, P., Birchwood, M. J., & Trower, P. (1996). *Cognitive therapy for delusions, voices, and paranoia*. New York: Wiley.

Clark, D. M. (1989). Anxiety states: panic and generalized anxiety. In K. Hawton, P. M. Salkovskis, J. Kirk, & D. M. Clark (Eds.), *Cognitive behaviour therapy for psychiatric problems: A practical guide*. New York: Oxford University Press.

Clark, D. A., & Beck, A. T. (2010). *Cognitive therapy of anxiety disorders: Science and practice*. New York: Guilford.

Collimore, K. C., & Asmundson, G. J. G. (2014). Fearful responding to interoceptive exposure in social anxiety disorder. *Journal of Anxiety Disorders*, *28*, 195–202.

Craske, M. G., & Barlow, D. H. (1993). Panic disorder and agoraphobia. In D. H. Barlow (Ed.), *Clinical handbook of psychological disorders (*2nd ed., pp. 1–47*)*. New York: Guilford.

Craske, M. G., Meadows, E. A., & Barlow, D. H. (1994). *Mastery of your anxiety and panic II and agoraphobia supplement: Therapist guide*. San Antonio, TX: Psychological Corporation.

Dixon, L. J., Kemp, J. J., Farrell, N. R., Blakey, S. M., & Deacon, B. J. (2015). Interoceptive exposure exercises for social anxiety. *Journal of Anxiety Disorders*, *33*, 25–34.

Ellard, K. K., Fairholme, C. P., Boisseau, C. L., Farchione, T. J., & Barlow, D. H. (2010). Unified protocol for the transdiagnostic treatment of emotional disorders: protocol development and initial outcome data. *Cognitive and Behavioral Practice*, *17*, 88–101.

Farchione, T. J., Fairholme, C. P., Ellard, K. K., Boisseau, C. L., Thompson-Hollands, J., Carl, J. R., ... Barlow, D. H. (2012). Unified protocol for transdiagnostic treatment of emotional disorders: a randomized controlled trial. *Behavior Therapy*, *43*, 666–678.

Farris, S. G., DiBello, A. M., Allan, N. P., Hogan, J., Schmidt, N. B., & Zvolensky, M. J. (2015). Evaluation of the Anxiety Sensitivity Index-3 among treatment-seeking smokers. *Psychological Assessment*, *27*, 1123–1128.

Fetzner, M. G., & Asmundson, G. J. G. (2015). Aerobic exercise reduces symptoms of posttraumatic stress disorder: a randomized controlled trial. *Cognitive Behaviour Therapy*, *44*, 301–313.

Holtz, K., Pane-Farre, C. A., Wendt, J., Lotze, M., & Hamm, A. O. (2012). Brain activation during anticipation of interoceptive threat. *NeuroImage*, *61*, 857–865.

Hunter, P. V., & Antony, M. M. (2009). Cognitive-behavioral treatment of emetophobia: the role of interoceptive exposure. *Cognitive and Behavioral Practice*, *16*, 84–91.

Jensen, D., Cohen, J. N., Mennin, D. S., Fresco, D. M., & Heimberg, R. G. (2016). Clarifying the unique associations among intolerance of uncertainty, anxiety, and depression. *Cognitive Behaviour Therapy*, *45*, 431–444.

Knapp, A. A., Frala, J., Blumenthal, H., Badour, C. L., & Leen-Feldner, E. W. (2013). Anxiety sensitivity and childhood learning experiences: impacts on panic symptoms among adolescents. *Cognitive Therapy and Research*, *37*, 1151–1159.

LeBouthillier, D. M., & Asmundson, G. J. G. (2015). A single bout of aerobic exercise reduces anxiety sensitivity but not intolerance of uncertainty or distress tolerance: a randomized controlled trial. *Cognitive Behaviour Therapy*, *44*, 252–263.

Lickel, J., Nelson, E., Lickel, A. H., & Deacon, B. (2008). Interoceptive exposure exercises for evoking depersonalization and derealization: a pilot study. *Journal of Cognitive Psychotherapy*, *22*, 321–330.

Limburg, K., Watson, H. J., Hagger, M. S., & Egan, S. J. (2016). The relationship between perfectionism and psychopathology: a meta-analysis. *Journal of Clinical Psychology*. https://doi.org/10.1002/jclp.22435.

Mansell, W., Carey, T. A., & Tai, S. J. (2013). *A transdiagnostic approach to CBT using method of levels therapy*. New York: Routledge.

Mantar, A., Yemez, B., & Alkin, T. (2010). Anksiyete Duyarlılığı İndeksi-3'ün Türkçe formunun geçerlik ve güvenilirlik çalışması. *Türk Psikiyatri Dergisi*, *21*, 225–234.

McKay, D., & Moretz, M. W. (2008). Interoceptive cue exposure for depersonalization: a case series. *Cognitive and Behavioral Practice*, *15*, 435–439.

Medina, J. L., DeBoer, L. B., Davis, M. L., Rosenfield, D., Powers, M. B., Otto, M. W., & Smits, J. A. J. (2014). Gender moderates the effect of exercise on anxiety sensitivity. *Mental Health and Physical Activity*, *7*, 147–151.

Naragon-Gainey, K. (2010). Meta-analysis of the relations of anxiety sensitivity to the depressive and anxiety disorders. *Psychological Bulletin*, *136*, 128–150.

Norton, P. J. (2012). *Cognitive-behavioral therapy of anxiety: A transdiagnostic treatment manual*. New York: Guilford Press.

Norton, P. J., & Paulus, D. J. (2017). Transdiagnostic models of anxiety disorder: theoretical and empirical underpinnings. *Clinical Psychology Review*. https://doi.org/10.1016/j.cpr.2017.03.004.

Olatunji, B. O., & Wolitzky-Taylor, K. B. (2009). Anxiety sensitivity and the anxiety disorders: a meta-analytic review and synthesis. *Psychological Bulletin*, *135*, 974–999.

Olthuis, J. V., Watt, M. C., Mackinnon, S. P., & Stewart, S. H. (2015). CBT for high anxiety sensitivity: alcohol outcomes. *Addictive Behaviors*, *46*, 19–24.

Otto, M. W. (2008). Anxiety sensitivity, emotional intolerance, and expansion of the application of interoceptive exposure: commentary on the special issue. *Journal of Cognitive Psychotherapy*, *22*, 379–384.

Otto, M. W., Jones, J. C., Craske, M. G., & Barlow, D. H. (1996). *Stopping anxiety medication: Panic control therapy for benzodiazepine discontinuation*. San Antonio, TX: Psychological Corporation.

Otto, M. W., & Pollack, M. H. (2009). *Stopping anxiety medication workbook* (2nd ed.). New York: Oxford University Press.

Poletti, S., Radaelli, D., Cucchi, M., Ricci, L., Vai, B., Smeraldi, E., & Benedetti, F. (2015). Neural correlates of anxiety sensitivity in panic disorder: a functional magnetic resonance imaging study. *Psychiatry Research: Neuroimaging*, *233*, 95–101.

Reinholt, N., Aharoni, R., Winding, C., Rosenberg, N., Rosenbaum, B., & Arnfred, S. (2017). Transdiagnostic group CBT for anxiety disorders: the unified protocol in mental health services. *Cognitive Behaviour Therapy*, *46*, 29–43.

Reiss, S. (1999). The sensitivity theory of aberrant motivation. In S. Taylor (Ed.), *Anxiety sensitivity: Theory, research, and treatment of the fear of anxiety* (pp. 35–58). Mahwah, NJ: Lawrence Erlbaum Associates Publishers.

Reiss, S., Peterson, R. A., Gursky, D. M., & McNally, R. J. (1986). Anxiety sensitivity, anxiety frequency and the predictions of fearfulness. *Behaviour Research and Therapy*, *24*, 1–8.

Reiss, S., Peterson, R., Taylor, S., Schmidt, N., & Weems, C. F. (2008). *Anxiety Sensitivity Index consolidated user manual: ASI, ASI-3, and CASI*. Ohio: IDS.

Sabourin, B. C., Stewart, S. H., Sherry, S. B., Watt, M. C., Wald, J., & Grant, V. V. (2008). Physical exercise as interoceptive exposure within a brief cognitive-behavioral treatment for anxiety-sensitive women. *Journal of Cognitive Psychotherapy*, *22*, 303–320.

Sabourin, B. C., Watt, M. C., Krigolson, O. E., & Stewart, S. H. (2016). Two interventions decrease anxiety sensitivity among high anxiety sensitive women: could physical exercise be the key? *Journal of Cognitive Psychotherapy*, *30*, 131–146.

Salkovskis, P. M., & Clark, D. M. (1991). Cognitive therapy for panic attacks. *Journal of Cognitive Psychotherapy*, *5*, 215–226.

Sandin, B., Valiente, R. M., Chorot, P., & Santed, M. A. (2007). ASI-3: Nueva escala para la evaluación de la sensibilidad ala ansiedad [ASI-3: a new scale for the assessment of anxiety sensitivity]. *Revista de Psicopatología y Psicología Clínica*, *12*, 91–104.

Schmidt, N. B., Keough, M. E., Mitchell, M. A., Reynolds, E. K., MacPherson, L., Zvolensky, M. J., & Lejuez, C. W. (2010). Anxiety sensitivity: prospective prediction of anxiety among early adolescents. *Journal of Anxiety Disorders*, *24*, 503–508.

Schmidt, N. B., Lerew, D. R., & Jackson, R. J. (1997). The role of anxiety sensitivity in the pathogenesis of panic: prospective evaluation of spontaneous panic attacks during acute stress. *Journal of Abnormal Psychology*, *106*, 355–364.

Schmidt, N. B., Lerew, D. R., & Jackson, R. J. (1999). Prospective evaluation of anxiety sensitivity in the pathogenesis of panic: replication and extension. *Journal of Abnormal Psychology*, *108*, 532–537.

Smits, J. A. J., Berry, A. C., Rosenfield, D., Powers, M. B., Behar, E., & Otto, M. W. (2008). Reducing anxiety sensitivity with exercise. *Depression and Anxiety*, *25*, 689–699.

Smits, J. A. J., Berry, A. C., Tart, C. D., & Powers, M. B. (2008). The efficacy of cognitive-behavioral interventions for reducing anxiety sensitivity: a meta-analytic review. *Behaviour Research and Therapy*, *46*, 1047–1054.

Stewart, S. H., Taylor, S., Jang, K. L., Cox, B. J., Watt, M. C., Fedoroff, I. C., & Borger, S. C. (2001). Causal modeling of relations among learning history, anxiety sensitivity, and panic attacks. *Behaviour Research and Therapy*, *39*, 443–456.

Taylor, S. (2000). *Understanding and treating panic disorder: Cognitive-behavioural approaches*. New York: Wiley.

Taylor, S. (2017). *Clinician's guide to PTSD: Cognitive-behavioral approaches* (2nd ed.). New York: Guilford.

Taylor, S., & Asmundson, G. J. G. (2004). *Treating health anxiety: A cognitive-behavioral approach*. New York: Guilford.

Taylor, S., Jang, K. L., Stewart, S. H., & Stein, M. B. (2008). Etiology of the dimensions of anxiety sensitivity: a behavioral-genetic analysis. *Journal of Anxiety Disorders, 22*, 899–914.

Taylor, S., Zvolensky, M. J., Cox, B. J., Deacon, B., Heimberg, R. G., Ledley, D. R., … Cardenas, S. J. (2007). Robust dimensions of anxiety sensitivity: development and initial validation of the Anxiety Sensitivity Index-3. *Psychological Assessment, 19*, 176–188.

Wald, J., & Taylor, S. (2007). Efficacy of interoceptive exposure therapy combined with trauma-related exposure therapy for posttraumatic stress disorder: a pilot study. *Journal of Anxiety Disorders, 21*, 1050–1060.

Wald, J., & Taylor, S. (2008). Responses to interoceptive exposure in people with posttraumatic stress disorder (PTSD): a preliminary analysis of induced anxiety reactions and trauma memories and their relationship to anxiety sensitivity and PTSD symptom severity. *Cognitive Behaviour Therapy, 37*, 90–100.

Wald, J., & Taylor, S. (2010). Implementation and outcome of combining interoceptive exposure with trauma-related exposure therapy in a patient with combat-related posttraumatic stress disorder. *Clinical Case Studies, 9*, 243–259.

Wald, J., Taylor, S., Chiri, L. R., & Sica, C. (2010). Posttraumatic stress disorder and chronic pain arising from motor vehicle accidents: efficacy of interoceptive exposure plus trauma-related exposure therapy. *Cognitive Behaviour Therapy, 39*, 104–113.

Walker, J. R., & Furer, P. (2008). Interoceptive exposure in the treatment of health anxiety and hypochondriasis. *Journal of Cognitive Psychotherapy, 22*, 366–378.

Wang, L., Liu, W.-T., Zhu, X.-Z., Wang, Y.-P., Li, L.-Y., Yang, Y.-L., & Ryder, A. G. (2014). Validity and reliability of the Chinese version of the Anxiety Sensitivity Index-3 in healthy adult women. *Chinese Mental Health Journal, 28*, 767–771.

Watt, M. C., Stewart, S. H., & Cox, B. J. (1998). A retrospective study of the learning history origins of anxiety sensitivity. *Behaviour Research and Therapy, 36*, 505–525.

Wolitzky-Taylor, K., McBeth, J., Guillot, C. R., Stone, M. D., Kirkpatrick, M. G., Zvolensky, M. J., … Leventhal, A. M. (2016). Transdiagnostic processes linking anxiety symptoms and substance use problems among adolescents. *Journal of Addictive Diseases, 35*, 266–277.

Zvolensky, M. J., Bogiaizian, D., Salazar, P. L., Farris, S. G., & Bakhshaie, J. (2014). An anxiety sensitivity reduction smoking-cessation program for Spanish-speaking smokers (Argentina). *Cognitive and Behavioral Practice, 21*, 350–363.

Optimizing outcomes for pain conditions by treating anxiety sensitivity

5

Janine V. Olthuis, Gordon J.G. Asmundson*†

*University of New Brunswick, Fredericton, NB, Canada, †University of Regina, Regina, SK, Canada

Chapter Outline

Introduction

During the mid- to late-1990s, a number of independent clinically focused research groups began research to understand and explain pain-specific presentations of fear and anxiety. These efforts led to the proposal of two theoretical accounts of the observed associations between fear and anxiety and chronic pain presentations, one by Asmundson, Norton, and Norton (1999) and the other by Vlaeyen and Linton (2000), which have evolved over the past decade and have led to innovative exposure-based treatments for chronic musculoskeletal pain (for reviews, see Bailey, Carleton, Vlaeyen,

The Clinician's Guide to Anxiety Sensitivity Treatment and Assessment. https://doi.org/10.1016/B978-0-12-813495-5.00005-X

& Asmundson, 2010; López-de-Uralde-Villaneuva et al., 2016). As it grew out of efforts to understand the influences of anxiety sensitivity on chronic pain, the theoretical account of Asmundson, Norton, and Norton (1999) is particularly germane to the application of anxiety sensitivity treatments to chronic pain.

In this chapter, we have four specific goals. First, we provide a brief overview of pain and chronic pain. Second, we define the construct of anxiety sensitivity, introduce models proposed to explain the association between it and persistent presentations of pain, and review the current evidence from related empirical investigations. Third, we provide an overview of clinical strategies as well as concrete and actionable clinical recommendations for optimizing pain outcomes through the application of techniques designed to reduce anxiety sensitivity. Finally, given that research in this area remains in its infancy, we provide a potential agenda to guide future research efforts.

Acute and chronic pain

Many people view pain as nothing more than an undesirable sensation. This idea dates back to the writings of Descartes and the traditional medical model, which limited the conceptualization of pain to a sensory experience stemming from injury or physical pathology (for a more detailed history, see Asmundson, Gómez-Perez, Richter, & Carleton, 2014). Contemporary models recognize that pain comprises biological, psychological, behavioral, and social determinants and that it can have adaptive as well as maladaptive functions (Asmundson & Wright, 2004). Acute pain, which has a sudden onset and is often the result of tissue damage or a disease process, is adaptive in that it signals the potential of physical damage and motivates action to limit damage and promote recovery (Wall, 1978). As physical recovery progresses, acute pain typically subsides; but, this is not always the case.

For approximately 20% of the population living in Westernized countries (Breivik, Collett, Ventafridda, Cohen, & Gallacher, 2006), acute pain moves through a complex interplay of biological, psychological, and social processes to become chronic (Katz, McCartney, & Rashiq, 2008), persisting 3 months or longer (International Association for the Study of Pain, 1986). Chronic pain may be related to injury or insult to body tissue or to damage to nerves (i.e., neuropathic pain). Unlike acute pain, chronic pain serves no adaptive function. And, while not necessarily maladaptive (Asmundson, Norton, & Allerdings, 1997; Turk & Rudy, 1987), a significant proportion of people who experience chronic pain also experience substantial emotional distress, limitations in social and occupational functioning, increased risk of developing psychiatric disorders (Asmundson & Katz, 2009), increased rates of suicide (El-Gabalawy, Asmundson, & Sareen, 2011), as well as increased medical service use and high-cost insurance claims (Gureje, Von Korff, Simon, & Gater, 1998; Stewart, Ricci, Chee, Morganstein, & Lipton, 2003).

Anxiety sensitivity and pain: Evidence and models

As detailed elsewhere in this volume, anxiety sensitivity refers to the fear of anxious arousal (e.g., racing heart, shortness of breath, fear of losing control) based on the belief that this may have harmful physical, psychological, or social consequences

(Reiss & McNally, 1985). There is evidence indicating that anxiety sensitivity amplifies fear reactions, thereby increasing vulnerability for the development and maintenance of common fears (Taylor, 1999). The vast majority of research and clinical interest in anxiety sensitivity has been relative to its association with panic attacks, panic disorder, posttraumatic stress disorder, and, to a lesser extent, several other mental health conditions (e.g., depression, substance abuse, social anxiety); however, there is now a fairly substantial literature implicating anxiety sensitivity as an important factor in the development and maintenance of morbidity associated with various disabling chronic health conditions (for review, see Asmundson, Wright, & Hadjistavropoulos, 2000), including asthma, gastrointestinal dysfunction, vestibular dysfunction, and chronic pain.

Of the chronic health conditions, it is the association between anxiety sensitivity and chronic pain that has received the majority of empirical attention. This research grew out of initial efforts by Asmundson and Norton (1995) to determine whether anxiety sensitivity, functioning in its capacity as a fear amplifier, had an influence on pain-related fear, anxiety, and avoidance behavior in chronic pain patients. In order to appreciate the implications of the amplifying effect of anxiety sensitivity on these pain-related factors, it is important to understand their role in the development and maintenance of chronic pain. According to fear-avoidance models of chronic pain (for review, see Asmundson, Norton, & Norton, 1999; Leeuw et al., 2007; Vlaeyen & Linton, 2000, 2012), there are two pathways one can take following the experience of pain. Individuals embark on the first pathway if they appraise their pain as unpleasant but transient and manageable (i.e., not catastrophic). This appraisal of pain may lead to engagement in appropriate restorative behaviors, starting with rest and gradually increasing activity in a safe but progressive fashion. In contrast, individuals may embark on the second pathway if they appraise their initial pain as catastrophic and threatening. These initial catastrophic appraisals of pain tend to be fed by negative affect and exposure to threatening illness information. Fear-avoidance models posit that these catastrophic interpretations of pain lead individuals to develop a fear of pain (i.e., a fearful reaction to an immediate pain threat) and pain-related anxiety (i.e., a negative emotional response in anticipation of pain threat), which then promotes both hypervigilance to pain (and, more broadly, to the body) and avoidance of activity that may provoke pain (Asmundson, Norton, & Vlaeyen, 2004). This intense focus on, and avoidance of, pain leads to negative affect, functional disability, and poor quality of life for the individual, and the cycle continues.

Anxiety sensitivity and pain catastrophizing, fear of pain, and pain-related anxiety

If we posit, then, that anxiety sensitivity acts as an amplifier of some of these key pain-related constructs in the fear-avoidance model, namely, pain-related anxiety, fear of pain, and pain catastrophizing, the importance of its role—and its need for clinical attention—becomes evident. Crucially, high anxiety sensitivity is theorized to increase the tendency of individuals to catastrophize about pain, increasing the chances that an individual will find themselves embroiled in the fear-avoidance cycle of pain rather than engaging in more helpful and appropriate rest and restoration behaviors (see, for example, Fig. 1). In support of this postulation, several studies have found a strong association between anxiety sensitivity and pain catastrophizing. Research with rheumatoid arthritis and chronic pain samples has shown that those with higher anxiety sensitivity also report significantly greater pain catastrophizing (Mehta, Rice, Janzen, et al., 2016; Mehta, Rice, McIntyre, et al., 2016; Rice et al., 2016). For example, Ramírez-Maestre, Esteve, Ruiz-Párraga, Gómez-Pérez, and López-Martínez (2017) recently investigated the association of pain catastrophizing and anxiety sensitivity among 232 acute back pain patients. Results revealed that anxiety sensitivity predicted pain catastrophizing, which subsequently predicted fear-avoidance beliefs, pain intensity, and pain-related disability. Similarly, Esteve, Marquina-Aponte, and Ramírez-Maestre (2014) found that among 102 children scheduled for outpatient surgery those with higher anxiety sensitivity reported higher levels of pain catastrophizing, which was in turn associated with higher estimated and reported pain levels.

Empirical evidence also supports the theoretical link between anxiety sensitivity and fear of pain. For instance, one of the initial investigations into the role of anxiety sensitivity in pain revealed that chronic back pain patients with high anxiety sensitivity reported greater fear of negative consequences of pain than those with low or

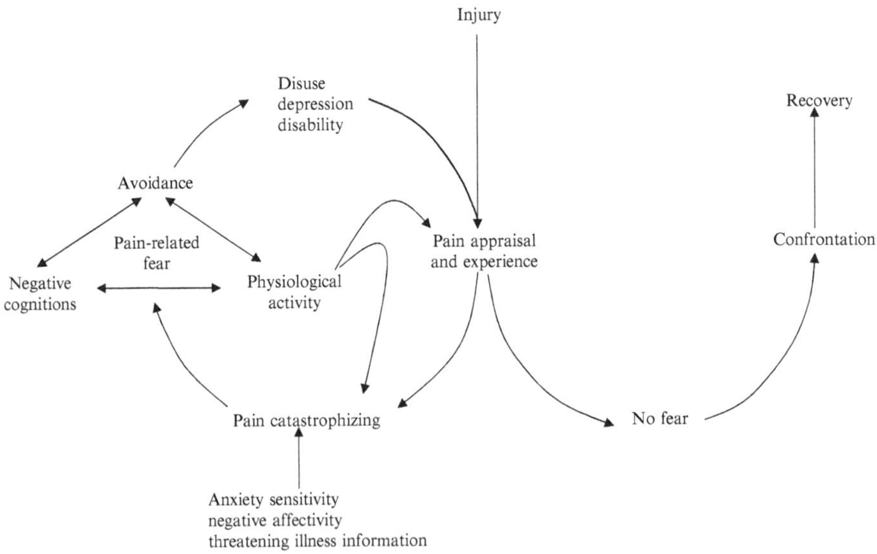

Fig. 1 The fear-avoidance model of chronic pain.
Reproduced with permission from Norton, P. J., & Asmundson, G. J. G. (2003). Amending the fear-avoidance model of chronic pain: what is the role of physiological arousal? *Behavior Therapy, 34*, 17–30, copyright 2003.

medium anxiety sensitivity (Asmundson & Norton, 1995). In subsequent studies with 259 individuals with chronic musculoskeletal pain (Asmundson & Taylor, 1996) and 72 patients with chronic headache (Asmundson, Norton, & Veloso, 1999), anxiety sensitivity was directly associated with fear of pain even after controlling for pain severity. Zvolensky, Goodie, McNeil, Sperry, and Sorrell (2001) also found that anxiety sensitivity physical concerns significantly predicted fear of pain (overall, medical pain, minor pain, and severe pain) in a heterogeneous pain sample, even after accounting for pain severity and depressive symptoms. A meta-analysis of the association between anxiety sensitivity and pain found a large effect size ($r = .50$; $g = 1.15$) between anxiety sensitivity and fear of pain in clinical pain samples (Ocañez, McHugh, & Otto, 2010); however, even in the case of acute pain, anxiety sensitivity has been shown to predict fear of childbirth in women in their final months of pregnancy (Jokić-Begić, Žigić, & Radoš, 2014).

Similar empirical support can be found for the theoretical link between anxiety sensitivity and pain-related anxiety. Studies have shown that high anxiety sensitivity predicts pain-related anxiety in chronic back pain patients (Asmundson & Norton, 1995), heterogeneous chronic pain samples (McCracken & Keogh, 2009; Zvolensky et al., 2001), individuals with HIV/AIDS (Brandt, Gonzalez, Grover, & Zvolensky, 2013), mental health samples (Olthuis, Watt, Mackinnon, Potter, & Stewart, 2015), and healthy university students (Carleton, Sharpe, & Asmundson, 2007; Vancleef, Peters, Roelofs, & Asmundson, 2006). In particular, anxiety sensitivity cognitive concerns have been associated with pain-related cognitive anxiety and fearful appraisals while anxiety sensitivity physical concerns have been linked to pain-related escape and avoidance behaviors and physiological symptoms (Zvolensky et al., 2001). Other work with a healthy university sample suggests that it is anxiety sensitivity physical concerns that are associated most strongly with pain-related anxiety (Carleton et al., 2007).

Anxiety sensitivity and functional impairment

With clear evidence that anxiety sensitivity amplifies pain catastrophizing, fear of pain, and pain-related anxiety, it is perhaps not surprising that anxiety sensitivity is also linked to pain-related functional impairment. Among patients with chronic pain, higher anxiety sensitivity predicts more physical and psychosocial disability (McCracken & Keogh, 2009), more pain disability (Mehta, Rice, Janzen, et al., 2016; Mehta, Rice, McIntyre, et al., 2016), and lower scores on several indices of physical and mental quality of life (Mehta, Rice, Janzen, et al., 2016; Plehn, Peterson, & Williams, 1998; Wong et al., 2014). In fact, anxiety sensitivity (physical and cognitive concerns) appears to predict functional disability even after accounting for pain intensity and severity as well as anxiety and depression symptoms (Smitherman, Davis, Walters, Young, & House, 2015). The meta-analysis by Ocañez et al. (2010) found a small-to-moderate effect size ($r = .22$; $g = .45$) between anxiety sensitivity and disability in clinical pain samples. Notably, high levels of anxiety sensitivity also predict higher levels of healthcare service use among individuals with pain. McCracken and Keogh (2009) found that anxiety sensitivity cognitive concerns predicted more frequent pain-related visits to general practitioners among 125 patients with chronic pain in a specialty pain clinic. Similarly, White, McDonnell, and Gervino (2011) found that anxiety sensitivity was positively associated with health care use among 231 patients with noncardiac chest pain.

Structural and hierarchical models of anxiety sensitivity and pain

The unique pathways from anxiety sensitivity to each of pain catastrophizing, fear of pain, pain-related anxiety, and pain-related disability have also been explored in the context of the fear-avoidance model of pain using structural equation and hierarchical linear modeling (for review, see Asmundson, Parkerson, Petter, & Noel, 2012). In one of the first studies in this area, Asmundson and Taylor (1996) used structural equation modeling with 259 chronic musculoskeletal pain patients and found that anxiety sensitivity indirectly predicted pain-related escape and avoidance behaviors by way of its impact on fear of pain, even after controlling for pain severity. These findings were replicated in a study of individuals with recurrent headaches (Asmundson, Norton, & Norton, 1999), with results demonstrating a direct link between anxiety sensitivity and pain-related fear and an indirect link between anxiety sensitivity and pain-related escape and avoidance via pain-related fear (again, even while accounting for pain severity). More recently, Olthuis et al. (2015) used hierarchical linear modeling to examine this model among a mental health treatment-seeking sample with high anxiety sensitivity, again showing that pain-related anxiety mediated the relation between anxiety sensitivity and escape/avoidance behaviors.

With respect to predicting disability, Thibodeau, Fetzner, Carleton, Kachur, and Asmundson (2013) investigated the association between anxiety sensitivity and disability using structural equation modeling with data from 78 chronic low back pain patients currently in treatment. They found that anxiety sensitivity indirectly predicted self-reported and behavioral (i.e., physical lifting ability, treatment outcomes, days absent from treatment) indicators of functional impairment by way of its impact on pain-related anxiety. In a study of acute back pain patients, Ramírez-Maestre et al. (2017) found that anxiety sensitivity was indirectly associated with disability by way of its impact on pain catastrophizing; pain catastrophizing was related to disability directly as well as indirectly via fear-avoidance beliefs and pain intensity. Results showing the indirect role of anxiety sensitivity on pain disability have also been found in pediatric populations; for instance, Cappucci and Simons (2015) found that fear of pain mediated the relation between anxiety sensitivity and disability using regression analyses among pediatric headache patients. Martin, McGrath, Brown, and Katz (2007) did not find a direct association between anxiety sensitivity and pain-related disability among a sample of chronic pain children and teens, but they did find that anxiety sensitivity accounted for significant variance in youth's fear of pain and fear of pain accounted for significant variance in pain-related disability.

Given evidence that anxiety sensitivity is associated with variables known to exacerbate chronic pain, it is perhaps not surprising that we see significantly higher anxiety sensitivity among chronic pain populations as compared to nonpain samples. This includes higher anxiety sensitivity among adults with versus without headaches (Drahovzal, Stewart, & Sullivan, 2006; Smitherman et al., 2015), children with noncardiac chest pain versus those with benign heart murmurs (Lee et al., 2013; Lipsitz et al., 2004), and nonclinical children with current pain problems as compared to those without pain problems (Tsao et al., 2009). Moreover, within pain samples, those with higher anxiety sensitivity seem to be more negatively affected by their pain. Higher anxiety sensitivity is associated with higher self-report pain levels in chronic pain patients (McCracken & Keogh, 2009; although not every study shows this link, see Asmundson & Norton, 1995), headache intensity, and number of headache symptoms among university students with headaches (Drahovzal et al., 2006), and more severe self-reported postconcussive symptoms among head trauma patients (Wood, McCabe, & Dawkins, 2011). In acute pain samples, anxiety sensitivity is positively associated with persistent pain post idiopathic scoliosis surgery in teens (Chidambaran et al., 2017), worse sexual pain (Gerrior, Watt, Weaver, & Gallagher, 2015; Meana & Lykins, 2009), and maximum sensory pain during labor (Curzik & Jokić-Begić, 2011; Lang, Sorrell, Rodgers, & Lebeck, 2006). The meta-analysis by Ocañez et al. (2010) found a small-to-moderate effect size ($r = .24$; $g = .49$) between anxiety sensitivity and pain severity in clinical pain samples.

It seems important to note that not every study of the association between pain and anxiety sensitivity follows this expected pattern of high anxiety sensitivity leading to worse pain experiences and outcomes. For example, in a study of surgical patients pre- and postoperative procedures (e.g., hip or knee replacement), high anxiety sensitivity actually predicted more rapid resolution of postsurgery pain (Carroll et al., 2015). Similarly, in a study of hand fracture patients, higher levels of anxiety sensitivity were associated with lower levels of disability (Keogh, Book, Thomas, Giddins, & Eccleston, 2010). There may be something unique about these pain populations that sets them apart from the literature on chronic pain populations. In these instances, where individuals are experiencing recovery-related pain from an acute injury or surgical procedure, high anxiety sensitivity may actually be somewhat protective. As Keogh et al. (2010) suggest, greater attention to and awareness of body sensations may actually lead these individuals to engage in more adaptive and appropriate protective behaviors postsurgery and postinjury that actually lead to better prognosis for healing. In contrast, these same behaviors engaged in by chronic pain populations, in response to high anxiety sensitivity, do not serve the same protective role, instead fostering avoidance of activity, which can worsen health outcomes.

Anxiety sensitivity and affective symptoms in individuals with pain

Negative effects of pain experiences among those with high anxiety sensitivity appear to also extend to affective symptoms. Cross-sectional studies suggest that among pain populations (e.g., heterogeneous chronic pain, unexplained back pain, rheumatoid arthritis samples), higher anxiety sensitivity is associated with greater negative affect and stress (Asmundson & Norton, 1995; McCracken & Keogh, 2009; Mehta, Rice,

Janzen, et al., 2016; Mehta, Rice, McIntyre, et al., 2016; Rice et al., 2016; Rice et al., 2017). These cross-sectional studies are supplemented by longitudinal research with a sample of individuals with musculoskeletal pain referred to a community physiotherapy clinic showing that anxiety sensitivity levels predicted emotional distress (e.g., depressed mood, irritability, tension) 3 months later (Hadjistavropoulos, Asmundson, & Kowalyk, 2004). The meta-analysis by Ocañez et al. (2010) found a moderate-to-large effect size ($r = .44$; $g = .95$) between anxiety sensitivity and negative affect in clinical pain samples.

Taken together then, well-established theories of chronic pain posit a theoretical link between anxiety sensitivity and chronic pain—both pain itself and pain-related disability, functional impairment, and reduced quality of life. Theory proposes that the link between anxiety sensitivity occurs via three important pain-related constructs: pain catastrophizing, fear of pain, and pain-related anxiety. As is evident here, considerable empirical evidence supports these theoretical connections, providing confidence in researchers' assertions that anxiety sensitivity plays an important role in chronic pain.

Anxiety sensitivity and pain: Clinical strategies and recommendations

Assessment

In light of the theoretical and empirical links between anxiety sensitivity and pain, considering anxiety sensitivity in the assessment and treatment of pain is important (Asmundson, Norton, & Norton, 1999). Best practice guidelines suggest that a comprehensive assessment of chronic pain follow a systematic approach using appropriate, validated tools to assess pain history, pain characteristics (e.g., severity, quality, timing, location, triggers), functional impact of pain (e.g., effects on work, sleep), psychosocial impacts of pain, and prior use of pain interventions (Registered Nurses Association of Ontario, 2013). Our work, and that of others, suggests that anxiety sensitivity, pain-related anxiety, fear of pain, and pain catastrophizing also be evaluated when assessing chronic pain patients. Ramírez-Maestre and Esteve (2013) posited the importance of assessing dispositional characteristics relevant to the pain experience, such as anxiety sensitivity, in the evaluation of chronic pain. They suggested that understanding the manifestation of anxiety sensitivity and other dispositional characteristics (specifically, neuroticism, experiential avoidance, optimism, resilience, and extraversion) could help in the design of intervention strategies for chronic pain patients as well as make predictions with respect to treatment outcome as patients with high levels of anxiety sensitivity (as well as neuroticism and experiential avoidance) will need targeted support from the outset of treatment to promote chronic pain adjustment.

The most widely accepted current measure of anxiety sensitivity is the Anxiety Sensitivity Index-3 (ASI-3; Taylor et al., 2007). The ASI-3 is an easily administered

18-item self-report measure that asks participants to indicate the extent to which they agree or disagree with a series of statements about their fear of physiological arousal sensations. The ASI-3 has good criterion validity and internal consistency (Taylor et al., 2007). The measure provides subscale scores for anxiety sensitivity physical (e.g., "When my chest feels tight, I get scared that I won't be able to breathe properly"), cognitive (e.g., "It scares me when I am unable to keep my mind on a task"), and social (e.g., "I worry that other people will notice my anxiety") concerns, the former two which would likely be of most interest to pain clinicians. The population mean anxiety sensitivity score is 12.8 ($SD = 10.6$; Reiss, Peterson, Taylor, Schmidt, & Weems, 2008), which can guide clinicians in understanding whether their patient's anxiety sensitivity is elevated. In cases where patients are showing elevated anxiety sensitivity, a comprehensive mental health screen may also be warranted. Research has repeatedly shown that high anxiety sensitivity, in addition to being linked to chronic pain, is associated with a number of anxiety and mood disorders and substance use problems (Naragon-Gainey, 2010; Olatunji & Wolitzky-Taylor, 2009). The comorbidity of chronic pain with mental health disorders, and its implications for the treatment of chronic pain, are well documented (Gatchel, 2004).

In addition to the ASI-3, there are a variety of measures that assess pain-related constructs that are associated with anxiety sensitivity, including pain-related anxiety, fear of pain, and pain catastrophizing. Pain-related anxiety is easily measured using the 20-item self-report Pain Anxiety Symptom Scale-20 (PASS-20; McCracken & Dhingra, 2002). The PASS-20 assesses cognitive symptoms due to pain, fearful thoughts about the consequences of pain, pain-related physiological arousal, and escape and avoidance behaviors evoked by pain. Fear of pain has traditionally been evaluated using the Fear of Pain Questionnaire-III (FPQ-III; McNeil & Rainwater, 1998). Recently, though, two groups have published brief versions of the FPQ-III, the FPQ-Short Form (FPQ-SF; Asmundson, Bovell, Carleton, & McWilliams, 2008) and the FPQ-9 (McNeil et al., 2018), that may be ideal for clinical practice. Finally, pain catastrophizing is typically assessed using Sullivan and colleagues' seminal Pain Catastrophizing Scale (PCS; Sullivan, Bishop, & Pivik, 1995). The PCS is a 13-item self-report measure of the three components of pain catastrophizing—helplessness, rumination, and magnification—that has been translated into many different languages. (A number of these measures are available on the online book companion site.)

The ease of administration of these self-report measures means they can be used not only during the initial assessment, but also through the course of treatment. They can be completed easily at the outset of a session to track progress through treatment. The subscale scores can be invaluable in identifying which components of anxiety sensitivity require particular treatment attention (i.e., physical and/or cognitive concerns) as well as which associated pain constructs are creating ongoing problems. Reductions in anxiety sensitivity, pain-related anxiety, fear of pain, and pain catastrophizing through the course of treatment may suggest that treatment goals are on track and that the intervention is having an impact on the patient.

Intervention: Emerging research evidence

When discussing pain treatments here, we focus on chronic (vs. acute) pain populations as these are typically the pain populations that seek, or are referred to, psychological interventions for pain. The literature on the treatment of anxiety sensitivity for the purposes of remediation of pain is still in its infancy; nevertheless, there are some promising studies in the field. As may be expected, given the indirect associations between anxiety sensitivity and pain outcomes, the targets of anxiety sensitivity interventions for pain are not always the severity and intensity of pain but, instead, often focus on reducing the cognitive variables related to pain (e.g., pain-related anxiety).

Much of the work on anxiety sensitivity treatment has targeted the efficacy of cognitive behavioral therapy (CBT) interventions in reducing anxiety sensitivity. As is evident elsewhere in this volume, research evidence overwhelmingly suggests that CBT can reduce anxiety sensitivity. In particular, a meta-analysis of CBT for anxiety sensitivity by Smits, Berry, Tart, and Powers (2008) found a large effect size ($g=1.40$) in favor of CBT relative to control conditions in reducing anxiety sensitivity. Importantly, several recent studies have shown that CBT-driven reductions in anxiety sensitivity have implications for pain-related anxiety. Watt, Stewart, Lefaivre, and Uman (2006) investigated the impact of a three-session CBT intervention for anxiety sensitivity on pain-related anxiety. The intervention was delivered in a group format, with three 1-h sessions on three consecutive days, and included (a) one session on psychoeducation related to anxiety sensitivity, mechanisms of anxiety, panic attacks, and the anxiety cycle, (b) one session on cognitive restructuring consistent with cognitive therapy for panic disorder (Craske & Barlow, 2001), and (c) one session on interoceptive exposure (IE) in the form of physical exercise (i.e., running). University women with high and low anxiety sensitivity (one standard deviation above or below the mean) were randomly assigned to either receive the CBT intervention or a nonspecific treatment condition involving a discussion of ethics that was designed to control for therapist contact. While participants in this study were selected for high anxiety sensitivity, not pain-related pathology, a comparison of pain-related anxiety scores suggested that their pain-related anxiety ($M = 46.60$, $SD = 18.37$) was comparable to pain-related anxiety in chronic pain samples ($M=38.62$, $SD=20.38$; McCracken & Dhingra, 2002). Results revealed that high anxiety sensitivity (but not low anxiety sensitivity) participants in the CBT condition (but not the nonspecific treatment condition) experienced significant reductions in self-reported pain-related anxiety from pre- to posttreatment. In addition, treatment effects on pain-related anxiety were eliminated when controlling for treatment-related changes in anxiety sensitivity, suggesting that changes in anxiety sensitivity may explain changes in pain-related anxiety.

As a follow-up study, Olthuis et al. (2015) extended the brief CBT intervention to an eight-session CBT treatment for anxiety sensitivity. The intervention involved psychoeducation about anxiety sensitivity, cognitive restructuring, IE, stress management, and relapse prevention. IE again consisted of physical exercise; participants were asked to run/walk briskly for 10 min, three times per week. Subsequent to the eight weekly sessions, the treatment also included 4 weeks of continued IE. To investigate the efficacy of this intervention, mental health treatment-seeking individuals with high anxiety sensitivity were randomized to either the CBT intervention or a waiting list control. Again, while not a pain sample, pain-related anxiety levels (CBT group: $M=37.36$, $SD=24.03$; waiting list: $M=40.42$, $SD=23.94$) were comparable to levels reported among chronic pain samples (McCracken & Dhingra, 2002). Multilevel modeling results showed that the intervention reduced anxiety sensitivity ($d=0.77$) and pain-related anxiety ($d=0.65$) from pre- to posttreatment (i.e., 8 weeks) and to a significantly greater degree than the waitlist control. Reductions were maintained at a 12-week assessment (i.e., post-IE). It was also found that anxiety sensitivity total and physical concerns were significant mediators of treatment-related changes in pain-related anxiety. Furthermore, a chained mediation model revealed that treatment-related reductions in anxiety sensitivity reduced pain-related anxiety (i.e., fearful thinking, cognitive anxiety, and physiological arousal), which in turn led to reductions in pain-related escape/avoidance behaviors. Taken together, these results suggest that treatment-related reductions in anxiety sensitivity and, subsequently, pain-related anxiety, may serve to reduce pain-related escape/avoidance behaviors.

Importantly, these CBT interventions did not directly target pain-related anxiety in their strategies or components and yet both resulted in significant reductions in pain-related anxiety. In fact, treatment-related reductions in pain-related anxiety were almost as strong as treatment-related reductions in panic symptoms ($d=0.74$) and substantially greater than treatment-related reductions in social phobia ($d=0.34$) and posttraumatic stress ($d=0.39$) symptoms (Olthuis, Watt, Mackinnon, & Stewart, 2014). At this stage, the active mechanism of change in the interventions remains unknown (Olthuis et al., 2014; Olthuis et al., 2015; Watt et al., 2006); however, common treatment ingredients between the two studies were psychoeducation, cognitive restructuring, and IE. IE, in particular, is suggested to be one of the key components of CBT for anxiety sensitivity (Olthuis et al., 2015; Watt et al., 2006). Indeed, the authors indicate that the IE exercises are intended to expose high anxiety sensitivity participants to feared arousal sensations to habituate them to these sensations and, consequently, reduce their fear. For instance, the physical act of jogging or running would likely expose individuals to sensations such as a racing heart, shortness of breath, muscle soreness and tension, and sweating. Continued exposure to these sensations would habituate participants to the sensations and reduce their elicitation of fear, theoretically generalizing to other nonexercise-related occasions when these sensations are experienced. Granted, it is important to note that this habituation model is only one possible mechanism of change behind IE. Stewart and Watt (2008) also describe models of cognitive restructuring, emotional processing, self-efficacy, and emotional acceptance that could help explain IE-related decreases in fear of physiological sensations.

Whereas IE is not clearly the mechanism of change in anxiety sensitivity in these studies by Watt et al. (2006) and Olthuis et al. (2015), other recent work has been able to pinpoint the role of IE somewhat more specifically. Wald, Taylor, Chiri, and Sica (2010) investigated the use of IE and trauma-related exposure therapy in the treatment of five women with posttraumatic stress disorder and chronic musculoskeletal pain stemming from a traumatic car accident in the prior year. Women were recruited for the study via local advertising and physician referral. Each participant received an initial four sessions of IE in the form of a series of exercises such as running for 1 min and hyperventilating for 1 min and then eight sessions of trauma-related exposure therapy. The rationale for preceding trauma-based exposure with IE was that if IE reduced fear of arousal-related sensations, women would be more willing to complete trauma-based exposure because they would be more able to tolerate its accompanying distress. Results showed that whereas trauma-related exposure led to more substantial changes in posttraumatic stress symptoms than IE, IE led to more substantial changes in anxiety sensitivity for four out of five participants. In terms of pain-related outcomes, this study showed that IE resulted in some small changes in pain severity; however, there was little change in pain interference. Three months after the end of treatment, pain severity and interference ratings had returned to pretreatment levels. This study extends findings from Watt et al. (2006) and Olthuis et al. (2015) by suggesting that IE exercises may lead to changes in anxiety sensitivity, and small, short-term changes in pain severity, among chronic pain patients. More work is needed, however, to understand the implications of these anxiety sensitivity reductions for pain-related anxiety, pain severity, and pain interference.

Intervention: Practical recommendations

Given the existing treatment literature and the empirical literature supporting the association between high anxiety sensitivity and chronic pain outcomes by way of fear of pain, pain-related anxiety, and pain escape and avoidance behaviors, we suggest that clinicians consider the direct treatment of anxiety sensitivity in their chronic pain patients with high anxiety sensitivity. In the context of existing treatments for chronic pain based on fear-avoidance models of chronic pain, exposure-based strategies are often used to decrease pain-related anxiety and fear (for review, see Bailey et al., 2010). Theoretically, less fear of pain and pain-related anxiety should, in turn, reduce the tendency and/or need for chronic pain patients to escape and avoid behaviors that may lead to arousal and/or pain, with positive outcomes for pain severity and disability (Lohnberg, 2007). Ramírez-Maestre and Esteve (2013) suggest, however, that individuals with high anxiety sensitivity may be less responsive to these psychological interventions as compared to those without high anxiety sensitivity, and may require a different approach to treatment.

The consideration of the role of anxiety sensitivity and its impact on fear of pain and pain-related anxiety suggests that it would benefit clinicians and their patients to tackle the reduction of high anxiety sensitivity before embarking on exposure activities targeting pain-related anxiety. The existing studies, as discussed earlier, support the use of CBT strategies in the reduction of anxiety sensitivity. Given the lack of dismantling treatment studies at this point, CBT strategies focused on psychoeducation, cognitive restructuring, and IE may be efficacious. Indeed, given that research shows that CBT (Olthuis et al., 2015; Watt et al., 2006) and IE (Wald, Taylor, Chiri, & Sica, 2010) for anxiety sensitivity result in reductions in pain-related anxiety, escape/avoidance behaviors, and perhaps even pain severity, and that reductions in anxiety sensitivity may mediate treatment-related reductions in both pain-related anxiety (Watt et al., 2006) and escape/avoidance behaviors (Olthuis et al., 2015), subsequent exposure exercises geared at pain-related anxiety and fear may prove to be redundant. De Peuter, Van Diest, Vansteenwegen, Van den Bergh, and Vlaeyen (2011), however, suggest that other nonarousal-related IE (i.e., sensations related to fear of pain) can be conducted subsequent to IE for anxiety sensitivity. Specific IE exercise suggestions for fear of pain (see Appendix A in the online book companion) might include tensing and releasing of specific muscle groups (e.g., clenching fists for 30 s, raising shoulders to ears and holding for 30 s), applying pressure to specific muscle groups (e.g., firmly pressing and holding hand on thigh for 30–60 s), or holding certain body postures for 30–60 s.

When working with patients with chronic pain, particularly those with high anxiety sensitivity, psychoeducation should involve providing information about anxiety sensitivity, its components (with a particular focus on cognitive and physical concerns), and its association with pain-related anxiety, escape/avoidance behaviors, and chronic pain. Helping patients to understand the anxiety cycle and the role of avoidance of physiological arousal sensations on the exacerbation of fear will also be important. Whereas psychoeducation in chronic pain treatment often includes helping patients understand the fear-avoidance model of pain (see Appendix B in the online companion), providing specific information on the role of anxiety sensitivity in this context will help patients gain insight into an important contributor to their fear of pain and a potential target for treatment goals. Because anxiety sensitivity is an unfamiliar construct to most patients, clearly explaining the construct and providing evidence of its direct link to pain is essential; in other words, a strong rationale for focusing on anxiety sensitivity in pain treatment is needed in order to gain "buy-in" from patients so they will engage in prescribed intervention strategies.

Subsequent to psychoeducation, cognitive restructuring may serve to provide some initial reductions is anxiety sensitivity. Watt and Stewart (2008) suggest focusing on two cognitive distortions when targeting high anxiety sensitivity: overestimation of the probability of a feared event occurring and catastrophizing about the consequences of the feared event. Individuals with high anxiety sensitivity and chronic pain are likely to catastrophize about the physical (e.g., "When my chest feels tight, I get scared that I won't be able to breathe properly") and cognitive (e.g., "When I cannot keep my mind on a task, I worry that I might be going crazy") consequences of arousal sensations. In a chronic pain population, it is likely that the patient may also catastrophize about the physical and cognitive consequences of pain. It is important, though, to remember that anxiety sensitivity is a distinct construct from pain-related anxiety, fear of pain, and pain catastrophizing. In efforts to reduce anxiety sensitivity, clinicians should remain focused on patient's feared consequences stemming from arousal sensations (e.g., rapid heart rate, sweating, shortness of breath, difficulty concentrating, dizziness). It is possible that feared consequences stemming from these arousal sensations may be pain-related; this is appropriate and can be targeted via the anxiety sensitivity intervention. There are certainly some pain-related nonarousal sensations (e.g., lower back pain, headaches) that remain distinct from anxiety sensitivity.

Nevertheless, there are a number of arousal sensations that are pain-related (e.g., chest pain, numbness/tingling) or that can increase pain (e.g., anxious arousal can increase pain through muscle tension, which, in turn, can increase anxious arousal) that would make it difficult to disentangle whether these were an anxiety sensitivity or pain-related fear. Targeting these fears through cognitive restructuring for anxiety sensitivity is appropriate and, even if they turn out to be more pain-related, will not hurt the patient or hinder treatment progress.

Cognitive restructuring for anxiety sensitivity in chronic pain patients will involve first helping patients identify when they are overestimating the probability that they will experience a feared consequence of arousal sensations and/or catastrophizing about the outcome. Practice identifying these negative automatic thoughts can be done through Socratic questioning with the therapist and subsequently through thought logs kept by the patient for homework. Subsequently, patients should be taught to challenge these cognitive distortions. Watt and Stewart (2008) recommend the use of targeted questioning to address probability overestimation (e.g., "What are the true odds of this happening? Has this ever happened before? What is the evidence that it will not happen?") and catastrophizing (e.g., "What is the worst possible thing that could happen? So what if that happened? What would you do? Could you survive?"). Many of these questions are appropriate to be asked of patients with chronic pain, though a patient's history of pain experiences stemming from physical exertion may not provide much disconfirming evidence. In these instances, it will be important to emphasize the transient nature of the discomfort stemming from arousal as well as the patient's ability to cope with distress. Ultimately, the goal is to replace dysfunctional thoughts with realistic hypotheses about arousal sensations (e.g., "My chest has felt tight like this before and I have always still been able to breathe"; "This feeling of dizziness will pass, it always does, I can handle it"; "I am feeling more pain because I am anxious; when I manage my anxiety I can better control my pain.").

Importantly, interventions for anxiety sensitivity in chronic pain populations should involve IE. As noted during our discussion of cognitive restructuring, patients may have a history of pain experiences that have been precipitated by the experience of arousal sensations. Subsequently, through interoceptive conditioning processes, described in detail by De Peuter et al. (2011), mild arousal-related sensations may elicit a fear response and can lead to false alarms (i.e., can induce fear even when they are not a sign of impending catastrophe). With this in mind, patients need disconfirming experiences in which the feared sensations are presented in absence of the anticipated feared responses so the sensations can be habituated to and the feared response extinguished (De Peuter et al., 2011).

Before beginning IE exercises, it is advisable to screen the participant for any health-related conditions that may contraindicate certain types of IE exercises so the selection of IE exercises maps onto the patient's specific health status (Asmundson, Gomez-Perez, & Fetzner, 2014). Typically, IE involves the identification of several (i.e., two to four) brief exercises (i.e., only a few minutes in length) that create arousal-related sensations that the patient perceives as distressing and that resemble those that the patient encounters in their daily life (or anticipates encountering, if their avoidance is pronounced). It is recommended that the patient complete these exercises in session with the therapist first, before they are assigned as homework for the patient to complete a number of times independently between sessions.

In the Watt et al. (2006) and Olthuis et al. (2015) studies, IE took the form of 10-min bouts of physical exercise (i.e., running/brisk walking) conducted 1–3 times per week over a period of 7–10 weeks. Though discussed at length in session in preparation, the IE exercises themselves were conducted outside of session with the exception of a single session in the Watt et al. (2006) intervention, which had participants engage in IE as a group in the final CBT session. Given that the majority of IE, in both studies, took place independently, participants were provided with heart rate monitors, which they were instructed to use to ensure they were exerting themselves to a sufficient extent to experience arousal-related physiological sensations (i.e., 60%–80% of maximal heart rate). For some patients with chronic pain, this could be an appropriate IE intervention. For others, their pain or broader physical disability may preclude them from being able to engage in running or brisk walking. These patients may be better served by more traditional IE exercises, such as those implemented by Wald et al. (2010).

In the context of traditional IE, patients are asked to engage in brief activities (i.e., for 1–2 min) both in session and at home that elicit feared physiological sensations. These activities might include 1 min of jogging on the spot, 1 min of hyperventilation, 1 min of breathing through a straw, or 30 s of shaking their head back and forth. Most panic disorder treatment manuals include sample IE activities, as do Watt and Stewart (2008). Again, with these exercises, the goal is to identify activities that the patient with chronic pain can execute that bring on the feared sensations but do not excessively exacerbate long-term pain. IE activities should be repeated until the distress they elicit has been reduced. For this reason, clinicians should ask patients to rate their level of distress (i.e., on a scale of 1–100) before, during, and after the activities; tracking this information can allow therapists to ascertain whether the IE exercises are having the desired effect. Whereas the sensations themselves may always be uncomfortable, the goal is for individuals to be able to experience the sensations without the accompanying heightened distress, including distress in anticipation of and following activities. In other words, individuals will learn to be comfortable being uncomfortable, and realize that being uncomfortable is not a catastrophic situation.

To best illustrate the assessment and treatment-related concepts we discuss here, we have provided a clinical case example of incorporating anxiety sensitivity intervention into chronic pain treatment. Consider the case of Ashley (in order to maintain patient anonymity, this case is a composite of several related clinical cases):

> *Ashley pursued treatment for chronic headache through the interdisciplinary pain management team at our local hospital. At the time of her referral, Ashley reported experiencing headaches of moderate-to-high severity several times per week. Medical reports accompanying her referral suggested no immediate concern about brain pathology that would need to be resolved to reduce Ashley's pain. She reported her headaches had been ongoing, with fluctuating frequency, for the prior four years, and were occasionally accompanied by fuzzy spots in her vision, an increased heart rate, and sweating. Her headache pain had significantly impacted her*

quality of life; for example, she and her partner were historically avid hikers and Ashley found herself unable to engage in this activity without pain. We conducted a comprehensive assessment of Ashley's pain including its frequency, severity, and associated disability, and measured Ashley's pain-related anxiety, fear of pain, and anxiety sensitivity. Ashley's scores across these measures were elevated. When these results were discussed with Ashley in the context of an assessment and treatment planning session, Ashley identified with a number of anxiety sensitivity concerns. She expressed concerns that any sensations of lightheadedness or dizziness were signs of impending headache, that her rapid heart rate and sweating were an indication that something else was seriously wrong with her body, and that her inability to get her mind off of her body sensations and potential pain might mean she was going crazy. With these concerns in mind, we hypothesized that Ashley would struggle to engage with the typical components of a chronic pain intervention without addressing her worries about these arousal sensations first. With Ashley's agreement, we worked through a brief five session intervention focused on reducing her anxiety sensitivity, assessing her anxiety sensitivity again at sessions three and five. In the first session, which was linked to her assessment and treatment planning session, we provided psychoeducation around normal arousal sensations and their course, anxiety sensitivity, the role of anxiety sensitivity in chronic pain, and examples of how anxiety sensitivity might be manifesting in Ashley's life (e.g., contributing to avoidance behaviors). When Ashley returned for a second session, she was taught cognitive strategies to help challenge her beliefs about the likelihood that the consequences she feared would occur and the seriousness of the possible consequences. For instance, Ashley's belief that the lightheadedness, rapid heart rate, and sweating she experienced were a sign of an approaching headache and potentially even symptoms of a major medical issue (e.g., brain tumor) was challenged by querying whether: (a) there were possible reasons why she might be feeling these sensations other than an approaching headache (e.g., physical exertion while hiking), (b) there were occasions when she had experienced these sensations and not experienced a subsequent headache, and (c) these sensations had ever resulted in serious physical catastrophe (e.g., dying from a brain tumor). In session three, Ashley began IE. Given Ashley's constellation of symptoms and concerns, two specific exercises were selected: 10 min sessions of brisk walking and hyperventilation for 60 seconds. The brisk walking was intended to bring on sweating and a rapid heart rate while hyperventilation is known to target some of the physiological sensations Ashley fears while also not exacerbating her chronic pain. We completed these activities in session together the first time; hyperventilation was done in the office while brisk walking was conducted through the halls of the hospital (with Ashley's consent). Ashley was somewhat apprehensive about the hyperventilation, predicting that it might bring on a headache. However, she understood the rationale that cognitive sensations such as lightheadedness, dizziness, and difficulty focusing could also be brought on for other reasons and be more temporary in nature and was willing to experiment with the hyperventilation. In-session practice confirmed that these exercises provoked sensations similar to those Ashley feared and allowed her to have a model of how IE exercises were properly conducted. She was sent home with homework to practice the IE exercises at least three times per week, and IE was reviewed and tweaked as needed (e.g., walking progressed to jogging) in sessions four and five. By session five, Ashley was reporting significantly reduced anxiety sensitivity, which was confirmed by her scores on the ASI-3. Although she continued to experience headaches, they were somewhat less frequent and she was not avoiding activities to the same degree. She found herself paying less attention to her arousal sensations and noted that a moment of lightheadedness (e.g., from standing up too quickly) no longer brought on anxiety about an oncoming headache. This, in turn, reduced the likelihood that a headache would develop. Subsequently, Ashley was able to pursue a more traditional CBT chronic pain program including psychoeducation, stress management, emotion regulation, cognitive restructuring, and IE targeted at fear of pain.

Future research directions

Given that research into the treatment of anxiety sensitivity for chronic pain and its related constructs is still in its infancy, there is substantial room for further advancement in the field. The existing studies of CBT and IE interventions for anxiety sensitivity have focused on high anxiety sensitivity (not chronic pain) samples (Olthuis et al., 2015; Watt et al., 2006) or have been case series (Wald et al., 2010). With this in mind, investigating the efficacy of CBT for anxiety sensitivity within chronic pain samples is much needed. Similarly, research on anxiety sensitivity interventions in chronic pain samples would benefit from a greater focus on functional pain outcomes, including escape/avoidance behaviors and functional impairment/disability; indeed, despite the importance of pain reduction for those with chronic pain and the fortunate outcome that this does occur in many chronic pain treatment protocols, improving function is often the primary outcome of interest (Woods & Asmundson, 2008). CBT for anxiety sensitivity could be tested as a standalone intervention and/or could be integrated as an aspect of a comprehensive chronic pain treatment package, in the manner of Wald et al. (2010), and as elaborated upon elsewhere by Asmundson (2014). Given that research shows that anxiety sensitivity reductions can have transdiagnostic implications (i.e., can reduce a range of mental health symptoms in addition to pain-related cognitions and behaviors; Olthuis et al., 2014; Olthuis et al., 2015), this type of intervention also warrants investigation among chronic pain samples with comorbid anxiety, trauma, depressive, and substance use disorders as a way to treat both problems with an integrated intervention.

Research is also needed to determine whether the addition of psychoeducation and cognitive restructuring leads to greater anxiety sensitivity reduction in pain-related cognitions and behaviors, as compared to IE alone. The empirical (Wald et al., 2010) and theoretical (De Peuter et al., 2011) emphasis has largely been on IE interventions to date; so, understanding whether the additional elements are needed will have implications not only for treatment efficacy but for the cost-effectiveness and practicalities of intervention delivery. Session-by-session tracking of anxiety sensitivity and pain-related cognitive and behavioral factors would also be helpful in confirming the mediating role of anxiety sensitivity reductions on these pain-related cognitions and behaviors. Similarly, research is needed to determine if additional graded in vivo exposure treatment focused on those behaviors and tasks chronic pain patients have been avoiding (de Jong et al., 2005), as suggested as a possibility by De Peuter et al. (2011) and Stewart and Asmundson (2006), is a necessary, beneficial, or unnecessary next step to anxiety sensitivity treatment when it comes to achieving optimal pain outcomes.

Finally, there is also always room in the field for innovative ideas as to how to include an anxiety sensitivity focus in chronic pain treatment. For instance, McCracken and Keogh (2009) suggest that perhaps anxiety sensitivity may be addressed via treatments that include acceptance, mindfulness, and values, such as Acceptance and Commitment Therapy (ACT; Hayes, Strosah, & Wilson, 1999). They suggested that this type of intervention, with its emphasis on reducing avoidance of anxious sensations and instead altering the meaning of these experiences and their influence on feelings and behavior, may serve to undermine anxiety sensitivity processes within the context of chronic pain. In support of this postulation, their research has shown that when acceptance of pain, mindfulness, and values-based action are considered, the variance in functioning among patients with chronic pain accounted for by anxiety sensitivity was significantly reduced (McCracken & Keogh, 2009). Future research that investigates specific therapeutic processes within the context of ACT that may serve to disrupt the impact of anxiety sensitivity on pain-related constructs may thus be worth investigating.

Appendix A Sample interoceptive exposure exercises for fear of pain

Interoceptive exposure exercise	Sample exercises
Tensing and releasing specific muscle groups	Clench fists for 30 s Raise shoulders to ears for 30 s Gently contract stomach muscles for 30 s Press lower back against chair or wall for 30 s
Applying pressure to specific muscle groups	Firmly pressing and holding hand to thigh for 30–60 s Firmly squeezing upper arm muscle for 30–60 s
Holding certain body postures	Pull shoulders back and hold for 30 s Sit up straight in chair for 30 s
Narrowing attentional focus to particular body parts	Focusing on lower back sensations for 60 s Focusing on sensations in neck for 60 s
Body checking via repeated palpation	Repeatedly palpating a spot on thigh for 30–60 s Repeatedly palpating temples for 30 s

Note. Learning objectives for each exercise are that pain can be generated through our own actions, does not necessarily portend catastrophe, can be managed, and dissipates with time.

Appendix B Fear-avoidance model of pain

This appendix is designed to provide clinicians with comprehensible psychoeducation about the fear-avoidance model of pain that can easily be provided to clients. The full handout, including a visual model of the fear-avoidance model, is available in the online companion.

Here you will find a model that can help us understand the development of pain. This model can help us understand a few important things about pain.

- The way that we think about and understand the pain we experience can influence whether we experience pain with or without fear.
- Negative thoughts about the pain that we experience can lead us to avoid activities that might bring on pain.
- Having high anxiety sensitivity, or a fear of arousal-related body sensations due to the belief that they will lead to catastrophe, seems to make it more likely that someone might experience negative thoughts about pain.
- Avoidance of activities and negative thoughts about pain can lead to the experience of pain-related disability, low mood, and lack of use of muscles and joints.

Appendix: Supplementary material

Supplementary material related to this chapter can be found online at https://www.elsevier.com/books-and-journals/book-companion/9780128134955.

References

Asmundson, G. J. G. (2014). The emotional and physical pains of trauma: contemporary and innovative approaches for treating co-occurring PTSD and chronic pain. *Depression and Anxiety*, *31*, 717–720.

Asmundson, G. J. G., Bovell, C. V., Carleton, R. N., & McWilliams, L. A. (2008). The Fear of Pain Questionnaire-Short Form (FPQ-SF): factorial validity and psychometric properties. *Pain*, *134*, 51–58.

Asmundson, G. J. G., Gomez-Perez, L., & Fetzner, M. (2014). Chronic pain and posttraumatic stress disorder. In N. Feeny & L. Zoellner (Eds.), *Facilitating resilience and recovery following trauma* (pp. 265–290). New York: Guilford.

Asmundson, G. J. G., Gómez-Perez, L., Richter, A., & Carleton, R. N. (2014). The psychology of pain: models and targets for comprehensive assessment. In H. van Griensven, J. Strong, & A. M. Unruh (Eds.), *Pain: A textbook for health professionals* (pp. 35–48). St. Louis, MO: Churchill Livingstone (Elsevier).

Asmundson, G. J. G., & Katz, J. (2009). Understanding the co-occurrence of anxiety disorders and chronic pain: State-of-the-art. *Depression and Anxiety*, *26*, 888–901.

Asmundson, G. J. G., & Norton, G. R. (1995). Anxiety sensitivity in patients with physically unexplained chronic back pain: a preliminary report. *Behaviour Research and Therapy*, *33*, 771–777.

Asmundson, G. J. G., Norton, G. R., & Allerdings, M. D. (1997). Fear and avoidance in dysfunctional chronic back pain patients. *Pain*, *69*, 231–236.

Asmundson, G. J. G., Norton, P. J., & Norton, G. N. (1999). Beyond pain: the role of fear and avoidance in chronicity. *Clinical Psychology Review*, *19*, 97–119.

Asmundson, G. J. G., Norton, P. J., & Veloso, F. (1999). Anxiety sensitivity and fear of pain in patients with recurring headaches. *Behaviour Research and Therapy*, *37*, 703–713.

Asmundson, G. J. G., Norton, P. J., & Vlaeyen, J. W. S. (2004). Fear-avoidance models of chronic pain: an overview. In G. J. G. Asmundson, J. W. S. Vlaeyen, & G. Crombez (Eds.), *Understanding and treating fear of pain* (pp. 3–24). Oxford, UK: Oxford University Press.

Asmundson, G. J. G., Parkerson, H. A., Petter, M., & Noel, M. (2012). What is the role of fear and escape/avoidance in chronic pain? Models, structural analysis and future directions. *Pain Management*, *2*, 295–303.

Asmundson, G. J. G., & Taylor, S. (1996). Role of anxiety sensitivity in pain-related fear and avoidance. *Journal of Behavioral Medicine*, *19*, 577–586.

Asmundson, G. J. G., & Wright, K. D. (2004). The biopsychosocial model of pain. In T. Hadjistavropoulos & K. D. Craig (Eds.), *Pain: Psychological perspectives* (pp. 35–57). New Jersey, NJ: Erlbaum.

Asmundson, G. J. G., Wright, K. D., & Hadjistavropoulos, H. D. (2000). Anxiety sensitivity and disabling chronic health conditions: state of the art and future directions. *Scandinavian Journal of Behaviour Therapy*, *29*, 100–117.

Bailey, K. M., Carleton, R. N., Vlaeyen, J. W., & Asmundson, G. J. G. (2010). Treatments addressing pain-related fear and anxiety in patients with chronic musculoskeletal pain: a preliminary review. *Cognitive Behaviour Therapy*, *39*, 46–63.

Brandt, C. P., Gonzalez, A., Grover, K. W., & Zvolensky, M. J. (2013). The relation between emotional dysregulation and anxiety and depressive symptoms, pain-related anxiety, and HIV-symptom distress among adults with HIV/AIDS. *Journal of Psychopathology and Behavioral Assessment*, *35*, 197–204.

Breivik, H., Collett, B., Ventafridda, V., Cohen, R., & Gallacher, D. (2006). Survey of chronic pain in Europe: prevalence, impact on daily life, and treatment. *European Journal of Pain*, *10*, 287–333.

Cappucci, S., & Simons, L. E. (2015). Anxiety sensitivity and fear of pain in paediatric headache patients. *European Journal of Pain*, *19*, 246–252.

Carleton, R. N., Sharpe, D. S., & Asmundson, G. J. G. (2007). Anxiety sensitivity and intolerance of uncertainty: requisites of the fundamental fears? *Behaviour Research and Therapy*, *45*, 2307–2316.

Carroll, I. R., Hah, J. M., Barelka, P. L., Wang, C. K. M., Wang, B. M., Gillespie, M. J., … Mackey, S. C. (2015). Pain duration and resolution following surgery: an inception cohort study. *Pain Medicine*, *16*, 2386–2396.

Chidambaran, V., Ding, L., Moore, D. L., Spruance, K., Cudilo, E. M., Pilipenko, V., … Sadhasivam, S. (2017). Predicting the pain continuum after adolescent idiopathic scoliosis surgery: a prospective cohort study. *European Journal of Pain*, *21*, 1252–1265.

Craske, M., & Barlow, D. H. (2001). Panic disorder and agoraphobia. In D. H. Barlow (Ed.), *Clinical handbook for psychological disorders: a step-by-step treatment manual* (3rd ed., pp. 1-59). New York, NY: Guilford Press.

Curzik, D., & Jokić-Begić, N. (2011). Anxiety sensitivity and anxiety as correlates of expected, experienced, and recalled labor pain. *Journal of Psychosomatic Obstetrics and Gynecology*, *32*, 198–203.

de Jong, J. R., Vlaeyen, J. W., Onghena, P., Goossens, M. E., Geilen, M., & Mulder, H. (2005). Fear of movement/(re)injury in chronic low back pain: education or exposure in vivo as mediator to fear reduction? *Clinical Journal of Pain*, *21*, 9–17.

De Peuter, S., Van Diest, I., Vansteenwegen, D., Van den Bergh, O., & Vlaeyen, J. W. (2011). Understanding fear of pain in chronic pain: Interoceptive fear conditioning as a novel approach. *European Journal of Pain, 15*, 888–894.

Drahovzal, D. N., Stewart, S. H., & Sullivan, M. J. L. (2006). Tendency to catastrophize somatic sensations: pain catastrophizing and anxiety sensitivity in predicting headache. *Cognitive Behaviour Therapy, 35*, 226–235.

El-Gabalawy, R., Asmundson, G. J. G., & Sareen, J. (2011). Suicide and chronic pain. In A. L. Berman & M. Pompili (Eds.), *Medical conditions associated with suicide risk* (pp. 75–86). Washington, DC: American Association of Suicidology.

Esteve, R., Marquina-Aponte, V., & Ramírez-Maestre, C. (2014). Postoperative pain in children: association between anxiety sensitivity, pain catastrophizing, and female caregivers' responses to children's pain. *The Journal of Pain, 15*, 157–168.

Gatchel, R. J. (2004). Comorbidity of chronic pain and mental health disorders: the biopsychosocial perspective. *American Psychologist, 59*, 795–805.

Gerrior, K. G., Watt, M. C., Weaver, A. D., & Gallagher, C. E. (2015). The role of anxiety sensitivity in the sexual functioning of young women. *Sexual and Relationship Therapy, 30*, 351–363.

Gureje, O., Von Korff, M., Simon, G. E., & Gater, R. (1998). Persistent pain and well-being: A World Health Organization study in primary care. *JAMA: The Journal of the American Medical Association, 280*, 147–151.

Hadjistavropoulos, H. D., Asmundson, G. J. G., & Kowalyk, K. M. (2004). Measures of anxiety: is there a difference in their ability to predict functioning at three-month follow-up among pain patients. *European Journal of Pain, 8*, 1–11.

Hayes, S. C., Strosah, K., & Wilson, K. G. (1999). *Acceptance and commitment therapy: an experiential approach to behavior change*. New York: Guilford.

International Association for the Study of Pain. (1986). Classification of chronic pain: descriptions of chronic pain syndromes and definitions of pain terms. *Pain Supplement, 3*, 1–222.

Jokić-Begić, N., Žigić, L., & Radoš, S. N. (2014). Anxiety and anxiety sensitivity as predictors of fear of childbirth: different patterns for nulliparous and parous women. *Journal of Psychosomatic Obstetrics and Gynecology, 35*, 22–28.

Katz, J., McCartney, C. J. L., & Rashiq, S. (2008). Why does pain become chronic? In S. Rashiqu, D. Schopflocher, P. Taenzer, & E. Jonsson (Eds.), *Chronic pain: A health policy perspective* (pp. 67–84). Weinheim, Germany: Wiley-Blackwell.

Keogh, E., Book, K., Thomas, J., Giddins, G., & Eccleston, C. (2010). Predicting pain and disability in patients with hand fractures: comparing pain anxiety, anxiety sensitivity and pain catastrophizing. *European Journal of Pain, 14*, 446–451.

Lang, A. J., Sorrell, J. T., Rodgers, C. S., & Lebeck, M. M. (2006). Anxiety sensitivity as a predictor of labor pain. *European Journal of Pain, 10*, 263–270.

Lee, J. L., Gilleland, J., Campbell, R. M., Johnson, G. L., Simpson, P., Dooley, K. J., & Blount, R. L. (2013). Internalizing symptoms and functional disability in children with noncardiac chest pain and innocent heart murmurs. *Journal of Pediatric Psychology, 38*, 255–264.

Leeuw, M., Goossens, M. E., Linton, S. J., Crombez, G., Boersma, K., & Vlaeyen, J. W. (2007). The fear-avoidance model of musculoskeletal pain: current scientific evidence. *Journal of Behavioral Medicine, 30*, 77–94.

Lipsitz, J. D., Masia-Warner, C., Apfel, H., Marans, Z., Hellstern, B., Forand, N., … Fyer, A. J. (2004). Anxiety and depressive symptoms and anxiety sensitivity in youngsters with noncardiac chest pain and benign heart murmurs. *Journal of Pediatric Psychology, 29*, 607–612.

Lohnberg, J. A. (2007). A review of outcome studies on cognitive-behavioral therapy for reducing fear-avoidance beliefs among individuals with chronic pain. *Journal of Clinical Psychology in Medical Settings*, *14*, 113–122.

López-de-Uralde-Villaneuva, I., Muñoz-García, D., Gil-Martínez, A., Pardo-Montero, J., Muñoz-Plata, R., Angulo-Díaz-Parreño, S., … La Touche, R. (2016). A systematic review and meta-analysis on the effectiveness of graded activity and graded exposure for chronic nonspecific low back pain. *Pain Medicine*, *17*, 172–188.

Martin, A. L., McGrath, P. A., Brown, S. C., & Katz, J. (2007). Anxiety sensitivity, fear of pain and pain-related disability in children and adolescents with chronic pain. *Pain Research and Management*, *12*, 267–272.

McCracken, L. M., & Dhingra, L. (2002). A short version of the Pain Anxiety Symptoms Scale (PASS-20): preliminary development and validity. *Pain Research and Management*, *7*, 45–50.

McCracken, L. M., & Keogh, E. (2009). Acceptance, mindfulness, and values-based action may counteract fear and avoidance of emotions in chronic pain: an analysis of anxiety sensitivity. *The Journal of Pain*, *10*, 408–415.

McNeil, D. W., Kennedy, S. G., Randall, C. L., Addicks, S. H., Wright, C. D., Hursey, K. G., & Vaglienti, R. (2018). Fear of Pain Questionnaire-9: brief assessment of pain-related fear and anxiety. *European Journal of Pain*, *22*, 39–48.

McNeil, D. W., & Rainwater, A. J. (1998). Development of the Fear of Pain Questionnaire-III. *Journal of Behavioral Medicine*, *21*, 389–410.

Meana, M., & Lykins, A. (2009). Negative affect and somatically focused anxiety in young women reporting pain with intercourse. *Journal of Sex Research*, *46*, 80–88.

Mehta, S., Rice, D., Janzen, S., Pope, J. E., Harth, M., Shapiro, A. P., & Teasell, R. W. (2016). Mood, disability, and quality of life among a subgroups of rheumatoid arthritis individuals with experiential avoidance and anxiety sensitivity. *Pain Research and Management*,7241856 [7 pages].

Mehta, S., Rice, D., McIntyre, A., Getty, H., Speechley, M., Sequeira, K., … Teasell, R. W. (2016). Identification and characterization of unique subgroups of chronic pain individuals with dispositional personality traits. *Pain Research and Management*,5187631 [7 pages].

Naragon-Gainey, K. (2010). Meta-analysis of the relations of anxiety sensitivity to the depressive and anxiety disorders. *Psychological Bulletin*, *136*, 128–150.

Ocañez, K. L. S., McHugh, R. K., & Otto, M. W. (2010). A meta-analytic review of the association between anxiety sensitivity and pain. *Depression and Anxiety*, *27*, 760–767.

Olatunji, B. O., & Wolitzky-Taylor, K. B. (2009). Anxiety sensitivity and the anxiety disorders: a meta-analytic review and synthesis. *Psychological Bulletin*, *135*, 974–999.

Olthuis, J. V., Watt, M. C., Mackinnon, S. P., Potter, S. M., & Stewart, S. H. (2015). The nature of the association between anxiety sensitivity and pain-related anxiety: evidence from correlational and intervention studies. *Cognitive Behaviour Therapy*, *44*, 423–440.

Olthuis, J. V., Watt, M. C., Mackinnon, S. P., & Stewart, S. H. (2014). Telephone-delivered cognitive behavioral therapy for high anxiety sensitivity: a randomized controlled trial. *Journal of Consulting and Clinical Psychology*, *82*, 1005–1022.

Plehn, K., Peterson, R. A., & Williams, D. A. (1998). Anxiety sensitivity: its relationship to functional status in patients with chronic pain. *Journal of Occupational Rehabilitation*, *8*, 213–222.

Ramírez-Maestre, C., & Esteve, R. (2013). Disposition and adjustment to chronic pain. *Current Pain and Headache Reports*, *17*, 312.

Ramírez-Maestre, C., Esteve, R., Ruiz-Párraga, G., Gómez-Pérez, L., & López-Martínez, A. E. (2017). The key role of pain catastrophizing in the disability of patients with acute back pain. *International Journal of Behavioral Medicine*, *24*, 239–248.

Registered Nurses' Association of Ontario. (2013). *Assessment and management of pain* (3rd ed.). Toronto, ON: Registered Nurses' Association of Ontario.

Reiss, S., & McNally, R. J. (1985). The expectancy model of fear. In S. Reiss & R. R. Bootzin (Eds.), *Theoretical issues in behavior therapy* (pp. 107–122). New York, NY: Academic Press.

Reiss, S., Peterson, R. A., Taylor, S., Schmidt, N., & Weems, C. F. (2008). *Anxiety Sensitivity Index consolidated user manual: ASI, ASI-3, and CASI*. Worthington, OH: IDS Publishing.

Rice, D., Mehta, S., Pope, J. E., Harth, M., Shapiro, A., & Teasell, R. W. (2016). Dispositional affect in unique subgroups of patients with rheumatoid arthritis. *Pain Research and Management*,1024985 [9 pages].

Rice, D. B., Mehta, S., Serrato, J., Pope, J. E., Harth, M., Sequeira, K., ... Teasell, R. W. (2017). Stress in patients diagnosed with rheumatoid arthritis compared to chronic pain. *Rehabilitation Psychology*, *62*, 571–579.

Smitherman, T. A., Davis, R. E., Walters, A. B., Young, J., & House, T. T. (2015). Anxiety sensitivity and headache: diagnostic differences, impact, and relations with perceived headache triggers. *Cephalalgia*, *35*, 710–721.

Smits, J. A. J., Berry, A. C., Tart, C. D., & Powers, M. B. (2008). The efficacy of cognitive-behavioral interventions for reducing anxiety sensitivity: a meta-analytic review. *Behaviour Research and Therapy*, *46*, 1047–1054.

Stewart, S. H., & Asmundson, G. J. G. (2006). Anxiety sensitivity and its impact on pain experiences and conditions: a state of the art. *Cognitive Behaviour Therapy*, *35*, 185–188.

Stewart, W. F., Ricci, J. A., Chee, E., Morganstein, D., & Lipton, R. (2003). Lost productive time and cost due to common pain conditions in the US workforce. *JAMA: The Journal of the American Medical Association*, *290*, 2443–2454.

Stewart, S. H., & Watt, M. C. (2008). Introduction to the special issue on interoceptive exposure in the treatment of anxiety and related disorders: novel applications and mechanisms of action. *Journal of Cognitive Psychotherapy: An International Quarterly*, *22*, 291–302.

Sullivan, M. J. L., Bishop, S. R., & Pivik, J. (1995). The pain catastrophizing scale: development and validation. *Psychological Assessment*, *7*, 524–532.

Taylor, S. (Ed.), (1999). *Anxiety sensitivity: Theory, research, and treatment of the fear of anxiety*. New Jersey: Erlbaum.

Taylor, S., Zvolensky, M. J., Cox, B. J., Deacon, B., Heimberg, R. G., Ledley, D. H., ... Cardenas, S. J. (2007). Robust dimensions of anxiety sensitivity: development and initial validation of the anxiety sensitivity index-3. *Psychological Assessment*, *19*, 176–188. https://doi.org/10.1037/1040-3590.19.2.176.

Thibodeau, M. A., Fetzner, M. G., Carleton, R. N., Kachur, S. S., & Asmundson, G. J. G. (2013). Fear of injury predicts self-reported and behavioral impairment in patients with chronic low back pain. *The Journal of Pain*, *14*, 172–181.

Tsao, J. C. I., Allen, L. B., Evans, S., Lu, Q., Myers, C. D., & Zeltzer, L. K. (2009). Anxiety sensitivity and catastrophizing: associations with pain and somatization in non-clinical children. *Journal of Health Psychology*, *14*, 1085–1094.

Turk, D. C., & Rudy, T. E. (1987). Towards a comprehensive assessment of chronic pain patients. *Behaviour Research and Therapy*, *25*, 237–249.

Vancleef, L. M., Peters, M. L., Roelofs, J., & Asmundson, G. J. G. (2006). Do fundamental fears differentially contribute to pain-related fear and pain catastrophizing? An evaluation of the sensitivity index. *European Journal of Pain*, *10*, 527–536.

Vlaeyen, J. W., & Linton, S. J. (2000). Fear-avoidance and its consequences in chronic musculoskeletal pain: a state of the art. *Pain*, *85*, 317–332.

Vlaeyen, J. W., & Linton, S. J. (2012). Fear-avoidance model of chronic musculoskeletal pain: 12 years on. *Pain*, *153*, 1144–1147.

Wald, J., Taylor, S., Chiri, L. R., & Sica, C. (2010). Posttraumatic stress disorder and chronic pain arising from motor vehicle accidents: efficacy of interoceptive exposure plus trauma-related exposure therapy. *Cognitive Behaviour Therapy*, *39*, 104–113.

Wall, P. D. (1978). The gate control theory of pain mechanisms: a re-examination and re-statement. *Brain*, *101*, 1–18.

Watt, M. C., & Stewart, S. H. (2008). *Overcoming the fear of fear: How to reduce anxiety sensitivity*. Oakland, CA: New Harbinger.

Watt, M. C., Stewart, S. H., Lefaivre, M.-J., & Uman, L. S. (2006). A brief cognitive-behavioral approach to reducing anxiety sensitivity decreases pain-related anxiety. *Cognitive Behaviour Therapy*, *35*, 248–256.

White, K. S., McDonnell, C. J., & Gervino, E. V. (2011). Alexithymia and anxiety sensitivity in patients with non-cardiac chest pain. *Journal of Behavior Therapy and Experimental Psychiatry*, *42*, 432–439.

Wong, W. S., Lam, H. M. J., Chow, Y. F., Chen, P. P., Lim, H. S., Wong, S., & Fielding, R. (2014). The effects of anxiety sensitivity, pain hypervigilance, and pain catastrophizing on quality of life outcomes of patients with chronic pain: a preliminary, cross-sectional analysis. *Quality of Life Research*, *23*, 2333–2341.

Wood, R. L. I., McCabe, M., & Dawkins, J. (2011). The role of anxiety sensitivity in symptom perception after minor head injury: an exploratory study. *Brain Injury*, *25*, 1296–1299.

Woods, M. P., & Asmundson, G. J. G. (2008). Evaluating the efficacy of graded in vivo exposure for the treatment of fear in patients with chronic back pain: a randomized controlled clinical trial. *Pain*, *136*, 271–280.

Zvolensky, M. J., Goodie, J. L., McNeil, D. W., Sperry, J. A., & Sorrell, J. T. (2001). Anxiety sensitivity in the prediction of pain-related fear and anxiety in a heterogeneous chronic pain population. *Behaviour Research and Therapy*, *39*, 683–696.

Further reading

Norton, P. J., & Asmundson, G. J. G. (2003). Amending the fear-avoidance models of chronic pain: what is the role of physiological arousal? *Behavior Therapy*, *34*, 17–30.

Integrative treatment program for anxiety sensitivity and smoking cessation

6

Michael J. Zvolensky, Lorra Garey, Brooke Y. Kauffman, Kara Manning
University of Houston, Houston, TX, United States

Chapter Outline

Tobacco: A modifiable health-risk behavior

Over 1 billion adults worldwide are current cigarette smokers (Jha, Ranson, Nguyen, & Yach, 2002), with approximately 37 million smokers residing in the United States (U.S.; CDC, 2011). Smoking is a robust risk factor for numerous diseases, including cardiovascular disease, pulmonary disease, and cancer (CDC, 2011). Given the negative health-related consequences of smoking and the large prevalence of smokers, it is not surprising that cigarette smoking remains the leading cause of preventable morbidity and mortality in the U.S., accounting for approximately 443,000 deaths each year (CDC, 2010). Importantly, quitting smoking substantially decreases risk of developing smoking-related health conditions and increases survival

The Clinician's Guide to Anxiety Sensitivity Treatment and Assessment. https://doi.org/10.1016/B978-0-12-813495-5.00006-1

time among those who have already developed smoking-related medical problems (Samet, 1991).

Anxiety sensitivity: Risk factor for poor smoking outcomes

In an effort to enhance smoking cessation treatment and outcomes, substantial work has been dedicated to elucidating individual difference risk factors for smoking maintenance and relapse processes. Convergent work has consistently implicated anxiety sensitivity as a prominent and unique individual difference factor relevant to smoking behavior and quit processes (Zvolensky, Lejuez, Kahler, & Brown, 2003). There are interrelated, but distinct, lines of independently replicated studies that have documented the role of anxiety sensitivity in a multitude of smoking maintenance and relapse processes (Leventhal & Zvolensky, 2015; Otto et al., 2016). Notably, within these studies, the effects of anxiety sensitivity for smoking processes were not explained by severity of tobacco dependence, gender, trait-like tendencies to experience negative affect states, or other types of substance use problems (e.g., alcohol; Leventhal & Zvolensky, 2015). For example, prior work has found that anxiety sensitivity is related to negative affect reduction motives and expectancies, and to a lesser extent, addictive as well as habitual motives (Farris, Leventhal, Schmidt, & Zvolensky, 2015; Gonzalez, Zvolensky, Vujanovic, Leyro, & Marshall, 2008; Gregor, Zvolensky, McLeish, Bernstein, & Morissette, 2008; Johnson, Farris, Schmidt, & Zvolensky, 2012; Leyro, Zvolensky, Vujanovic, & Bernstein, 2008). These subjective expectations and motives may be linked to actual smoking effects, as high anxiety sensitivity smokers also report greater smoking-induced reductions in subjective anxiety after stressful laboratory situations (Evatt & Kassel, 2010; Perkins, Karelitz, Giedgowd, Conklin, & Sayette, 2010) and more positive subjective benefits of smoking (Farris & Zvolensky, 2016; Wong et al., 2013).

Anxiety sensitivity is also related to the tendency to smoke in an inflexible manner when one is confronted with interoceptive stress (e.g., bodily tension; Zvolensky, Farris, Schmidt, & Smits, 2014). Other empirical work has demonstrated that anxiety sensitivity is associated with the tendency to perceive quitting as more difficult (Langdon, Farris, Hogan, Grover, & Zvolensky, 2016; Zvolensky et al., 2007) and to expect periods of smoking deprivation to be personally threatening (Farris, Paulus, et al., 2015; Guillot, Leventhal, Raines, Zvolensky, & Schmidt, 2016). In fact, anxiety sensitivity is related to greater negative affect, craving, and nicotine withdrawal symptoms (Johnson, Stewart, Rosenfield, Steeves, & Zvolensky, 2012; Langdon et al., 2013), shorter time to lapse/relapse, and lower overall abstinence; findings that have been observed during aided (i.e., pharmacological and psychosocial treatment; Zvolensky, Stewart, Vujanovic, Gavric, & Steeves, 2009) and unaided (Marshall, Johnson, Bergman, Gibson, & Zvolensky, 2009) quit attempts. The effects of anxiety sensitivity on lapse/relapse behavior have been found to operate through negative affect states and craving/withdrawal. Other studies demonstrate that anxiety sensitivity mediates the relation between emotional disorders and severity of smoking behavior (Olvera et al., 2015; Powers et al., 2016; Zvolensky, Farris, Leventhal, & Schmidt, 2014).

Treatment conceptualization: Anxiety sensitivity reduction for smoking

We have developed an integrated treatment protocol for targeting anxiety sensitivity among smokers informed by an integrated theoretical model of their relation (see Fig. 1). This theoretically derived intervention program integrates anxiety sensitivity reduction cognitive-behavioral therapeutic strategies with evidence-based smoking cessation counseling strategies. This program, termed the Anxiety Sensitivity Reduction Program for Smoking (ASRP-S), is structured around the theoretically relevant cognitive risk factor, anxiety sensitivity. By structuring the intervention around anxiety sensitivity, the program is expected to simultaneously improve mental health *and* smoking behavior. The program focuses on three elements: (1) psychoeducational provision of an integrated therapeutic rationale, (2) decreasing emotional sensitivity and reactivity to anxiety, bodily cues, and nicotine withdrawal via cognitive-behavioral

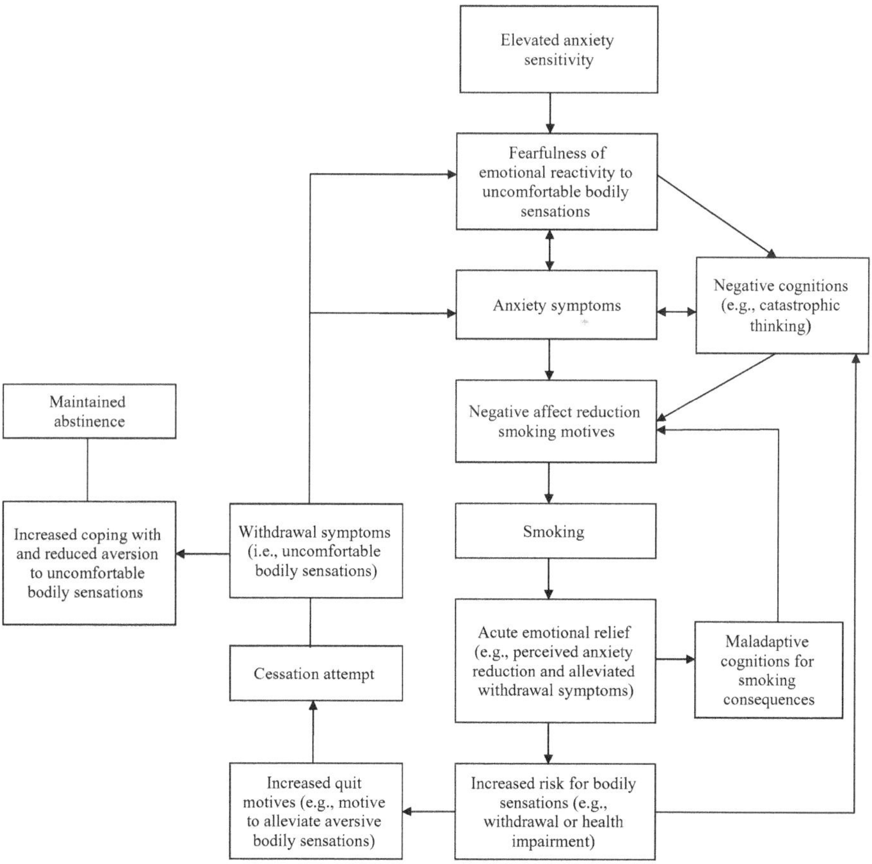

Fig. 1 Theoretical model for anxiety sensitivity and smoking.

Table 1 Treatment elements and associated components

Element	Components
1. Integrated therapeutic rationale	• How smoking promotes or exacerbates mental health problems • Rationale for targeting anxiety sensitivity and smoking together • Fear of anxiety, catastrophic thinking, and smoking are maladaptive coping mechanisms • 2–3 Sessions focused on anxiety sensitivity exclusively, but embedded throughout the whole treatment
2. Decreasing anxiety sensitivity via cognitive-behavioral methods	• Decrease emotional sensitivity and reactivity to interceptive stimuli • Help smokers learn a sense of tolerance, control, and safety when experiencing anxiety symptoms • Interoceptive exposure, cognitive restructuring, and acceptance strategies • Clinical practice guidelines from *Treating Tobacco Use and Dependence*
3. Specialized smoking-oriented psychoeducation and relapse prevention	• Provide positive reinforcement and social support for quitting • Discuss past quit experiences • Set a quit date • Self-monitoring program for smoking and coping behaviors • Identify high-risk smoking situations • Discuss abstinence violation effect • Teach adaptive coping strategies • Enlist social support for quitting • Remove all tobacco from environment

methods, and (3) specialized smoking-oriented psychoeducation and relapse prevention. See Table 1 for an overview of these elements.

Element one: Integrated therapeutic rationale

Persons with high anxiety sensitivity are likely to believe that smoking helps them manage and/or cope with negative affect and do not understand that smoking may promote or exacerbate mental health problems. This issue is perhaps not surprising given that many professionals who specialize in the treatment of anxiety and its disorders do not understand or address the role of smoking in terms of mental health functioning (Zvolensky et al., 2005). As a result, clients have limited knowledge of the interaction between smoking and anxiety problems. To address this limitation of current practice, the current treatment emphasizes the importance of providing clients with a thorough psychoeducational rationale for targeting smoking and anxiety sensitivity. An aspect of this discussion needs to address the targeting these behaviors concurrently because of their negative bidirection relation and compounded impact on one's health. This rationale is particularly important because it provides a foundation for the treatment to not only focus on proven strategies for smoking cessation, but also on helping the individual learn and practice strategies to better manage interpreting, coping, and tolerating emergent withdrawal symptoms and anxiety symptoms. Specifically, we introduce the concepts of fear of anxiety and smoking as a maladaptive way of coping with anxiety-related distress. We pay attention to highlighting the process of the forward-feeding anxiety cycle, whereby catastrophic thinking and anxiety sensitivity can lead to both subjective threat evaluations and heightened attention to threatening stimuli, resulting in a greater risk for panic attacks as well as the exacerbation of interoceptive states like withdrawal symptoms. We also indicate such reactions may sensitize a person to the interoceptive and environmental cues that signal such distress in the future, leading to smoking as a way of coping. Finally, we articulate that targeting anxiety sensitivity and modifying it via thinking and behavioral exercises is important in enhancing *both* smoking and mental health. We emphasize that practicing cognitive-behavioral exercises both in and out of session is an important element of the intervention that directly contributes to each individual's ultimate success.

Element two: Decreasing anxiety sensitivity via cognitive-behavioral methods

The second core element involves using empirically derived cognitive-behavioral strategies developed for anxiety sensitivity to decrease emotional sensitivity and reactivity to interoceptive stimuli. Importantly, exposure exercises are adapted to target interoceptive cues across varying intensity levels of nicotine withdrawal (elicited via deprivation from smoking for various time periods). This intervention component is aimed to help smokers learn (or relearn) a sense of tolerance, control, and safety in the presence of anxiety-related sensations: a task presumably accomplished through helping individuals directly experience sensations in a controlled fashion, where emotionally corrective outcomes are facilitated, rather than in the naturally occurring context where catastrophic misinterpretation of these symptoms may occur (e.g., during cessation or smoking abstinence).

Accordingly, we integrate (1) interoceptive exposure with (2) corrective information about anxiety and cognitive interventions designed to teach clients alternatives to catastrophic misinterpretations of the sensations and their feared consequences ("I will lose control"), as well as (3) continued use of situational exposure. Specifically, we use cognitive restructuring aimed at targeting the elimination of catastrophic beliefs about the meaning and consequences of anxiety sensations and symptoms of withdrawal. In addition to cognitive-restructuring strategies, acceptance-based strategies are employed to foster increased tolerance for anxiety and related sensations. Furthermore, we systematically employ interoceptive exposure to extinguish fears of aversive internal sensations, with specific preparation for sensations that would be experienced as part of smoking discontinuation (withdrawal). Clients are explicitly taught that the goal of such therapeutic work is not to attempt the impossible task of eliminating anxiety or emotion-laden withdrawal sensations, but rather to ensure that these internal cues are not interpreted fearfully, escalating bothersome sensations into debilitating anxiety. Exposure to somatic and other interoceptive symptoms in advance of cessation theoretically should help ensure that participants have practice with an alternative model of symptom management well before the characteristic symptoms of smoking discontinuation are encountered.

Interoceptive exposure is described, demonstrated, and practiced in session and individuals are encouraged to practice the exercises outside of session (as part of assigned between session work). The importance of varying practice contexts to facilitate the "unlearning" of fear responses across settings is emphasized as a rationale for frequently practicing exercises out of session. Three interoceptive exposure exercises (e.g., head rolling, voluntary hyperventilation, and chair spinning) are typically completed each session, which is generally feasible within the given time constraints. For example, dizziness is induced by a head-rolling exercise in which clients gently swing their heads around in circles with their eyes closed for 1 min. The repeated use of such exercises provides adaptation to the sensations (habituation) and reduces the probability that such sensations will trigger anxiety in future circumstances. While performing these exercises, we pay attention to drawing a clear connection between aversive anxiety-related states and somatic changes and discuss such experiences in the context of changing smoking behavior (e.g., during a cessation attempt). Once participants can identify and isolate bodily sensations, they are coached to change their cognitive reactions to these sensations by reframing them in more adaptive ways and accepting them as "normal" reactions.

As the client progresses through the interoceptive exposure exercises, we increase exposure intensity by incorporating periods of smoking deprivation into the interoceptive exposure exercises. By adapting existing exposure-based interventions to withdrawal symptoms, it may be possible to decrease withdrawal symptoms, a primary factor in poor cessation outcomes (Kenford et al., 2002). Participants are asked to practice at least one self-exposure per day out of session along with monitoring their performance using an exposure monitoring data recording card. It also is emphasized to individuals these exercises are useful in terms of maintaining treatment goals and relapse prevention.

Element three: Specialized smoking-oriented psychoeducation and relapse prevention

The final element of the treatment program provides evidenced-based information for altering smoking behavior that is specifically designed for an anxiety vulnerable population. We base our discussion generally on clinical practice guidelines from the U.S. Department of Health and Human Services, *Treating Tobacco Use and Dependence* (Fiore et al., 2008).

This component includes a variety of information, representing nine separate aspects. First, we provide positive reinforcement and social support for quitting. For example, therapists are instructed to congratulate participants for deciding to quit smoking, review the positive health consequences of quitting, and express their willingness to help the participant succeed. Second, we discuss past quit experiences. These past quit attempts are reviewed to identify what strategies contributed to success and what factors hindered previous attempts. Third, we work with the client to set a quit date. This quit date occurs only after the client has demonstrated progress in interoceptive exposure exercises in and outside of session (i.e., successfully and regularly completing between session work). Here, it is important to have observed progress both for the exposure exercises in withdrawal and nonwithdrawal states. Fourth, we initiate a formal self-monitoring program for smoking and other (alternative) coping behaviors (e.g., physical exercise). Specifically, participants track each cigarette they smoke through their quit date and note situational cues for smoking as well as alternative strategies that they could have used instead of smoking.

Fifth, we work with the client to identify idiographic high-risk situations for smoking. The focus of this topic is to anticipate situations that likely will place them at risk for relapse and plan how to handle such situations ahead of time (without smoking). Sixth, we present and discuss the abstinence violation effect (Marlatt & Gordon, 1985). Namely, clients are prepared for the possibility of lapsing and given strategies for coping with the potential negative emotional reactions to lapsing. For example, clients are encouraged to identify and alter maladaptive thinking patterns about lapsing (e.g., altering thoughts such as "I might as well give up because I just had a cigarette" to "I just smoked, but this is not an excuse to alter my longer-term effort of changing my smoking behavior"). Seventh, we help clients identify and develop skills to support adaptive coping strategies. Due to the unique psychological concerns of individuals with high anxiety sensitivity, these coping strategies often reflect three key aspects of self- and emotion-regulation. The first pertains to coping behaviors that would alter negative emotional experiences in the short-term, particularly anxiety. The second pertains to longer-term health-oriented lifestyle behaviors such as physical exercise. Therapists assist the client in developing behavioral and cognitive strategies for coping with emotionally salient events in the short term and help develop plans for evoking longer-term health-oriented change. Third, therapists help each client identify specific high-risk situations for smoking and provide support to avoid them altogether. For example, therapists advise clients to avoid the use of alcohol or other substances to assist in smoking quit attempts or management of affect.

Eighth, we attempt to help clients enlist social support for quitting. Therapists advise clients to tell their friends and family about their quit date and discuss ways to increase social support during the quit attempt. For example, clients often are encouraged to share with friends and family that their "weak moments" tend to be related to dysregulated affect (e.g., worry, anxiety) and that they are trying to quit smoking by responding differently to such affective events. We believe this approach enhances the psychological environment for behavior change while explicitly recognizing the role of anxiety-specific processes in such behavior change. Clients also are encouraged, when applicable, to ask smokers in their household to avoid smoking in their presence. Finally, clients are encouraged to prepare for quitting by removing all tobacco products from their environment. This strategy helps remove unnecessary risks for tobacco use prior to vulnerable time periods and acts as a "behavioral index" of commitment to change.

Practical guide to treatment implementation: ASRP-R

ASRP-S consists of four in-person, individually delivered 90-min sessions. The treatment can easily be adapted for small groups by including group process issues (confidentiality, group guidelines, etc.) during the first session. ASRP-S is a prevention program; thus, all therapy sessions are presented prior to quit day/treatment session 4. Each session includes specific objectives (see Table 2), handouts, and between session work assignments. The structure consists of reviewing between session work and past session content, outlining and addressing current session objectives, assigning between session work, and previewing topics covered in the upcoming session. Clients are provided a client binder during the first session to help guide their treatment. In the following, we provide a practical clinical guide for implementing ASRP-S. This guide serves as a model for administering ASRP-S, but therapists should exercise clinical judgment when utilizing this manualized treatment. Indeed, the program was intentionally developed to be flexible and easily adapted to fit the unique needs of clients.

There are several clinical tactics that therapists should incorporate into each session. To decrease redundancy, these tactics are not discussed in the guidelines for each session, but reviewed here. First, the overall goal and integrated nature of this treatment should be reiterated at each session. This will serve to reinforce the client's involvement in treatment and openness to new and different skills. Consistent with this approach, it will be necessary for therapists to revisit and link themes throughout treatment. Doing so will provide clients with a thorough, coherent understanding of the treatment as well as the function of different strategies and skills. As a result, clients may better assimilate treatment elements and have greater success. Second, the flexible nature of ASRP-S supports a client-centered, motivational interviewing directive. As such, therapists are to personalize the treatment to the client's unique experiences as much as possible. This will include drawing from the client's cigarette use history, past quit experiences, and specific anxiety-related symptoms and distress. In some instances, however, personalized examples may not be appropriate. Thus, when necessary, therapists may provide generic examples to help illustrate complex topics. Therapists should employ open-ended and reflective questioning to obtain information from clients and encourage clients to ask questions during treatment.

Session 1

The introduction session consists of obtaining informed consent, therapist introduction, and an overview of the treatment. To begin, the therapist orients the client to the goal-oriented nature of the treatment and the overall structure of treatment, including time commitment, confidentiality, and assignments. It is critical that the therapist stress the importance of treatment attendance and participation during treatment as well as outside of treatment. During this session, the therapist should provide reinforcement and empathetic support for client's decision to quit and emphasize that the goal of this treatment is to assist with smoking abstinence. This is achieved by

Table 2 Overview of session objectives

Session 1 Introduction	**Session 2 Exposure exercises**	**Session 3 Preparing to quit**	**Session 4 Quit day**
• Program introduction • Therapist introduction • *Discuss role of smoking in anxiety and panic development* • *Introduce concepts of anxiety sensitivity, catastrophizing, and smoking as maladaptive coping* • *Identify anxiety sensitivity as a target of intervention and discuss importance of IE exercises* • Provide reinforcement and empathic support for quitting smoking • Discuss nicotine use and prior abstinence attempts • Discuss common reasons for smoking and quitting smoking • Discuss common barriers to successful cessation	• Greetings, overview, and homework review • *Revisit psychoeducation on anxiety and smoking* • *Learn and practice IE exercises: observe, describe, express* • *Define, differentiate, and discuss feelings, thoughts and behaviors* • *Cognitive restructuring: identify and address maladaptive thoughts. define, differentiate and discuss: feelings, thoughts and behaviors* • Discuss HRS for smoking relapse *and CBT-oriented coping strategies for HRS* • Introduce procedures for enlisting social support • Review self-help materials • *Emphasize identifying HRS while monitoring cigarette use via monitoring sheets*	• Greetings, overview, and homework review • *Discuss practice and monitoring of IE exercises (and withdrawal symptoms) as opportunities to increase resilience and practice IE exercises in session* • *Review anxiety psychoeducation and maladaptive cognitions* • Review social support • Review HRS and CBT-oriented coping strategies for smoking relapse • Discuss guidelines for quit day preparation, including environmental control and fading. emphasize continued self-monitoring and preparation for quit day • Coping card • Review and discuss proper use of quit smoking medication (if applicable)	• Greetings, overview, and homework review • Discuss quitting experiences and withdrawal symptoms • *Emphasize anxiety-relevant coping during urges to smoke; explicitly recognize link between withdrawal symptoms, distress/anxiety, and urge while practicing IE exercises* • Discuss common barriers to maintaining abstinence and relapse prevention. (emphasize waiting 15 min after an urge and that a lapse is not a reason to revert to regular behavior.) • Review HRS plan for smoking relapse • Discuss lifestyle changes to maintain abstinence • Review social support • Quitting benefits and relapse prevention

Continued

Table 2 Continued

Session 1 Introduction	**Session 2 Exposure exercises**	**Session 3 Preparing to quit**	**Session 4 Quit day**
• Review and recommend smoking cessation medications • *Set quit date for session 4* • *Reiterate self-monitoring of cigarette use and anxiety via monitoring sheets* • *Provide self-help materials* • *Final comments and reminders and distribution of monitoring sheets*	*and maladaptive thoughts while practicing IE exercises* • *Final comments and reminders*	• *Emphasize continued self-monitoring and preparation for quit day* • *Final comments and reminders*	• Explicitly emphasize long-term benefits of quitting smoking • *Highlight importance of utilizing anxiety coping strategies during cessation* • *Final comments and reminders*

Note: *IE*, interoceptive exposure; *HRS*, high-risk situations; *CBT*, cognitive behavioral therapy. Italics are specific to the Anxiety Sensitivity Reduction Program for Smoking (ASRP-S).

candidly discussing the potential difficulties associated with smoking (i.e., stress, withdrawal) and pitting them again client's goals and values for improved physical and mental health.

The therapist presents the need to address specific mental health risk factors in the context of smoking cessation. Specifically, anxiety sensitivity is introduced as a targetable, malleable risk factor for quit failure and emotional distress that may complicate quit success. The client is informed of theoretical and empirical data for targeting anxiety sensitivity in the context of smoking cessation treatment to assist with quit success. Subsequently, the integrated treatment goal is presented: to achieve smoking abstinence through integrating anxiety sensitivity reduction with the most valid smoking cessation practices. Moreover, to assuage potential client resistance, the therapist should emphasize that this novel treatment contains activities that may be unfamiliar to the client. The therapist should encourage client to practice flexibility by suggesting that they be willing to try exercises and activities "outside of their comfort zone" or different from what they have tried in the past.

The therapist facilitates a discussion on cigarette use and history, including typical use and past quit attempts. With regards to past quit attempts, the therapist will want to obtain a thorough understanding of the client's quit history. Factors that assisted with the quit, quit-related benefits, and factors that contributed to relapse should be discussed and summarized. Consistent with a Motivational Interviewing approach (Miller & Rollnick, 2012; Rollnick & Miller, 1995), reasons for smoking followed by reasons for quitting should be reviewed with each client. If appropriate, the therapist briefly introduces the paradoxical effects of withdrawal and the smoking cycle; handouts 1 and 2 illustrate these effects. This is followed by a discussion of barriers to cessation.

The next part of this session presents a more in-depth explanation of smoking as a maladaptive coping mechanism for anxiety-related symptoms. The paradoxical effect of smoking is reviewed in further detail. Components covered should include the influence of cigarette use severity and dependence on withdrawal; the overlap between withdrawal and distress and other negative feelings; the relation between long-term smoking and increased aversive physical sensation as a consequence of poorer physical health; the misinterpretation of withdrawal and physical sensation as anxiety when they are actually consequences of cigarette use; and the use of cigarettes to alleviate misinterpreted experiences.

Anxiety sensitivity is then introduced as a factor related to both smoking and anxiety. The therapist should provide a formal, well-defined definition of anxiety sensitivity and the catastrophizing nature of anxiety sensitivity. It will be necessary for the therapist to ensure the client understands (a) the concept of anxiety sensitivity, (b) the malleability of anxiety sensitivity, and (c) the relation between anxiety sensitivity and catastrophizing as it relates to the anxiety and smoking cycle. Specifically, the therapist should relate anxiety sensitivity back to the paradoxical effect of smoking and emphasize the additive influence of elevated anxiety sensitivity on the misinterpretation of nicotine-related withdrawal and aversive physical sensations. Psychoeducation on anxiety sensitivity and smoking is followed by an explanation of and rationale for interoceptive exposures to treat anxiety sensitivity. The client is informed that interoceptive exposures will begin the following treatment session.

The last section of this session includes psychoeducation on quit smoking medications, setting a quit date, and assignment of between session work. A rationale for including a quit smoking medication as an adjunct to therapy should be provided to each client. Over-the-counter quit smoking medications (nicotine replacement therapy [NRT] patches, NRT gum, NRT lozenge, etc.) can be purchased by the client directly. Other medications, including bupropion and varenicline, require a prescription and should be monitored by a physician. The therapist should educate their client on potential side effects of different medications and possible contraindications. Consultation with a caring physician is advised when applicable. The therapist and client should then identify the date of the fourth treatment session and schedule that as the quit day. As mentioned earlier in the chapter, the quit date depends on the client's progress; thus, the date should be adjusted as needed to best meet the client's needs. The pharmacotherapy agent selected will determine the appropriate time to initiate use, but use should commence either on or before the scheduled quit date. Lastly, the client is provided with cigarette consumption and mood monitoring forms to use over the next week (handout 3). The therapist should provide a rationale for importance of careful and thorough monitoring.

The client is then provided quit smoking self-help materials (see handouts 4 for example) and a client binder. The therapist should encourage the client to review the provided materials and ask questions at the following treatment session. At this stage, the therapist ensures the client's understanding of the material and invites any additional questions before concluding the session.

Session 2

Between session work is reviewed at the beginning of the sessions. Barriers to completing the assignments should be addressed to prevent further difficulties and enhance effectiveness. After, the therapist outlines goals for the present session and reviews topics discussed at the previous session. Particular attention should be dedicated to revisiting smoking effects on the body, anxiety sensitivity as a construct and a targetable risk factor, and the paradoxical effect of smoking.

Following the overview and review, exposure exercises are reintroduced. Similarities between physical sensations experienced during periods of anxiety and attempting to quit are discussed. The therapist first explains that exposure exercises are intended to elicit uncomfortable physical sensations that mimic those experienced when attempting to quit and that these sensations, albeit uncomfortable, are not harmful. Interoceptive exposure exercises should be presented as a method to increase tolerance to uncomfortable sensation by purposefully inducing them in a controlled, safe environment. The therapist's goal is to ensure the client understands that it is the interpretation of these physical sensations that determines the client's response and experience, and that through repeated exposure and practice one can better understand and interpret the benign physical sensations that often accompany quitting smoking. Subsequently, a more accurate, appropriate interpretation of these sensations may positively impact their smoking.

Prior to introducing the exposure exercises, the therapist will want to explain the subjective units of distress metric and inform the client that they will be asked to give their distress rating after each exposure. The therapist should reiterate that the exposure exercises are not harmful and that they are intended to elicit physical sensations associated with quitting smoking such as dizziness, lightheadedness, shortness of breath, etc. Three example exercises include chair spinning, straw breathing, and hyperventilation. For each of these exercises, the therapist should demonstrate the exercise, then ask the client to engage in the exercise, and finally reinforce that the client observe, describe, and express the sensations (this is accompanied by a distress rating). The therapist will want to emphasize that these sensations are *Normal* reactions to this behavior that are *OK* and we want to *Accept*, even though they are uncomfortable (because they are not causing us harm and experiencing them in this fashion will help to make them less intense in the future, such as after quit day; NOA). After selecting the exercise that elicited a moderate amount of distress, have the client complete repeated trials until extinction has been reached. The client is shown how to monitor and track their exposure exercises using handout 5.

Next, the client is taught cognitive-behavioral strategies to identify cognitions, emotions, and behaviors. The therapist provides psychoeducation on the interconnectedness of these constructs and the importance of differentiating them, particularly in the context of quitting smoking. Considering the complexity of this topic, the therapist may want to offer examples for how to differentiate cognitions, emotions, and behaviors and their relatedness. The client should be encouraged to monitor and practice differentiated these three facets with an understanding that through repeated identification one can begin to appreciate the impact of thoughts on emotions and behaviors and therefore appropriately adjust thoughts that might interfere with their quit success. Such work has the benefit to facilitate quit success. As a final aspect to this topic, the therapist will want to relate this skill back to the exposure exercises. Specifically, the therapist should communicate that skills to identify and change negative thoughts about one's ability to tolerate uncomfortable feelings and situations, whether general anxiety-related or quit-related, will be critical to their eventual success because it involves repeated exposure to these uncomfortable sensations and restructuring how one perceives and tolerates these sensations.

To further assist with smoking cessation, high-risk situations and social support warrant discussion in treatment. The therapist should work with the client to identify high-risk situations and develop a plan for how the client will respond to these situations. The therapist should provide a rationale for this exercise and ensure an appropriate, feasible plan is documented. In addition, the importance of social support during a quit attempt is discussed in this session. The key is for the client to understand that easily available cigarettes, often supported by smokers at social or other gatherings, significantly increase the likelihood of relapse.

For between session work, the client is asked to continue monitoring their smoking behavior as well as their mood and its relation to smoking using handout 3. This will provide a useful tool for the client to consider the interconnectedness among cognition, emotion, and behavior. In addition to the high-risk situations identified during treatment, the client should use time outside of the session to identify and plan for additional situations that might lead to smoking, and discuss their forthcoming quit attempt with friends and family. Additionally, the client is assigned to monitor and practice exposure exercises at least every other day for 15–20 min and record their exercises using handout 5. The therapist will want to remind the client of the NOA acronym and encourage them to observe, describe, and express sensations as well as identify maladaptive thoughts they experience during their practice. The therapist ensures the client's understanding of the material, answers questions about the self-help materials, and invites any additional questions. The therapist also requests that the client arrive to the next session having abstained from cigarettes for at least 6 h and explains that this will help the in-session exposure practices be more effective. Following this request and answering all questions, the therapist concludes the session.

Session 3

The focus of the third session is to practice interoceptive exposure exercises, develop adaptive coping strategies, and challenge maladaptive cognitions. This is the last session prior to the scheduled quit day; therefore, the therapist should take time to reflect the connection between the content of the current and previous sessions and the scheduled quit attempt. At the beginning of the session, between session work is evaluated for completeness and new insights are discussed. Barriers in completing the assignments are addressed to prevent further difficulties and enhance effectiveness. After, the therapist outlines goals for the present session and review topics discussed at the previous session.

The first topic covered is the client's interoceptive exposure practice and monitoring. The therapist will want to gain an in-depth understanding of the client's experience with the exercises. Indeed, it will be important for the therapist and client to discuss the frequency and length of the practice, the length of smoking withdrawal before and after the practice, any noticeable changes in sensations, and how their thoughts about the sensations influenced their experience. Regarding cognitive interpretation of the sensations, the therapist and client should devote time to developing alternative thoughts that help decrease the intensity and impact of the exercises, if necessary.

Following the discussion of the client's out of session practice, the client is instructed to practice two of the most anxiety-provoking exercises in session. As before, the therapist first demonstrates the exercise. Then, the client practices the exercise, but is instructed to raise their hand when they feel sensations and continue the exercise for 5–10 s beyond that point. The therapist should reinforce the use of NOA and encourage the client to use these exercises as an opportunity to increase their resilience in preparation for possible withdrawal symptoms/sensations they may experience when they quit or reduce their cigarettes.

A brief review of the influence of cognitions on emotions and behavior is provided. Discussions should focus on how the client's thoughts during their out-of-session exposure practice impacted their anxiety. The therapist should emphasize the role of cognitive interpretation of symptoms on symptom severity and type. The goal is for the client to identify that changing their thoughts about the exercises and symptoms may lead to improvements in the severity of anxiety symptoms. The connection among cognitions, emotions, and behaviors should then be extended smoking. In particular, the therapist and client should work together to identify maladaptive thoughts about smoking, discuss how such thoughts influence quit behavior, and generate alternative thoughts to aid cessation.

Next, the therapist and client revisit the importance of social support and planning for high-risk situations. The therapist will want to use the client's between session work related to social support as a way to broach this topic. Evocative questions regarding the client's experience talking to family and friends about quitting, and family and friends' reactions to discussions about quitting will help facilitate this discussion. The goal is to help the client understand the importance of and enlist social support when attempting to quit. Another important topic of discussion is high-risk situations and coping strategies. During this discussion, the therapist should elicit 1–2 additional high-risk situations and work with the client to document appropriate behavioral coping plans. The therapist also should use this opportunity to discuss the importance of making healthy lifestyle changes to reduce the impact of high-risk situations, and encourage the client to consider short- and long-term lifestyle changes that will reduce the risk of a relapse.

The next section focuses on preparing one's environment for quitting. The client is instructed to remove all smoking paraphernalia from their home, car, and workplace. They should develop a plan for making cigarettes unavailable to them, activities to do instead of smoking, and tactics to manage stress without smoking (see handouts 6 and 7). It is recommended that clients keep their schedules filled and busy during the first few weeks following quit day as this will support the quit attempt. The therapist and client should work together to develop a list of activities that the client will do prior to smoking during periods of intense cravings. The therapist should work with the client to document this information using handout 8. For heavy-smoking clients or clients with strong concern about cravings, the therapist may want to introduce fading wherein the client practices reducing their cigarette consumption prior to the scheduled quit date. Fading can be helpful to attenuate craving intensity following the quit. To synthesize this information, the client receives a coping card that summarizes many of the discussed ideas, including avoiding triggers, substitute behaviors, social support, mental coping, and stress reduction. The client is encouraged to create a personalized quit-smoking coping card that they can reference after quit day to help curb intense urges. The therapist should explain that waiting 5 min after the initial urge and referencing their coping card may significantly increase the chance of remaining abstinent.

The therapist should reinforce the client's commitment and preparedness to quit by highlighting specific knowledge and skills the client has to support the quit. The therapist encourages the client to review the self-help materials information and practice the newly learned skills. Indeed, the client will want to continue monitoring their smoking and mood over the next week as well as continue practicing and challenging themselves with the exposure exercises at least every other day for 15–20 min; practices should be tracked using handout 5. At least one set of exposure exercises should occur during a period of cigarette withdrawal. The therapist also may encourage the client to enlist additional support before the next appointment. Further, if the client opts to use NRT, the therapists should review proper use with the client.

At the end of the session, the therapist should answer any additional questions regarding the present session. Moreover, it is important that the therapist clearly outlines the agenda for the next week and state that it is the client's scheduled quit date. The client should be informed that the quit begins the morning of the day regardless of when the therapy appointment is scheduled; thus, the client should not use cigarettes, but practice their skills as soon as wakening the day of their quit. Finally, the therapist should take this time to recognize the difficulty in quitting smoking, congratulate the client on their accomplishments and commitment, and reinforce the client's ability to quit given their skills.

Session 4

Prior to reviewing between session work, client compliance is evaluated. Specifically, the therapist assesses if the client has abstained from smoking, removed smoking paraphernalia from their home, car, and workplace, and used the quit smoking medication appropriately, if applicable. Following this, the between session work is checked for completeness. Difficulties completing the assignments are addressed. After, the therapist outlines goals for the present session and briefly reviews topics discussed at the previous session.

The client's current withdrawal symptoms/urges and current anxiety level are assessed using subjective units of distress. The therapist and client review the client's anxiety monitoring and discuss its relation to smoking and smoking urges (handout 3). This provides an opportunity to focus on specific interpretations and meanings of nicotine cravings and/or anxiety. If the client is struggling with resisting smoking when experiencing uncomfortable sensations, the therapist should assist with providing corrective feedback and emphasize NOA. As needed, address maladaptive smoking-related cognitions with the client (e.g., future oriented concerns about inability to get through cravings—emphasize present mindfulness). The therapist should work with the client to derive additional strategies to refrain from smoking. The therapist should introduce a handout to track their cravings (handout 9). In session, the client should confirm that the client explicitly recognizes the link between withdrawal, distress/anxiety, and urge to smoke. The therapist should review anxiety psychoeducation and the role of maladaptive cognitions, as needed. The therapist should work with the client to relate present experiences to exposure exercises while emphasizing behavior and thought change. Therapists should remind clients that symptoms are opportunities to increase tolerance.

As a next step, common barriers to maintaining abstinence and relapse prevention are reviewed. Emphasize the importance of preemptively developing a strategy and plan for how to cope with urges and high-risk situations, and identify the maladaptive belief that smoking will help reduce anxiety/stress as a risk factor for relapse. The therapist should highlight additional factors to consider, including social support, staying focused on short-term quit goals, and openness to experience withdrawal symptoms rather than avoidance.

The therapist and client then should thoroughly review the client's between session work on high-risk situations (handout 6), coping card development, and lifestyle changes (handout 7). Therapists should reiterate how each of these facets contributes to quit success and failure. Any important final discussion points or suggestions regarding these area, including developing a plan for lapse and the importance of staying busy, should be discussed. Additionally, the therapist should reemphasize the importance of enlisting social support prior to quit day and as needed, problem-solve with those who are still reluctant to do so.

Following, the therapist reviews smoking cessation benefits and the positive impact of smoking cessation on health. Attention should be directed to both the short- and long-term benefits of quitting. To encourage sustained abstinence, the client should be provided with a sample relapse prevention plan. Both the client's abstinence plan (see handout 8) and the sample relapse prevention plan should be discussed in detail. Any concerns or questions should be thoroughly addressed to prevent relapse.

Prior to concluding the session, the therapist should highlight the important aspect of the treatment program. Specifically, the therapist should review the harmful consequences of smoking including increasing the risk of developing problems with anxiety. The therapist should review the rationale for reducing anxiety sensitivity to facilitate quit success. Emphasize the importance of continuing to monitor anxiety in relationship to smoking urges. Review skills learned in treatment that will help the client manage stress adaptively, including alternative coping strategies. Reiterate the importance of practicing skills learned in treatment outside of treatment for the skill to become "second nature." Elicit the client's personalized feedback on the program. Finally, build self-efficacy by congratulating the client and provide words of encouragement moving forward.

Status of efficacy

The ASRP-S program has been developed in a theoretically driven manner and is supported indirectly by a relatively large body of empirical literature. Existing work has evaluated the treatment, in various formats, on well over 800 individuals. The results of such work generally suggest reducing anxiety sensitivity improves mental health and smoking behavior. These effects are evident when compared to other gold standard treatments that do not focus on anxiety sensitivity reduction. Ongoing studies are currently evaluating the efficacy of mobile personalized care (e.g., feedback based on participant responses) and pharmacological methods (e.g., D-cycloserine) for anxiety sensitivity reduction treatment, which may provide more robust effects. Other work is exploring for whom the treatment works best and by what mechanism of change. These lines of research will have important implications for treating anxiety sensitivity in the context of smoking. A critical next step for this work will be to explore the generalizability of the ongoing, novel research to diverse populations (e.g., low-income smokers) most prone to chronic tobacco-related disease.

Summary

Tobacco use is a major public health concern. Better understanding of transdiagnostic risk factors for tobacco use can be a highly efficient clinical strategy for increasing smoking cessation. This chapter focused on one transdiagnostic approach to addressing smoking cessation through an integrated anxiety sensitivity and smoking treatment, ASRP-S. ASRP-S can be completed over a period of four in-person sessions aimed to target a number of cognitive and behavioral facets known to be associated with tobacco use. Clinicians should exercise their clinical judgment when administering ASRP-S to provide a personalized and flexible treatment approach that best addresses client needs.

Appendix: Supplementary material

Supplementary material related to this chapter can be found online at https://www.elsevier.com/books-and-journals/book-companion/9780128134955.

Disclosure

All authors have no conflict of interest to disclose. All authors have contributed to and approved the final manuscript.

References

Centers for Disease Control and Prevention (CDC) (2010). *2010 Surgeon general's report-how tobacco smoke causes disease: The biology and behavioral basis for smoking-attributable disease*. Atlanta, GA: CDC.

Centers for Disease Control and Prevention (CDC) (2011). Vital signs: current cigarette smoking among adults aged ≥ 18 years-United States, 2005-2010. *Morbidity and Mortality Weekly Report*, *60*(33), 1207–1212.

Evatt, D. P., & Kassel, J. D. (2010). Smoking, arousal, and affect: the role of anxiety sensitivity. *Journal of Anxiety Disorders*, *24*(1), 114–123.

Farris, S. G., Leventhal, A. M., Schmidt, N. B., & Zvolensky, M. J. (2015). Anxiety sensitivity and pre-cessation smoking processes: testing the independent and combined mediating effects of negative affect-reduction expectancies and motives. *Journal of Studies on Alcohol and Drugs*, *76*(2), 317–325.

Farris, S. G., Paulus, D. J., Gonzalez, A., Mahaffey, B. L., Bromet, E. J., Luft, B. J., … Zvolensky, M. J. (2015). Anxiety sensitivity mediates the association between post-traumatic stress symptom severity and interoceptive threat-related smoking abstinence expectancies among World Trade Center disaster-exposed smokers. *Addictive Behaviors*, *51*, 204–210.

Farris, S. G., & Zvolensky, M. J. (2016). An experimental test of the effect of acute anxious arousal and anxiety sensitivity on negative reinforcement smoking. *Journal of Psychopharmacology*. https://doi.org/10.1177/0269881116642880.

Fiore, M. C., Jaen, C. R., Baker, T., Bailey, W., Benowitz, N., Curry, S. E., ... Healton, C. (2008). *Treating tobacco use and dependence: 2008 update*. Rockville, MD: US Department of Health and Human Services.

Gonzalez, A., Zvolensky, M. J., Vujanovic, A. A., Leyro, T. M., & Marshall, E. C. (2008). An evaluation of anxiety sensitivity, emotional dysregulation, and negative affectivity among daily cigarette smokers: relation to smoking motives and barriers to quitting. *Journal of Psychiatric Research*, *43*(2), 138–147. https://doi.org/10.1016/j.jpsychires.2008.03.002.

Gregor, K. L., Zvolensky, M. J., McLeish, A. C., Bernstein, A., & Morissette, S. (2008). Anxiety sensitivity and perceived control over anxiety-related events: associations with smoking outcome expectancies and perceived cessation barriers among daily smokers. *Nicotine & Tobacco Research*, *10*(4), 627–635.

Guillot, C. R., Leventhal, A. M., Raines, A. M., Zvolensky, M. J., & Schmidt, N. B. (2016). Anxiety sensitivity facets in relation to tobacco use, abstinence-related problems, and cognitions in treatment-seeking smokers. *Addictive Behaviors*, *56*, 30–35.

Jha, P., Ranson, M. K., Nguyen, S. N., & Yach, D. (2002). Estimates of global and regional smoking prevalence in 1995, by age and sex. *American Journal of Public Health*, *92* (6), 1002–1006.

Johnson, K. A., Farris, S. G., Schmidt, N. B., & Zvolensky, M. J. (2012). Anxiety sensitivity and cognitive-based smoking processes: testing the mediating role of emotion dysregulation among treatment-seeking daily smokers. *Journal of Addictive Diseases*, *31*(2), 143–157.

Johnson, K. A., Stewart, S., Rosenfield, D., Steeves, D., & Zvolensky, M. J. (2012). Prospective evaluation of the effects of anxiety sensitivity and state anxiety in predicting acute nicotine withdrawal symptoms during smoking cessation. *Psychology of Addictive Behaviors*, *26* (2), 289–297. https://doi.org/10.1037/a0024133.

Kenford, S. L., Smith, S. S., Wetter, D. W., Jorenby, D. E., Fiore, M. C., & Baker, T. B. (2002). Predicting relapse back to smoking: contrasting affective and physical models of dependence. *Journal of Consulting and Clinical Psychology*, *70*(1), 216.

Langdon, K. J., Farris, S. G., Hogan, J. B. D., Grover, K. W., & Zvolensky, M. J. (2016). Anxiety sensitivity in relation to quit day dropout among adult daily smokers recruited to participate in a self-guided cessation attempt. *Addictive Behaviors*, *58*, 12–15.

Langdon, K. J., Leventhal, A. M., Stewart, S., Rosenfield, D., Steeves, D., & Zvolensky, M. J. (2013). Anhedonia and anxiety sensitivity: prospective relationships to nicotine withdrawal symptoms during smoking cessation. *Journal of Studies on Alcohol & Drugs*, *74* (3), 469–478.

Leventhal, A. M., & Zvolensky, M. J. (2015). Anxiety, depression, and cigarette smoking: a transdiagnostic vulnerability framework to understanding emotion–smoking comorbidity. *Psychological Bulletin*, *141*(1), 176.

Leyro, T. M., Zvolensky, M. J., Vujanovic, A. A., & Bernstein, A. (2008). Anxiety sensitivity and smoking motives and outcome expectancies among adult daily smokers: replication and extension. *Nicotine & Tobacco Research*, *10*(6), 985–994. https://doi.org/10.1080/14622200802097555.

Marlatt, G. A., & Gordon, J. R. (1985). *Relapse prevention: Maintenance strategies in addictive behavior change*. New York: Guilford Press.

Marshall, E. C., Johnson, K., Bergman, J., Gibson, L. E., & Zvolensky, M. J. (2009). Anxiety sensitivity and panic reactivity to bodily sensations: relation to quit-day (acute) nicotine withdrawal symptom severity among daily smokers making a self-guided quit attempt. *Experimental and Clinical Psychopharmacology*, *17*(5), 356.

Miller, W. R., & Rollnick, S. (2012). *Motivational interviewing: Helping people change*. New York, NY: Guilford Press.

Olvera, H., Bakhshaie, J., Garey, L., Jardin, C., Schmidt, N. B., & Zvolensky, M. J. (2015). The role of anxiety sensitivity in the relation between trait worry and smoking behavior. *Nicotine & Tobacco Research*, *17*(6), 682–689.

Otto, M. W., Eastman, A., Lo, S., Hearon, B. A., Bickel, W. K., Zvolensky, M., ... Doan, S. N. (2016). Anxiety sensitivity and working memory capacity: risk factors and targets for health behavior promotion. *Clinical Psychology Review*, *49*, 67–78.

Perkins, K. A., Karelitz, J. L., Giedgowd, G. E., Conklin, C. A., & Sayette, M. A. (2010). Differences in negative mood-induced smoking reinforcement due to distress tolerance, anxiety sensitivity, and depression history. *Psychopharmacology*, *210*(1), 25–34. https://doi.org/10.1007/s00213-010-1811-1.

Powers, M. P., Davis, M. L., Kauffman, B. Y., Baird, S. O., Zvolensky, M., ... Rosenfield, D. Smits, J. A. J. (2016). Anxiety sensitivity, smoking variability, and nicotine addiction among treatment seeking smokers. *Addictive Disorders and Their Treatment*, *15*(3), 136–142. http://doi.org/10.1097/ADT.0000000000000075.

Rollnick, S., & Miller, W. R. (1995). What is motivational interviewing? *Behavioural and Cognitive Psychotherapy*, *23*(4), 325–334.

Samet, J. (1991). Health benefits of smoking cessation. *Clinics in Chest Medicine*, *12*(4), 669–679.

Wong, M., Krajisnik, A., Truong, L., Lisha, N. E., Trujillo, M., Greenberg, J. B., ... Leventhal, A. M. (2013). Anxiety sensitivity as a predictor of acute subjective effects of smoking. *Nicotine & Tobacco Research*, *15*(6), 1084–1090.

Zvolensky, M. J., Baker, K., Yartz, A. R., Gregor, K., Leen-Feldner, E. W., & Feldner, M. T. (2005). Mental health professionals with a specialty in anxiety disorders: knowledge, training, and perceived competence in smoking cessation practices. *Cognitive and Behavioral Practice*, *12*(3), 312–318.

Zvolensky, M. J., Farris, S. G., Leventhal, A. M., & Schmidt, N. B. (2014). Anxiety sensitivity mediates relations between emotional disorders and smoking. *Psychology of Addictive Behaviors*, *28*(3), 912.

Zvolensky, M. J., Farris, S. G., Schmidt, N. B., & Smits, J. A. (2014). The role of smoking inflexibility/avoidance in the relation between anxiety sensitivity and tobacco use and beliefs among treatment-seeking smokers. *Experimental and Clinical Psychopharmacology*, *22*(3), 229–237. https://doi.org/10.1037/a0035306.

Zvolensky, M. J., Lejuez, C. W., Kahler, C. W., & Brown, R. A. (2003). Integrating an interoceptive exposure-based smoking cessation program into the cognitive-behavioral treatment of panic disorder: theoretical relevance and case demonstration. *Cognitive and Behavioral Practice*, *10*(4), 347–357.

Zvolensky, M. J., Stewart, S. H., Vujanovic, A. A., Gavric, D., & Steeves, D. (2009). Anxiety sensitivity and anxiety and depressive symptoms in the prediction of early smoking lapse and relapse during smoking cessation treatment. *Nicotine & Tobacco Research*, *11*(3), 323–331.

Zvolensky, M. J., Vujanovic, A. A., Miller, M. O. B., Bernstein, A., Yartz, A. R., Gregor, K. L., ... Gibson, L. E. (2007). Incremental validity of anxiety sensitivity in terms of motivation to quit, reasons for quitting, and barriers to quitting among community-recruited daily smokers. *Nicotine & Tobacco Research*, *9*(9), 965–975.

Anxiety sensitivity treatment for children and adolescents

7

Jamie A. Sherman, Dylan A. Braun, Jill Ehrenreich-May
University of Miami, Miami, FL, United States

Chapter Outline

Anxiety sensitivity treatment for children and adolescents

Prevalence rates of anxiety disorders increase significantly during late childhood and adolescence (Ollendick, Shortt, & Sander, 2005). The increased incidence of anxiety in youth is concerning, as such disorders impair development across multiple domains (e.g., social, academic, family) (Bittner et al., 2007; Brunner et al., 2014; Garber & Weersing, 2010; Goodwin, Fergusson, & Horwood, 2004; Strauss, Last, Hersen, & Kazdin, 1988). Anxiety sensitivity, or the fear of the bodily sensations that typically accompany anxious experiences, is known to be a particularly relevant construct to consider when treating panic symptoms in youth and adults (Taylor, 1999). However, results from Olatunji and Wolitzky-Taylor's (2009) meta-analysis on the prevalence of anxiety sensitivity suggest that youth with all types of anxiety and related disorders present with elevated levels of anxiety sensitivity. Within the child literature, specifically, evidence supports the expectation that children with clinically diagnosed anxiety and related disorders (i.e., panic disorder, agoraphobia, generalized anxiety disorder, social anxiety, separation anxiety, specific phobias, OCD and PTSD, etc.) report higher levels of anxiety sensitivity compared to their nonanxious peers

The Clinician's Guide to Anxiety Sensitivity Treatment and Assessment. https://doi.org/10.1016/B978-0-12-813495-5.00007-3

(Chorpita, Albano, & Barlow, 1996a; Silverman, Goedhart, Barrett, & Turner, 2003; Weems, Hammond-Laurence, Silverman, & Ginsburg, 1998; Weems, Hammond, Silverman, & Ferguson, 1997). Since anxiety sensitivity appears to cooccur with a wide variety of anxiety disorders in child and adolescent populations, anxiety sensitivity is worth examining as a focus of treatment as we seek to better understand and address symptoms of youth.

Anxiety sensitivity has been conceptualized as a risk factor for the development of an anxiety disorder in adolescence (Hale & Calamari, 2006; Weems, Hayward, Killen, & Taylor, 2002). The tripartite model of anxiety and depression, first developed by Clark and Watson (1991), proposed high negative affect (NA), as a higher-order factor across both anxiety and depression, with low levels of positive affect (PA) to be more characteristic of depression, and high levels of physiological hyperarousal (pH) to be more specific to anxiety. Empirical work continues to disentangle the relative contributions of other related constructs, including anxiety sensitivity, to the development and maintenance of internalizing disorders (Allan et al., 2014; Hayward, Killen, Kraemer, & Taylor, 2000; Muris, Roelofs, Rassin, Franken, & Mayer, 2005; Weems et al., 2002). Citing Piaget's theory of cognitive development (Piaget, 1971), Chorpita, Albano, and Barlow (1996b) suggest that the relationship between anxiety sensitivity and anxiety emerges as older children and adolescents begin to connect internal sensations associated with anxiety (APA, 2013) to future consequences, especially more abstract ones. Those who are already more cognizant of their symptoms may become more distressed by the potential consequences that their worrying might have on their lives.

In line with this theory, Chorpita and Daleiden (2000) suggest that anxiety sensitivity serves as a measure of autonomic arousal in younger children but that it characterizes both autonomic arousal and high negative affect in adolescents. If this holds true, the relationship between anxiety sensitivity and anxiety disorders should increase during adolescence. Weems et al. (2002) found that adolescents with stable high scores on a measure of anxiety sensitivity over time were more likely to experience panic attacks compared to adolescents with stable low scores. Similarly, in a study examining the developmental trajectories of anxiety sensitivity, Allan et al. (2014) found that, in a community sample of adolescents, those with high anxiety sensitivity were more likely to report worsening anxiety symptoms over time, despite a general decrease in anxiety symptoms during development their sample. This suggests that anxiety sensitivity may serve as a pertinent risk or maintaining factor for anxiety disorders in youth. Thus, treatments focusing on reducing levels of anxiety sensitivity in childhood may help prevent at-risk youth high in anxiety sensitivity from developing anxiety disorders or anxiety disorder symptoms from worsening later in adolescence or early adulthood. Increasing our understanding of how to best conceptualize anxiety sensitivity in youth may be highly valuable as we seek to develop such targeted treatments.

Measurement of anxiety sensitivity in youth

As mentioned, heightened anxiety sensitivity is associated with physical, social, and cognitive consequences in youth. (Reiss, 1991; Reiss, Peterson, Gursky, & Mcnally, 1986; Taylor, 1999). For example, children with high levels of anxiety sensitivity may fear that a rapid heartbeat indicates a heart attack; worry that worrying itself will lead to losing control of one's mind or "going crazy"; or state that "funny feelings in my body scare me." Valid and reliable clinical measures can be helpful in assessing the degree to which a child is experiencing elevated anxiety sensitivity. As discussed in earlier chapters, the Anxiety Sensitivity Index for adults (ASI; Reiss et al., 1986) was developed to study the construct of anxiety sensitivity. In order to measure anxiety sensitivity in children and adolescents, the Child Anxiety Sensitivity Inventory (CASI; Silverman, Fleisig, Rabian, & Peterson, 1991) was created as a downward adaptation of the adult measure. The CASI consists of 18 items assessing the extent to which children and adolescents believe that experiencing anxiety will result in negative consequences, as well as the fear of the numerous physical symptoms of anxiety. Items from the CASI include, "It scares me when I feel 'shaky'," "When my stomach hurts, I worry that I might be really sick," and "When I am afraid, I worry that I might be crazy." CASI items are scored as 1 (none), 2 (some), and 3 (a lot). Total scores range from 18 to 54, with higher scores reflecting higher levels of anxiety sensitivity.

The CASI has satisfactory reliability and validity (Silverman et al., 1991). Many studies have treated anxiety sensitivity, as measured by the CASI, as a unitary construct, using only the total composite score as the means of determining levels of anxiety sensitivity, and while it was developed to be a unidimensional measure, factor analyses in adults and children (using the ASI and CASI, respectively) support a hierarchical multidimensional model of anxiety sensitivity (Adornetto et al., 2008; Chorpita et al., 1996a; Essau, Sasagawa, & Ollendick, 2010; Silverman et al., 2003). At this time, a lack of consensus exists about which facets of anxiety sensitivity can be discriminated by the measure.

While there is much that remains to be learned about how anxiety sensitivity may maintain and influence the development of anxiety disorders in youth, there are numerous potential benefits to directly addressing anxiety sensitivity within the framework of cognitive-behavioral therapy, the most commonly used evidence-based treatment for anxiety disorders in youth (Ishikawa, Okajima, Matsuoka, & Sakano, 2007; Kendall, Furr, & Podell, 2010; Kennedy, Mash, Tawfik, & Ehrenreich-May, 2017). This is especially true during exposure, one major purported active treatment component of cognitive-behavioral treatments for anxiety disorders (Ale, McCarthy, Rothschild, & Whiteside, 2015; Ishikawa et al., 2007; Spielmans, Pasek, & McFall, 2007). During exposure therapy, children and adolescents are tasked with facing difficult or emotionally triggering situations and using coping skills learned during CBT to handle their emotions following these activities. Since individuals with high levels of anxiety sensitivity must contend not only with their feared stimuli but also with the perceived threat of their own bodily arousal, incorporating treatment for the anxiety sensitivity itself may help enhance treatment efficacy for these individuals (Blakey, Abramowitz, Reuman, Leonard, & Riemann, 2017). Reducing anxiety sensitivity in youth may, in turn, lead to improved overall responses to available evidence-based therapies.

How do we target anxiety sensitivity in youth?

As noted, anxiety sensitivity, broadly referring to an individual's tendency to fear consequences of anxiety (Taylor, 2014), appears elevated in many youth and adults with clinical anxiety disorders (Chorpita et al., 1996a; Naragon-Gainey, 2010; Noel &

Francis, 2011; Olatunji & Wolitzky-Taylor, 2009; Reiss et al., 1986; Taylor, 2014). However, while a bulk of recent work has been done conceptualizing the relevance of anxiety sensitivity as a mediator of treatment-based change in adults (Boswell et al., 2013; Gallagher et al., 2013; Smits, Berry, Tart, & Powers, 2008), little work has been done to examine anxiety sensitivity as a mechanism of change in youth treatment. Preliminary work proposes that, in adults, anxiety sensitivity is a modifiable construct exhibited most markedly by individuals with panic disorder and/or agoraphobia but is also apparent in adults with various other anxiety disorders (Taylor, 2014). Since anxiety sensitivity refers to the belief that physiological sensations are dangerous and panic disorder results in the worsening of such sensations due to catastrophic thinking in response to them, typical interventions for both problems are similar. One particular recent intervention study involved delivery of the Anxiety Sensitivity Education and Reduction Training (ASERT) program to undergraduates with varying levels of anxiety sensitivity. ASERT consisted of psychoeducation on the nature of symptoms arising from stress and anxiety as well as a brief interoceptive exposure. Results suggest that this treatment targeting anxiety sensitivity in adults effectively reduces symptoms of anxiety sensitivity, anxiety, and other internalizing symptoms, thereby increasing individuals' ability to tolerate distress (Norr, Allan, Macatee, Keough, & Schmidt, 2014).

This study and other similar ones have shown that treatments akin to those used to treat panic disorder in adults might prove most effective in targeting elevated anxiety sensitivity. However, although panic-focused treatments do exist in youth (e.g., Mastery of Anxiety and Panic for Adolescents, Riding the Wave; Pincus, Ehrenreich, & Mattis, 2008), it remains unclear whether anxiety sensitivity is tied directly to panic presentations in youth and it is resultantly also uncertain whether treatment components typically introduced within panic treatment packages would effectively reduce anxiety sensitivity in youth. However, considering anxiety sensitivity's clear role in panic etiology, implementing effective therapies for panic disorder appears to be one reasonable approach to the treatment of anxiety sensitivity in youth.

The logical next step, therefore, along the road to attempting to target anxiety sensitivity in youth would be to present components of evidence-based panic disorder treatments for youth to those with heightened anxiety sensitivity. One problem with treating individuals with heightened anxiety sensitivity using interventions designed to solely target panic disorder (shown to simultaneously target anxiety sensitivity in adults) is that, if used as standalone treatments, the implementation of such approaches might miss the mark on addressing additional symptom sets that share anxiety sensitivity elements but also require additional cognitive and behavioral techniques to promote change across the symptom set. Therefore, targeting both anxiety sensitivity and disorder-specific symptoms (e.g., symptoms of generalized anxiety disorder, social anxiety disorder, separation anxiety disorder, specific phobias, selective mutism) may be particularly helpful for effectively treating individual youth with both anxiety disorders and heightened anxiety sensitivity.

Whether incorporating aspects of treatment targeting panic symptoms and anxiety sensitivity more broadly in a transdiagnostic CBT package (e.g., Unified Protocol for Treatment of Emotional Disorders in Children and Adolescents; Ehrenreich-May,

Kennedy, Sherman, Bilek, Buzzella, et al., 2018) or presenting standalone CBT for panic disorder and commonly cooccurring heightened anxiety sensitivity (e.g., Mastery of Anxiety and Panic for Adolescents, Riding the Wave; Pincus, Ehrenreich, & Mattis, 2008), clinicians will find several common treatment components essential to the treatment of anxiety sensitivity in youth. While both approaches incorporate anxiety sensitivity-related treatment components, transdiagnostic treatments are particularly helpful for youth with multiple emotional disorder treatment targets (i.e., one or more nonpanic anxiety disorders) while panic-specific treatments might be better suited for youth with crystalized panic disorder symptoms. Since the average age of onset for panic disorder is mid-late to late adolescence (APA, 2013), youth who would benefit most from panic-specific approaches might be relatively older than those who might benefit more from transdiagnostic approaches. See the following content for a summary of how these key treatment components are presented in each of these packages.

Evidence-based treatments targeting anxiety sensitivity in youth

Mastery of anxiety and panic for adolescents, riding the wave (MAP-A; Pincus, Ehrenreich, & Mattis, 2008)

The *Mastery of Anxiety and Panic for Adolescents, Riding the Wave* (MAP-A; Pincus, Ehrenreich, & Mattis, 2008) is a treatment program geared toward adolescents with panic disorder, with or without agoraphobia, is particularly relevant to the treatment of anxiety sensitivity in youth. For more detailed instruction on the administration of the MAP-A, refer to the published manual and supplementary materials (Pincus, Ehrenreich, & Mattis, 2008).

Mastery of Your Anxiety and Panic (MAP) was developed by Drs. Michelle Craske and David Barlow (2006a). It has been established as an effective treatment for adults with panic disorder and agoraphobia. MAP-A is a developmentally appropriate, downward adaptation of MAP with established efficacy for adolescents (Pincus, Ehrenreich-May, Whitton, Mattis, & Barlow, 2010). The core treatment program consists of 11 guided therapy sessions. While it was created for use with youth aged 12–17, it can also, with some adjustments, be utilized with younger patients as well, although little empirical work has been done to evaluate the MAP-A for younger youth. This makes sense considering that MAP-A is particularly helpful for youth with primary panic disorder, which typically onsets in late-mid to late adolescence (APA, 2013). MAP-A calls for an experienced therapist with a strong foundation in cognitive behavioral therapy, and specifically, exposure therapy for adolescents with panic disorder and agoraphobia. The goals of MAP-A include reducing the strong conditioned fear responses that patients with panic disorder experience as a reaction to their bodily sensations, as well as addressing the anxiety-provoking beliefs that youth hold about the risks of their physiological symptoms.

Prior to the development of the MAP-A, few studies had evaluated the efficacy of psychotherapy for panic disorder (Ollendick, 1995). As the onset of panic disorder peaks in adolescence, the development of an effective panic/agoraphobia treatment manual was considered a top priority. As previously mentioned, anxiety sensitivity is most often associated with panic disorder (Kearney, Albano, Eisen, Allan, & Barlow, 1997). Criterion B1 of the DSM-5 lists the persistent worry about the consequences of physiological sensations of panic as a core symptom of the disorder (APA, 2013). Therefore, tested and proven panic disorder manuals like the MAP-A are an appropriate starting point when exploring options for the treatment of anxiety sensitivity. We felt it would be most valuable to discuss the components of MAP-A in that the principles could be applied to an anxiety-sensitivity-specific treatment.

Psychoeducation sessions

When the considering the challenges of providing psychoeducation to youth, it is important to remember that children and adolescents may present with relatively less insight into the triggers of their emotional experiences and how their responses to bodily sensations may influence behavioral choices. This can make it more difficult, compared to adults, to assess for symptom severity and level of functional impairment, as adolescents may lack the insight and flexibility required to understand that, although distressing, uncomfortable body sensations are a normal and natural component of the experience of anxiety or fear. It can be helpful, therefore, to incorporate the adolescent's caretakers in this process.

One of the primary goals of the psychoeducation component of MAP-A, which is typically concentrated in the first two sessions, is to provide youth (and parents) with accurate information about the origin and function of physiological fear responses. The therapist reinforces the idea that the anxiety they experience is a reaction to, and not inherently a part of, the physical sensations associated with panic. Helping youth understand this point can be helpful later on in the treatment when youth attempt, through exposure exercises, to separate their natural sensations from their associated fear response. The psychoeducation sessions also emphasize that there are situations when it might be beneficial to feel anxious, such as when the fight-or-flight response activates in truly dangerous situations. The goal of MAP-A, and any feasible treatment of anxiety sensitivity, is not to extinguish the anxiety response entirely, but rather to help the patient experience unhelpful anxiety at a diminished level. By starting the therapy with an extensive psychoeducation component, the therapist can help correct faulty understandings of their symptoms before launching into the other aspects of the treatment. This could be especially relevant to the youth with high anxiety sensitivity who have been misinterpreting the actual risks of their bodily sensations like heart palpitations or shortness of breath. Initial psychoeducation appears to be important for targeting anxiety sensitivity in youth. In fact, one study investigating the efficacy and week-to-week symptom change during administration of the Panic Control Treatment for Adolescents, an early version of MAP-A (Hoffman & Mattis, 2000), provided evidence that panic disorder symptoms decrease during the initial psychoeducational period alone (Micco, Choate-Summers, Ehrenreich, Pincus, & Mattis, 2007).

Cognitive work sessions

With the goal of reducing anxiety-provoking thoughts, the next two sessions in the treatment program (3 and 4) are primarily focused on the cognitive components of the treatment. Cognitive restructuring of catastrophic appraisals of anxiety-related bodily sensations is a second important component of treatments targeting panic symptoms and anxiety sensitivity in youth. Micco et al. (2007) provided empirical evidence that, following cognitive restructuring, adolescents with panic disorder demonstrated a drastic drop in anxiety symptoms. In these sessions and beyond, the therapist helps youth develop strategies to recognize and subsequently challenge their less realistic concerns about the expected fallout of panic sensations. Cognitive restructuring techniques are employed to help youth reframe the way they view their uncomfortable symptoms of anxiety. For example, youth are taught strategies for identifying and challenging anxiety-provoking thoughts (e.g., "What if I faint right now?") by evaluating the evidence (e.g., "How many times have I fainted a result of these sensations?") as well as their ability to cope (e.g., "Even if I did faint, how bad would it be? Could I get through it?"). These exercises are used to address two major thinking errors to which youth with panic and anxiety sensitivity are highly susceptible, including probability overestimation, where the child expects an unlikely threatening outcome, and catastrophic thinking, where youth are inclined to expect the worst-case scenario. It's important that youth with unrealistic concerns understand that not only is their feared outcome highly unlikely or impossible, but even if it did happen, (e.g., fainting in front of one's peers due to hyperventilation) they are capable of moving past it. By thinking critically about their worries related to their anxiety symptoms, youth are equipped to face their symptoms more confidently during the latter half of the treatment program. Please refer to Fig. 1 (Pincus, Ehrenreich, & Spiegel, 2008), which exemplifies use of this skill with youth.

Exposure therapy sessions

Once youth are more aware of any illogical beliefs that they hold about their bodily sensations, they are ready to start building tolerance of these uncomfortable feelings through interceptive and, and later, situational exposure exercises. Typically starting at session 5, youth are taught to induce their feared physiological symptoms outside of the context of an anxiety-provoking situation by using interoceptive exposures. These exercises, in which naturalistic activities, such as head-shaking to cause dizziness or breathing through a thin straw to induce breathlessness, are used to decondition fear reactions. These exposures also allow youth to discover for themselves that the bodily sensations can be controlled and that they are not necessarily harmful, or harbingers of a greater feared outcome. Once youth can recognize and provoke their conditioned fear to natural bodily sensations, the therapist guides them through multiple sessions of situational, or in vivo, exposures where patients face situations that they typically avoid to further extinguish the fear response. In MAP-A, youth develop a hierarchy of feared, agoraphobic situations with the guidance of their therapist (e.g., if crowded elevator is a chronically avoided situation, being in an elevator alone, with one other person, with two other people, with three other people, etc.). This hierarchy is

Situation	Automatic thought(s)	Emotions	Thinking trap (overestimating catastrophic thinking)	Evidence for	Evidence against	Alternative thought

Fig. 1 Thinking like a detective.
Handout from Mastery of Anxiety and Panic for Adolescents workbook.

employed as the patient and therapist gradually move up the list. Both interoceptive exposures and situational exposures are utilized in the later sessions (6–10), and youth are instructed to attempt additional exposures as homework between sessions. Interoceptive and in vivo exposure exercises allow youth to become more accustomed to uncomfortable physiological sensations and to begin to increase their ability to experience physical sensations without an intense automatic fear reaction and/or using problematic avoidance or escape behaviors. The exercises also help youth separate the idea of physical sensations from that of conceptualization of harm in order to learn that such sensations are not truly dangerous (Pincus, Ehrenreich, & Mattis, 2008).

Breathing retraining

The rationale for including breathing retraining in panic treatments is based on the hyperventilation model of panic disorder, which theorizes that subtle, chronic hyperventilation in people with panic disorder leads to physical symptoms that, when noticed, can lead to panic attacks (Ley, 1985). Studies used to support this model have evidenced that people with panic disorder have lower basal pCO_2 levels (Papp et al., 1997; Roth, Wilhelm, & Trabert, 1998) and greater subjective responses to voluntary hyperventilation (Rapee, Brown, Antony, & Barlow, 1992). The purpose of breathing retraining is to correct youths' tendency toward subtle hyperventilation, and resultantly decrease physical sensations that make youth more likely to experience panic attacks.

During breathing retraining, the role of hyperventilation in panic attacks is discussed, and youth are taught slow, diaphragmatic breathing as a coping skill to reduce the frequency and intensity of physical sensations that trigger and maintain panic. However, the idea of incorporating breathing retraining into treatments for panic disorder is a debated topic. Specifically, in a review on the efficacy of breathing retraining for adults with panic disorder, Meuret, Wilhelm, Ritz, and Roth (2003, 2008) noted that studies of breathing retraining are limited and do not provide sufficient evidence indicating whether the technique is helpful. Thus, although some work has shown beneficial effects of breathing retraining on panic treatment outcome, evidence is inconclusive, with other work suggesting that breathing retraining does not produce expected changes in respiration rate or quality for individuals with panic disorder (Wollburg, Roth, & Kim, 2011). Few studies have examined this treatment component in isolation, indicating continued uncertainty among experts regarding the true efficacy of breathing retraining as a treatment for panic disorder for adults. Within the youth literature, Micco et al. (2007) examined efficacious treatment components within an early version of the MAP-A itself. While psychoeducation and cognitive restructuring were found to have the strongest effects on treatment outcome, breathing retraining did not appear to contribute to the efficacy of this CBT package (Micco et al., 2007).

Breathing retraining is thought to backfire when youth begin to use this skill as an avoidance strategy, even when not faced with significant panic symptoms that may lead to hyperventilation. Overuse of the strategy can be problematic when youth with high levels of anxiety sensitivity. First, youth might begin to conceptualize the breathing retraining as a "quick fix" for panic sensations, decreasing self-efficacy about their ability to handle distressing sensations on their own and relying only on the breathing to feel safe. Second, monitoring physical sensations in order to decide when to use the breathing exercises can inadvertently increase youth's focus on internal sensations and resultant panic reactions.

Parental involvement

As in many treatments geared toward adolescent, parents play an important role in the MAP-A. Throughout the program, the clinician empowers parents to support their children as coaches and cotherapists. Parents are typically involved in a portion of each session, typically for at least 10–15 min each week. In session 5, parents are asked to participate in an interoceptive exposure to demonstrate that these bodily feelings are uncomfortable for everyone, regardless of whether or not the person has panic disorder. Parents also have opportunities to model to their children that our bodies naturally habituate to these symptoms. As many parents of anxious children practice the same catastrophic thinking as their children, it is important to encourage caregivers to practice thoughtful parenting, helping them to recognize the example they are setting for their children when faced with anxiety-provoking situations. We have included a handout from MAP-A with guidance on how best to encourage parents to support their anxious children in their efforts to be brave. Fig. 2 (Pincus, Ehrenreich, & Spiegel, 2008) presents one commonly incorporated handout for parents.

Push compassionately:

Help your child push through the anxiety, and hold firm to expectations about her following through with the situation. But be equally sure to include empathy for the amount of distress the situation is causing her.

Focus on competency:

Reiterate (as many times as necessary) that your child has the ability to handle the situation. Help her to focus on the skills needed to complete the task rather than on the anxiety.

Downplay physical feelings:

Express compassion for the physical feelings, but no longer react to your child as you would if she were truly ill (e.g., if she had the stomach flu). Remind her that anxiety is causing the sensation, the sensation is time-limited (i.e., it won't last forever, it will end as soon as the anxiety does), and it is not harmful.

Be realistic:

If something is really hard (or perhaps is the first time the child is trying something new), keep the situation manageable in length and intensity, but with the understanding that each time the child tries it, she should push herself to stay a little longer.

Some of this may be different from your typical response to situations, and may feel uncomfortable at first. Also, you may wonder why your other children have responded just fine to your usual interventions. It is important to note that your interventions weren't "bad parenting"; they simply were not the ideal way to handle a child with an anxious temperament. It is important to find a parenting style that fits with your child's temperament— since each child is different, your parenting may have to adjust slightly to best meet each child's needs.

Fig. 2 Parenting anxious youth: 101.
Excerpt from Parenting Handout 1; Mastery of Anxiety and Panic for Adolescents.

Unified protocols for transdiagnostic treatment of emotional disorders in children and adolescents (UP-C and UP-A; Ehrenreich-May, Kennedy, Sherman, Bilek, Buzzella, et al., 2018)

The Unified Protocols for Transdiagnostic Treatment of Emotional Disorders in Children and Adolescents (UP-C and UP-A; Ehrenreich-May, Kennedy, Sherman, Bilek, Buzzella, et al., 2018) are transdiagnostic, evidence-based approaches for treating children and adolescents with a range of cooccurring emotional concerns, including anxiety, depression, and related emotional disorders (Bilek & Ehrenreich-May, 2012; Ehrenreich, Goldstein, Wright, & Barlow, 2009; Ehrenreich-May et al., 2017;

Ehrenreich-May, Queen, Bilek, Remmes, & Marciel, 2014; Kennedy, Bilek, & Ehrenreich-May, 2018; Queen, Barlow, & Ehrenreich-May, 2014). Importantly, youth with anxiety and depressive disorders have been found to exhibit certain cross-cutting processes, which has allowed for the development of transdiagnostic approaches such as the UP-A and UP-C (Barlow, Sauer-Zavala, Carl, Bullis, & Ellard, 2014; Tonarely, Sherman, & Ehrenreich-May, 2017). Anxiety sensitivity, in fact, represents one such transdiagnostic factor as it has been found to be elevated in youth exhibiting a variety of internalizing symptoms (Noel & Francis, 2011; Weems et al., 1997). Implementation of the UP-A or the UP-C may provide the optimal combinative treatment approach for simultaneously targeting anxiety sensitivity and symptoms of a variety of different anxiety and depressive disorders that may not be effectively treated by anxiety sensitivity-specific treatments alone. With that being said, components of the UP-A and UP-C discussed here are specifically theorized to target anxiety sensitivity and panic symptoms in youth.

Getting to know your emotions and behaviors

The second module of the UP-A (session 2 in UP-C), Getting to Know Your Emotions and Behaviors, has two major components applicable to the treatment of anxiety sensitivity in youth. First, youth receive psychoeducation about emotional experiences, and learn to identify thoughts, physiological sensations, and behaviors involved in emotional experiences including happiness, anger, sadness, and anxiety/fear. Youth specifically learn about how all of the components of emotional experiences interrelate and influence one another and that emotional experiences are often initiated by a triggering event, physiological sensation, or thought. If targeting anxiety sensitivity, it may be particularly important to emphasize the "physiological sensations" piece of this psychoeducation, and particularly, the fact that physiological sensations interact with other components of an intense emotional experience and can even serve as triggers of emotional experiences. One example of a physiological sensation as a trigger follows: A child or adolescent grows increasingly worried about what might be wrong with him or her after realizing that his or her heart is beating quickly for no apparent reason. Although physiological sensations are not always the triggers for the youth with emotional disorders, catastrophic thinking in response to physiological sensations typical in youth with heightened anxiety sensitivity can intensify a strong or uncomfortable emotional experience. Overall, the role of physiological sensations, as triggers and also as components of emotional experiences more generally (especially the experiences of anxiety and fear) should be emphasized when working with youth experiencing high levels of anxiety sensitivity.

Second, cycles of avoidance (avoiding situations, feelings, or thoughts that cause uncomfortable emotions) and anger (quickly/impulsively responding with aggression when experiencing uncomfortable emotions) are introduced as maladaptive behavioral responses in which individuals with intense emotional experiences often engage to quickly reduce uncomfortable emotions. During this section of treatment, youth are taught that, although these strategies for reducing discomfort often work in the short term, they can be maladaptive overall and lead to more prolonged, intense, and frequent emotional discomfort over time. For individuals with heightened anxiety sensitivity, this idea of avoidance in response to distress is important. Youth with emotional disorders typically respond to uncomfortable emotions that might seem intolerable (secondary to anxiety sensitivity and related difficulty with tolerating distress) by using avoidant strategies. Within the UP-A and UP-C treatments, youth learn that these avoidant strategies are maladaptive and not helpful for learning to handle difficult emotional experiences in the long term. This avoidance-focused framework sets the stage for the anxiety sensitivity-related coping skills presented later in UP-A or UP-C treatment. See Fig. 3 (Ehrenreich-May, Kennedy, Sherman, Bennett, & Barlow, 2018) for a reproduction of one primary worksheet used to conceptualize emotional experiences as a combination of thoughts, physiological sensations, and behaviors.

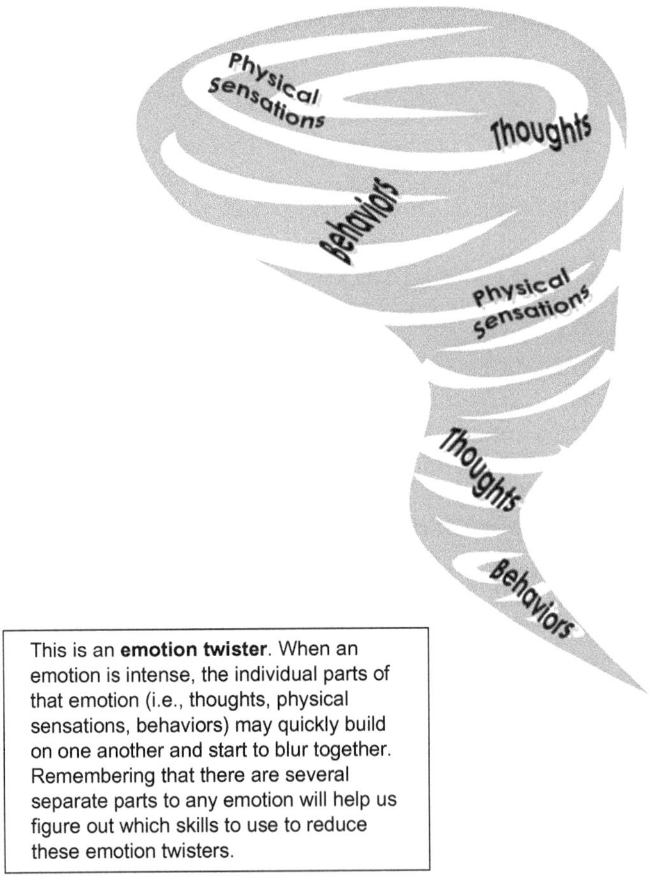

Fig. 3 Emotion twister.
Reproduced from Unified Protocol for Transdiagnostic Treatment of Emotional Disorders in Adolescents: Workbook.

Awareness of physical sensations

Module 4 in the UP-A (session 4 in UP-C), Sensational Awareness, which may be construed as the most applicable portion of UP-A or UP-C for the treatment of anxiety sensitivity, also contains two subsections. First, youth receive additional psychoeducation about the physical sensations that typically occur within one's body when having an emotional experience, with therapists employing an explanation of the body's adaptive "fight or flight response" as a launching point into this discussion of physiological sensations. At this point, youth are encouraged to increase awareness of such physical sensations through a body-drawing activity. Specifically, using the outline of a body as a reference point, youth work to record different physiological sensations associated with strong emotions, including fear, anxiety, and even anger and sadness (although, for treating anxiety sensitivity, the experiences of fear and anxiety should be emphasized here). In the UP-A and UP-C, physiological sensations associated with strong emotions are commonly referred to as "body clues" due to the fact that they can serve as signals, allowing one to recognize that he or she is having an emotional experience.

Second, the clinician introduces youth to the concept behind sensational exposures (i.e., interoceptive exposures), or the idea that certain physical activities can induce the same physical sensations caused by emotional experiences. These activities are similar to those introduced in treatments discussed here that target panic disorder more directly. Through in-session and home-based practice of such exposures and discussion with their clinician, youth learn that these sensations, whether caused by physical activity (e.g., running in place, breathing through a coffee straw, spinning in a chair, shaking one's head back and forth) or emotions, are harmless, and while uncomfortable, they resolve on their own.

In order to target anxiety sensitivity and distress tolerance more directly, the UP-A and UP-C place an emphasis on the fact that, even if sensations do not go away and remain present for a while, the physical sensations themselves are not dangerous and can be coped with simply by allowing them to be present and observing them without judgment. This important component of the sensational awareness section of treatment involves teaching youth to "body scan." Body scanning, simply put, is an awareness strategy used to help youth tolerate uncomfortable physical sensations and resist performing any emotional behaviors (e.g., looking at hands to refocus, stopping activity midway, or sitting down) to make the feelings go away more quickly. Instead, youth are taught that the sensations are not harmful and do dissipate with time on their own, without youth having to perform emotional behaviors. Please refer to Fig. 4 (Ehrenreich-May, Kennedy, Sherman, Bennett, & Barlow, 2018) for one primary worksheet used to allow youth to track interoceptive exposure activities and their experiences during such activities. Please see Fig. 5 (Ehrenreich-May, Kennedy, Sherman, Bilek, & Barlow, 2018) for a downward-adapted child-friendly version of a handout introducing this treatment component.

Rating scale:

None **Slight** **Medium** **A lot** **Extreme**

Name of sensational exposure task	Physical sensations	Intensity of sensation (0-8)	Notes (e.g., thoughts, emotions, desire to engage in emotional behaviors)

Fig. 4 Monitoring how my body feels.
From Unified Protocol for Transdiagnostic Treatment of Emotional Disorders in Adolescents: Workbook.

Being flexible in your thinking (thinking traps and detective thinking)

The first two sections of Module 5 in the UP-A (sessions 5 and 6 in UP-C) each serve to increase cognitive flexibility and also more indirectly serve to target anxiety sensitivity. These portions of treatment serve a similar purpose to that of cognitive restructuring, a common component of panic disorder treatments mentioned here that is thought to target anxiety sensitivity in youth. However, one major difference between "Cognitive Restructuring" and "Detective Thinking" is that, when youth are taught cognitive restructuring, they are specifically tasked with reframing and modifying maladaptive thinking patterns, while youth engaging in detective thinking

Hi again! Jack here. Today we are going to work together to become **body detectives**. Now that we have learned what body clues are, we are ready to get to work!

Body detectives are super cool Emotion Detectives who are really good at knowing what body clues they feel when they are having different emotions! Work with your therapist to think of some emotions like the ones listed here and if those emotions makeyou feel any of these common body clues. Then, write down which body clues you have the most at the bottom of this figure!

Emotion	Body clues
Happiness	Feel like smiling, feel warm inside, heart beating fast
Fear	Feel dizzy, heart beating fast, face feels hot, feel sweaty, muscles feel tight or hot, shaking, mouth feels dry, out of breath
Sadness	Feel heavy, chest feels tight, feel like crying, shaking, throat feels tight, eyes hurt, feel tired, feel like moving slowly
Anger	Face feels hot, muscles feel tight and hot, mouth feels dry, hands and feet feel tight, hot or shaky, throat feels tight, chest feels tight, feel like yelling, screaming
Anxiety	Brain feels full, heart beating fast, face feels hot, muscles feel tight, feel like yelling, screaming, stomach hurts or head hurts, feel nauseous
Which body clue do you have the most?	

Fig. 5 Becoming a body detective.
From Unified Protocol for Transdiagnostic Treatment of Emotional Disorders in Children: Workbook.

are asked not to completely reject an interpretation, but rather, to entertain the fact that there might be another way to look at or understand a situation. Youth are also encouraged to try to tolerate multiple potential explanations of a situation and to cope with any of the possible explanations.

The skill of cognitive flexibility is introduced first using an optical illusions task in which youth are taught to recognize that situations (like optical illusions) can be interpreted in many ways, with multiple explanations being understandable and making sense. Then, youth are introduced to the concept of maladaptive automatic thoughts/thinking errors (referred to as "thinking traps" in the UP-A and UP-C) that often contribute to uncomfortable emotional experiences. When working with youth who might be experiencing heightened levels of anxiety sensitivity, automatic thoughts or thinking traps discussed during this section of treatment might relate directly to physiological sensations (e.g., "If my heart is beating fast, maybe I am having a heart attack," "If I feel like I can't breathe I might hyperventilate," "If I feel dizzy I may faint").

Second, antecedent cognitive reappraisal (referred to as "detective thinking" in the UP-A) is taught and practiced in order to encourage youth to increase his/her cognitive flexibility, or the ability to consider more than one explanation of a given situation and that one's automatic cognition is not always the most accurate one (e.g., "If I feel dizzy, I may faint, but I also may not faint. In fact, I have felt dizzy many times in the past and have only fainted once"). Finally, the idea of being able to tolerate or handle even the most difficult possible explanation is introduced (e.g., "If I do feel dizzy and faint, how can I cope with that?"). This way, youth with heightened anxiety sensitivity are taught that, even if physiological sensations do, on rare occasions, result in difficult situations, the sensations themselves are not dangerous in the long term and the situations can be handled.

Situational emotion exposure

Module 7 in the UP-A (sessions 9–14 in UP-C) incorporates the ideas of gradually exposing oneself to stimuli that cause emotional distress (e.g., fear, anxiety, sadness, anger) and learning that one can tolerate these difficult situations. Gradual exposure has been shown to be one of the most effective, if not the most effective components of CBT for anxiety (Butler, Chapman, Forman, & Beck, 2006; Ishikawa et al., 2007). During this portion of treatment, youth are introduced to the theory behind exposure, including the rationale for repeated exposure practice, and learning that something feared or avoided is often not as aversive as one imagines once it is endured, concepts which can easily be tied into lessons learned during the previous interoceptive exposure section of treatment. The remainder of situational emotion exposure sessions are spent creating and revising exposure stepladders and hierarchies (meant to structure steps to be taken toward facing fears as well as accompanying contingent reinforcement for youth facing difficult emotional triggers) and completing activities in-session and at home to formally place youth in situations that cause distress. For example, an adolescent typically experiencing physiological sensations and fear of these sensations in social situations with unfamiliar adults (e.g., waiters, school principal, store clerks) might be supported in making small talk with the barista at a coffee shop, instructed by the therapist to order a pizza over the phone, or asked to order his/her own food at a restaurant. One of the goals of the situational emotion exposure module in the UP-A is to help youth generalize and apply the skills that they have learned throughout the earlier modules to a broader range of settings and situations that provoke their distressing physiological sensations.

While one additional way to further increase the effectiveness of this portion of treatment for youth experiencing heightened anxiety sensitivity would be to continue to practice interoceptive exposures, situational exposures should be incorporated as well. As mentioned earlier in this chapter, most youth with heightened anxiety sensitivity do not solely experience nontriggered panic disorder symptoms, but rather, display difficulty with troubling physiological sensations arising in many different situations. Therefore, what may be most helpful when administering the UP-A or UP-C to youth with heightened anxiety sensitivity is pairing interoceptive exposures with situations that typically cause youth to experience troubling physiological sensations (e.g., running in place before entering a crowded store in the mall). Of course. One additional approach that can help youth with heightened anxiety sensitivity benefit from exposures more generally is emphasizing the ways in which habituation and other learning processes occurring during situational and interoceptive exposures relate to physiological sensations (e.g., "The first time you did the speech, you spoke about experiencing many distressing body clues. By the sixth speech you made, you noted those body clues felt less intense, dissipated more quickly, and were not even as distressing to you as before.").

Unique challenges in treating youth with high anxiety sensitivity

Finally, when treating youth and working with parents of youth with high levels of anxiety sensitivity, clinicians must keep certain risks in mind. Working with youth and their caregivers presents unique challenges. First, it is especially important to be sure that the youth's symptoms are, in fact, resultant of anxiety and not another medical cause. Second, youth often attend treatment only as long as their caregivers remain engaged in or convinced of the benefits of therapy. Therefore, parental understanding and acceptance of the therapeutic approach is imperative to successful youth treatment. Additionally, youth with heightened anxiety sensitivity are often required to face difficult situations daily, even at the start of treatment. For example, youth commonly experience troubling physiological sensations at school or in other social settings, but are often required tolerate such situations regularly. Thus, the therapist must be aware and able to help the youth essentially face naturalistic exposures from the very beginning of therapy.

The first unique challenge involves ensuring the safety of the youth in treatment. As is the case with adults who experience many troubling physiological sensations associated with anxiety, youth with high levels of anxiety sensitivity are likely to attribute physiological sensations to medical causes. Although it is important for the therapist to consider that, in all likelihood, these sensations are harmless results of anxiety, it is also imperative for the therapist to work with parents and youth to make sure that the physiological sensations are not due to a medical condition. This might involve receiving clearance from a pediatrician or specialist prior to initiating therapy or early in the course of therapy. Even once medical causes of physiological sensations are ruled out, therapists may find that youth and their parents remain concerned about the youth feeling physically uncomfortable in therapy. Thus, when working with children, it is extremely important to provide thorough psychoeducation to the youth and his/her caregivers about distress that the youth might be expected to experience following exposures and to communicate often with caregivers about difficult exposures.

Second, parental distress can become a barrier in youth treatment, especially when youth are experiencing physiological sensations that the youth might appraise as dangerous, as is often the case for youth with heightened anxiety sensitivity. If parents are unable to cope with their child's physiological distress and interpretation of such, parents could avoid completing exposures with their children or even discontinue services. Should parents have difficulty dealing with their child's distress following exposure sessions, the therapist may choose to take precautions to increase parents' comfort with the therapeutic approach in order to decrease the likelihood of treatment dropout. Such precautions might include involving the caregivers in some interoceptive and/or situational exposures, taking exposure slightly more slowly, and warning caregivers about potential reactions that the youth might have when first experiencing exposure, while reiterating that this distress will decrease over time, through review of the concepts of habituation and learning as mechanisms of change within the treatment.

Another unique challenge therapists will come across in the treatment of youth with heightened anxiety sensitivity is that children who attend school typically experience frequent and naturalistic exposures to troubling stimuli or situations prior to learning any skills to deal with these situations. For example, a child or adolescent with agoraphobia may still have to attend school each day, even before interoceptive or situational exposures have been covered in therapy. Similarly, youth may experience negative social feedback in response to his/her physiological symptoms (e.g., peers making fun of them for blushing, teachers reprimanding them for avoiding presentations or freezing up when asked questions, etc.). When treating youth experiencing these or similar challenges, therapists may choose to have youth gradually approach these difficult situations as soon as possible within the course of therapy, as tolerated. Home-based exposure assignments may involve gradually increasing approach toward these situations and tolerating physiological sensations along the way (e.g., taking a bathroom break every other period instead of every period in school, entering the cafeteria for 5 min each day if the youth typically eats in the office or bathroom, answering an easy question in class).

Concluding remarks

The most commonly used treatments for anxiety sensitivity in adults are designed to target panic disorder, an anxiety disorder most commonly associated with heightened anxiety sensitivity (Olatunji & Wolitzky-Taylor, 2009; Smits et al., 2008). Little work has been done to investigate the efficacy of treatments for reducing anxiety sensitivity in youth. This may be due in part to the fact that panic disorder is uncommon in young children. However, panic disorder typically develops in early to midadolescence (Costello, Mustillo, Erkanli, Keeler, & Angold, 2003; Craske & Waikar, 1994; Ollendick & Pincus, 2008) and serves as a debilitating disorder, often comorbid with additional functionally impairing disorders including agoraphobia, other anxiety disorders, and depression (Kessler et al., 2005; Kessler, Chiu, Demler, & Walters, 2005). Many clinically anxious children and adolescents who do not meet diagnostic criteria for panic disorder do exhibit elevated anxiety sensitivity (Noel & Francis, 2011; Olatunji & Wolitzky-Taylor, 2009). While the relationship between anxiety sensitivity and panic disorder appears to be less crystalized in children and adolescents, the fact that youth with various anxiety disorders display heightened anxiety sensitivity suggests that treating anxiety sensitivity in youth may help prevent the future development of panic disorder and agoraphobia. Further, anxiety sensitivity itself serves as a risk factor for the development of a range of different anxiety-related problems in youth and adults (Schmidt et al., 2010; Schmidt, Lerew, & Jackson, 1997) and reducing anxiety sensitivity could help prevent the development of additional anxiety disorders as well.

Another viewpoint on the treatment of anxiety sensitivity in youth involves seeing anxiety sensitivity as a transdiagnostic factor presenting across a range of emotional disorders in youth, including anxiety and depression. In line with this theory, research has suggested that children with a range of emotional disorders display heightened anxiety sensitivity (Noel & Francis, 2011). While transdiagnostic treatments including the UP-A and UP-C do not focus on the treatment of anxiety sensitivity alone, youth with heightened anxiety sensitivity, as well as multiple anxiety and/or depressive disorders, may benefit from an approach that targets anxiety sensitivity as well as other transdiagnostic factors of emotional disorders in youth, including distress tolerance, cognitive inflexibility, negative affect, and experiential avoidance (Barlow et al., 2014; Kennedy & Ehrenreich-May, 2017; Leyro, Zvolensky, & Bernstein, 2010; MacDermott, Betts, Gullone, & Allen, 2009; Maner & Schmidt, 2006; McLaughlin & Nolen-Hoeksema, 2011; Muris et al., 2005; Tonarely, & Ehrenreich-May, under review; Wong & Moulds, 2011).

Considering the potential efficacy of anxiety sensitivity interventions in youth, both from treatment and prevention perspectives, we propose several important next steps in research on the treatment of anxiety sensitivity in youth. First, it will be important for future research efforts to focus on testing the hypothesis that a treatment package comprised psychoeducation, cognitive restructuring, and interceptive exposures could serve as an efficacious personalized treatment for children and adolescents with heightened anxiety sensitivity in particular. It will also be necessary to investigate the potential utility of broader, transdiagnostic treatment programs such as the UP-A and UP-C for targeting anxiety sensitivity as a transdiagnostic factor of emotional disorders in youth.

References

Adornetto, C., Hensdiek, M., Meyer, A., In-Albon, T., Federer, M., & Schneider, S. (2008). The factor structure of the Childhood Anxiety Sensitivity Index in German children. *Journal of Behavior Therapy and Experimental Psychiatry*, *39*(4), 404–416.

Ale, C. M., McCarthy, D. M., Rothschild, L. M., & Whiteside, S. P. (2015). Components of cognitive behavioral therapy related to outcome in childhood anxiety disorders. *Clinical Child and Family Psychology Review*, *18*(3), 240–251. https://doi.org/10.1007/s10567-015-0184-8.

Allan, N. P., Capron, D. W., Lejuez, C. W., Reynolds, E. K., MacPherson, L., & Schmidt, N. B. (2014). Developmental trajectories of anxiety symptoms in early adolescence: the influence of anxiety sensitivity. *Journal of Abnormal Child Psychology*, *42*(4), 589–600. https://doi.org/10.1007/s10802-013-9806-0.

APA (2013). *Diagnostic and statistical manual of mental disorders* (5th ed.). Washington, DC: Author.

Barlow, D. H., Sauer-Zavala, S., Carl, J. R., Bullis, J. R., & Ellard, K. K. (2014). The nature, diagnosis, and treatment of neuroticism back to the future. *Clinical Psychological Science*, *2*(3), 344–365.

Bilek, E. L., & Ehrenreich-May, J. (2012). An open trial investigation of a transdiagnostic group treatment for children with anxiety and depressive symptoms. *Behavior Therapy*, *43*(4), 887–897. https://doi.org/10.1016/j.beth.2012.04.007.

Bittner, A., Egger, H. L., Erkanli, A., Jane Costello, E., Foley, D. L., & Angold, A. (2007). What do childhood anxiety disorders predict? *Journal of Child Psychology and Psychiatry*, *48*(12), 1174–1183. https://doi.org/10.1111/j.1469-7610.2007.01812.x.

Blakey, S. M., Abramowitz, J. S., Reuman, L., Leonard, R. C., & Riemann, B. C. (2017). Anxiety sensitivity as a predictor of outcome in the treatment of obsessive-compulsive disorder. *Journal of Behavior Therapy and Experimental Psychiatry*, *57*, 113–117. https://doi.org/10.1016/j.jbtep.2017.05.003.

Boswell, J. F., Farchione, T. J., Sauer-Zavala, S., Murray, H. W., Fortune, M. R., & Barlow, D. H. (2013). Anxiety sensitivity and interoceptive exposure: a transdiagnostic construct and change strategy. *Behavior Therapy*, *44*(3), 417–431.

Brunner, R., Kaess, M., Parzer, P., Fischer, G., Carli, V., Hoven, C. W., … Wasserman, D. (2014). Life-time prevalence and psychosocial correlates of adolescent direct self-injurious behavior: a comparative study of findings in 11 European countries. *Journal of Child Psychology and Psychiatry*, *55*(4), 337–348. https://doi.org/10.1111/Jcpp.12166.

Butler, A. C., Chapman, J. E., Forman, E. M., & Beck, A. T. (2006). The empirical status of cognitive-behavioral therapy: a review of meta-analyses. *Clinical Psychology Review*, *26*(1), 17–31. https://doi.org/10.1016/j.cpr.2005.07.003.

Chorpita, B. F., Albano, A. M., & Barlow, D. H. (1996a). Child anxiety sensitivity index: considerations for children with anxiety disorders. *Journal of Clinical Child Psychology*, *25*(1), 77–82. https://doi.org/10.1207/s15374424jccp2501_9.

Chorpita, B. F., Albano, A. M., & Barlow, D. H. (1996b). Cognitive processing in children: relation to anxiety and family influences. *Journal of Clinical Child Psychology*, *25*(2), 170–176.

Chorpita, B. F., & Daleiden, E. L. (2000). Properties of the Childhood Anxiety Sensitivity Index in children with anxiety disorders: autonomic and nonautonomic factors. *Behavior Therapy*, *31*(2), 327–349.

Clark, L. A., & Watson, D. (1991). Tripartite model of anxiety and depression: psychometric evidence and taxonomic implications. *Journal of Abnormal Psychology*, *100*(3), 316.

Costello, E. J., Mustillo, S., Erkanli, A., Keeler, G., & Angold, A. (2003). Prevalence and development of psychiatric disorders in childhood and adolescence. *Archives of General Psychiatry*, *60*(8), 837–844. https://doi.org/10.1001/archpsyc.60.8.837.

Craske, M. G., & Barlow, D. H. (2006a). Mastery of your anxiety and worry. New York, NY: Oxford University Press.

Craske, M. G., & Waikar, S. V. (1994). Panic disorder. In *Handbook of prescriptive treatments for adults* (pp. 135–155). Boston, MA: Springer.

Ehrenreich, J. T., Goldstein, C. M., Wright, L. R., & Barlow, D. H. (2009). Development of a unified protocol for the treatment of emotional disorders in youth. *Child and Family Behavior Therapy*, *31*(1), 20–37. https://doi.org/10.1080/07317100802701228.

Ehrenreich-May, J., Kennedy, S. M., Sherman, J. A., Bennett, S. M., & Barlow, D. H. (2018). *Unified protocol for transdiagnostic treatment of emotional disorders in adolescents: Workbook*. New York: Oxford University Press.

Ehrenreich-May, J., Kennedy, S. M., Sherman, J. A., Bilek, E. L., & Barlow, D. H. (2018). *Unified protocol for transdiagnostic treatment of emotional disorders in children: Workbook*. New York: Oxford University Press.

Ehrenreich-May, J., Kennedy, S. M., Sherman, J. A., Bilek, E. L., Buzzella, B. A., Bennett, S. M., & Barlow, D. H. (2018). *Unified protocols for the transdiagnostic treatment of emotional disorders in children and adolescents: Therapist guide*. New York: Oxford University Press.

Ehrenreich-May, J., Queen, A. H., Bilek, E. L., Remmes, C. S., & Marciel, K. K. (2014). The unified protocols for the treatment of emotional disorders in children and adolescents. In J. Ehrenreich-May & B. C. Chu (Eds.), *Transdiagnostic treatments for children and adolescents principles and practice* (pp. 267–293). New York, NY: Guilford Press.

Ehrenreich-May, J., Rosenfield, D., Queen, A. H., Kennedy, S. M., Remmes, C. S., & Barlow, D. H. (2017). An initial waitlist-controlled trial of the unified protocol for the treatment of emotional disorders in adolescents. *Journal of Anxiety Disorders*, *46*, 46–55.

Essau, C. A., Sasagawa, S., & Ollendick, T. H. (2010). The facets of anxiety sensitivity in adolescents. *Journal of Anxiety Disorders*, *24*(1), 23–29.

Gallagher, M. W., Payne, L. A., White, K. S., Shear, K. M., Woods, S. W., Gorman, J. M., & Barlow, D. H. (2013). Mechanisms of change in cognitive behavioral therapy for panic disorder: the unique effects of self-efficacy and anxiety sensitivity. *Behaviour Research and Therapy*, *51*(11), 767–777.

Garber, J., & Weersing, V. R. (2010). Comorbidity of anxiety and depression in youth: implications for treatment and prevention. *Clinical Psychologist (New York)*, *17*(4), 293–306. https://doi.org/10.1111/j.1468-2850.2010.01221.x.

Goodwin, R. D., Fergusson, D. M., & Horwood, L. J. (2004). Association between anxiety disorders and substance use disorders among young persons: results of a 21-year longitudinal study. *Journal of Psychiatric Research*, *38*(3), 295–304. https://doi.org/10.1016/j.jpsychires.2003.09.002.

Hale, L. R., & Calamari, J. E. (2006). Panics symptoms and disorder in youth: what role does anxiety sensitivity play? In C. M. Velotis (Ed.), *New developments in anxiety disorder research* (pp. 131–162). New York: Nova Biomedical Books.

Hayward, C., Killen, J. D., Kraemer, H. C., & Taylor, C. B. (2000). Predictors of panic attacks in adolescents. *Journal of the American Academy of Child and Adolescent Psychiatry*, *39*(2), 207–214. https://doi.org/10.1097/00004583-200002000-00021.

Hoffman, E. C., & Mattis, S. G. (2000). A developmental adaptation of panic control treatment for panic disorder in adolescence. *Cognitive and Behavioral Practice*, *7*(3), 253–261.

Ishikawa, S., Okajima, I., Matsuoka, H., & Sakano, Y. (2007). Cognitive behavioural therapy for anxiety disorders in children and adolescents: a meta-analysis. *Child and Adolescent Mental Health*, *12*(4), 164–172. https://doi.org/10.1111/j.1475-3588.2006.00433.x.

Kearney, C. A., Albano, A. M., Eisen, A. R., Allan, W. D., & Barlow, D. H. (1997). The phenomenology of panic disorder in youngsters: an empirical study of a clinical sample. *Journal of Anxiety Disorders*, *11*(1), 49–62.

Kendall, P. C., Furr, J. M., & Podell, J. L. (2010). Child-focused treatment of anxiety. In J. R. Weisz & A. E. Kazdin (Eds.), *Evidence-based psychotherapies for children and adolescents* (2nd ed., pp. 45–59). New York: Guilford Press.

Kennedy, S. M., Bilek, E. L., & Ehrenreich-May, J. A. (2018). A randomized controlled pilot trial of the unified protocol for the treatment of emotional disorders in children (UP-C). *Behavioral Modification.*

Kennedy, S. M., & Ehrenreich-May, J. (2017). Assessment of emotional avoidance in adolescents: Psychometric properties of a new multidimensional measure. *Journal of Psychopathology and Behavioral Assessment*, *39*(2), 279–290.

Kennedy, S. M., Mash, J. A., Tawfik, S. H., & Ehrenreich-May, J. (2017). Anxiety disorders. In C. Flessner & J. Piacentini (Eds.), *Clinical handbook of psychological disorders in children and adolescents: A step-by-step manual* (pp. 122–168). New York: Guilford Press.

Kessler, R. C., Berglund, P., Demler, O., Jin, R., Merikangas, K. R., & Walters, E. E. (2005). Lifetime prevalence and age-of-onset distributions of DSM-IV disorders in the national comorbidity survey replication (vol 62, pg 593, 2005). *Archives of General Psychiatry*, *62*(7), 768.

Kessler, R. C., Chiu, W. T., Demler, O., & Walters, E. E. (2005). Prevalence, severity, and comorbidity of 12-month DSM-IV disorders in the National Comorbidity Survey Replication. *Archives of General Psychiatry*, *62*(6), 617–627.

Ley, R. (1985). Blood, breath, and fears: a hyperventilation theory of panic attacks and agoraphobia. *Clinical Psychology Review*, *5*(4), 271–285.

Leyro, T. M., Zvolensky, M. J., & Bernstein, A. (2010). Distress tolerance and psychopathological symptoms and disorders: a review of the empirical literature among adults. *Psychological Bulletin*, *136*(4), 576.

MacDermott, S. T., Betts, J., Gullone, E., & Allen, J. S. (2009). *Emotion regulation in childhood and adolescence: A revised version of the emotion regulation questionnaire (ERQ-CA).* Australia: Monash University (Forthcoming).

Maner, J. K., & Schmidt, N. B. (2006). The role of risk avoidance in anxiety. *Behavior Therapy*, *37*(2), 181–189.

McLaughlin, K. A., & Nolen-Hoeksema, S. (2011). Rumination as a transdiagnostic factor in depression and anxiety. *Behaviour Research and Therapy*, *49*(3), 186–193.

Meuret, A. E., Wilhelm, F. H., Ritz, T., & Roth, W. T. (2003). Breathing training for treating panic disorder. Useful intervention or impediment? *Behavioral Modification*, *27*(5), 731–754.

Meuret, A. E., Wilhelm, F. H., Ritz, T., & Roth, W. T. (2008). Feedback of end-tidal pCO_2 as a therapeutic approach for panic disorder. *Journal of Psychiatric Research*, *42*(7), 560–568.

Micco, J. A., Choate-Summers, M. L., Ehrenreich, J. T., Pincus, D. B., & Mattis, S. G. (2007). Identifying efficacious treatment components of panic control treatment for adolescents: a preliminary examination. *Child & Family Behavior Therapy*, *29*(4), 1–23.

Muris, P., Roelofs, J., Rassin, E., Franken, I., & Mayer, B. (2005). Mediating effects of rumination and worry on the links between neuroticism, anxiety and depression. *Personality and Individual Differences*, *39*(6), 1105–1111.

Naragon-Gainey, K. (2010). Meta-analysis of the relations of anxiety sensitivity to the depressive and anxiety disorders. *Psychological Bulletin*, *136*(1), 128.

Noel, V. A., & Francis, S. E. (2011). A meta-analytic review of the role of child anxiety sensitivity in child anxiety. *Journal of Abnormal Child Psychology*, *39*(5), 721–733. https://doi.org/10.1007/s10802-011-9489-3.

Norr, A. M., Allan, N. P., Macatee, R. J., Keough, M. E., & Schmidt, N. B. (2014). The effects of an anxiety sensitivity intervention on anxiety, depression, and worry: mediation through affect tolerances. *Behaviour Research and Therapy, 59*, 12–19. https://doi.org/10.1016/j.brat.2014.05.011.

Olatunji, B. O., & Wolitzky-Taylor, K. B. (2009). Anxiety sensitivity and the anxiety disorders: a meta-analytic review and synthesis. *Psychological Bulletin, 135*(6), 974–999. https://doi.org/10.1037/A0017428.

Ollendick, T. H. (1995). Cognitive behavioral treatment of panic disorder with agoraphobia in adolescents: a multiple baseline design analysis. *Behavior Therapy, 26*(3), 517–531.

Ollendick, T. H., & Pincus, D. (2008). Panic disorder in adolescents. In R. G. Steele, T. D. Elkin, & M. C. Roberts (Eds.), *Handbook of evidence-based therapies for children and adolescents. Issues in clinical child psychology* (pp. 83–102). Boston, MA: Springer.

Ollendick, T. H., Shortt, A. L., & Sander, J. B. (2005). Internalizing disorders of childhood and adolescence. In J. E. Maddux & B. A. Winstead (Eds.), *Psychopathology: Foundations for a contemporary understanding* (pp. 353–376). Mahwah, NJ: Lawrence Erlbaum Associates Publishers.

Papp, L. A., Martinez, J. M., Klein, D. F., Coplan, J. D., Norman, R. G., Cole, R., ... Gorman, J. M. (1997). Respiratory psychophysiology of panic disorder: three respiratory challenges in 98 subjects. *American Journal of Psychiatry, 154*(11), 1557–1565.

Piaget, J. (1971). The theory of stages in cognitive development. In D. R. Green, M. P. Ford, & G. B. Flamer (Eds.), *Measurement and Piaget*. New York: McGraw-Hill.

Pincus, D. B., Ehrenreich, J. T., & Mattis, S. G. (2008). *Mastery of anxiety and panic for adolescents, riding the wave: Therapist guide*. New York: Oxford University Press.

Pincus, D. B., Ehrenreich, J. T., & Spiegel, D. A. (2008). *Riding the wave: Workbook*. New York: Oxford University Press.

Pincus, D. B., Ehrenreich-May, J., Whitton, S. W., Mattis, S. G., & Barlow, D. H. (2010). Cognitive-behavioral treatment of panic disorder in adolescence. *Journal of Clinical Child & Adolescent Psychology, 39*(5), 638–649.

Queen, A. H., Barlow, D. H., & Ehrenreich-May, J. (2014). The trajectories of adolescent anxiety and depressive symptoms over the course of a transdiagnostic treatment. *Journal of Anxiety Disorders, 28*(6), 511–521.

Rapee, R. M., Brown, T. A., Antony, M. M., & Barlow, D. H. (1992). Response to hyperventilation and inhalation of 5.5% carbon dioxide-enriched air across the DSM-III-R anxiety disorders. *Journal of Abnormal Psychology, 101*(3), 538.

Reiss, S. (1991). Expectancy model of fear, anxiety, and panic. *Clinical Psychology Review, 11*(2), 141–153. https://doi.org/10.1016/0272-7358(91)90092-9.

Reiss, S., Peterson, R. A., Gursky, D. M., & Mcnally, R. J. (1986). Anxiety sensitivity, anxiety frequency and the prediction of fearfulness. *Behaviour Research and Therapy, 24*(1), 1–8. https://doi.org/10.1016/0005-7967(86)90143-9.

Roth, W. T., Wilhelm, F. H., & Trabert, W. (1998). Voluntary breath holding in panic and generalized anxiety disorders. *Psychosomatic Medicine, 60*(6), 671–679.

Schmidt, N. B., Keough, M. E., Mitchell, M. A., Reynolds, E. K., MacPherson, L., Zvolensky, M. J., & Lejuez, C. W. (2010). Anxiety sensitivity: prospective prediction of anxiety among early adolescents. *Journal of Anxiety Disorders, 24*(5), 503–508.

Schmidt, N. B., Lerew, D. R., & Jackson, R. J. (1997). The role of anxiety sensitivity in the pathogenesis of panic: prospective evaluation of spontaneous panic attacks during acute stress. *Journal of Abnormal Psychology, 106*(3), 355.

Silverman, W. K., Fleisig, W., Rabian, B., & Peterson, R. A. (1991). Childhood Anxiety Sensitivity Index. *Journal of Clinical Child Psychology, 20*(2), 162–168. https://doi.org/10.1207/s15374424jccp2002_7.

Silverman, W. K., Goedhart, A. W., Barrett, P., & Turner, C. (2003). The facets of anxiety sensitivity represented in the Childhood Anxiety Sensitivity Index: confirmatory analyses of factor models from past studies. *Journal of Abnormal Psychology*, *112*(3), 364–374. https://doi.org/10.1037/0021-843x.112.3.364.

Smits, J. A. J., Berry, A. C., Tart, C. D., & Powers, M. B. (2008). The efficacy of cognitive-behavioral interventions for reducing anxiety sensitivity: a meta-analytic review. *Behaviour Research and Therapy*, *46*(9), 1047–1054.

Spielmans, G. I., Pasek, L. F., & McFall, J. P. (2007). What are the active ingredients in cognitive and behavioral psychotherapy for anxious and depressed children? A meta-analytic review. *Clinical Psychology Review*, *27*(5), 642–654. https://doi.org/10.1016/j.cpr.2006.06.001.

Strauss, C. C., Last, C. G., Hersen, M., & Kazdin, A. E. (1988). Association between anxiety and depression in children and adolescents with anxiety disorders. *Journal of Abnormal Child Psychology*, *16*(1), 57–68. https://doi.org/10.1007/Bf00910500.

Taylor, S. (1999). *Anxiety sensitivity: Theory, research, and treatment of the fear of anxiety*. Mahwah, NJ: Lawrence Erlbaum Associates Publishers.

Taylor, S. (2014). *Anxiety sensitivity: Theory, research, and treatment of the fear of anxiety*. New York: Routledge.

Tonarely, N. A. and Ehrenreich-May, J. (under review). Confirming the factor structure and psychometrics of the distress tolerance scale (DTS) in youth. Assessment.

Tonarely, N. A., Sherman, J. A., & Ehrenreich-May, J. (2017). Neuroticism as a higher order factor in youth emotional disorders. In: *Poster presented at the American Behavioral and Cognitive Therapy (ABCT) conference, San Diego, CA*.

Weems, C. F., Hammond, L. K., Silverman, W. K., & Ferguson, C. (1997). The relation between anxiety sensitivity and depression in children and adolescents referred for anxiety. *Behaviour Research and Therapy*, *35*(10), 961–966. https://doi.org/10.1016/S0005-7967(97)00049-1.

Weems, C. F., Hammond-Laurence, K., Silverman, W. K., & Ginsburg, G. S. (1998). Testing the utility of the anxiety sensitivity construct in children and adolescents referred for anxiety disorders. *Journal of Clinical Child Psychology*, *27*(1), 69–77. https://doi.org/10.1207/s15374424jccp2701_8.

Weems, C. F., Hayward, C., Killen, J., & Taylor, C. B. (2002). A longitudinal investigation of anxiety sensitivity in adolescence. *Journal of Abnormal Psychology*, *111*(3), 471–477. https://doi.org/10.1037/0021-843x.111.3.471.

Wollburg, E., Roth, W. T., & Kim, S. (2011). Effects of breathing training on voluntary hypo- and hyperventilation in patients with panic disorder and episodic anxiety. *Applied Psychophysiology and Biofeedback*, *36*(2), 81–91.

Wong, Q. J. J., & Moulds, M. L. (2011). The relationship between the maladaptive self-beliefs characteristic of social anxiety and avoidance. *Journal of Behavior Therapy and Experimental Psychiatry*, *42*(2), 171–178.

Further reading

Craske, M. G., & Barlow, D. H. (2006b). *Mastery of your anxiety and panic*. New York: Oxford University Press.

Targeting anxiety sensitivity as a prevention strategy

8

Norman B. Schmidt, Nicholas P. Allan†, Ashley A. Knapp‡, Dan Capron§*
*Florida State University, Tallahassee, FL, United States, †Ohio University, Athens, OH, United States, ‡Dartmouth College, Hanover, NH, United States, §University of Southern Mississippi, Hattiesburg, MS, United States

Chapter Outline

Psychopathology in general and anxiety disorders in particular represent massive public health burdens due to their prevalence (Achenbach, Howell, McConaughy, & Stanger, 1995) and chronicity (Pine, Cohen, Gurley, Brook, & Ma, 1998), which results in substantial impairment across the lifespan (Ferdinand & Verhulst, 1995). A multifaceted approach is needed to effectively address issues that require increased attention to prevention efforts. Indeed, there have been numerous calls to increase efforts to address mental health problems from a preventive perspective (e.g., American Academy of Child and Adolescent Psychiatry, 1990). In a review of prevention for anxiety and related psychopathology, Feldner and Zvolensky (2004)

The Clinician's Guide to Anxiety Sensitivity Treatment and Assessment. https://doi.org/10.1016/B978-0-12-813495-5.00008-5

concluded that most existing prevention efforts fail to investigate the effects of modifying specific risk factors on the incidence of anxiety psychopathology. Instead, prevention programs for anxiety disorders have typically modified existing treatment strategies rather than targeting a specific risk factor or collection of theorized risk factors. Thus, prevention approaches tend to be symptom driven versus being based on theoretical models of psychopathology. These authors argued that there are several key reasons to incorporate risk-factor research into prevention programs but foremost is that prevention programs designed to target specific risk factors could be enormously helpful in providing causal tests of putative risk factors and thereby directly inform our understanding of these conditions (Holden & Black, 1999; Kellam & Rebok, 1992). Work on anxiety sensitivity represents one such opportunity for risk factor focused preventative efforts.

Anxiety sensitivity reflects the belief that anxious arousal is indicative of impending cognitive, physical, or social harm. Anxiety sensitivity has been included in the latest iteration of the diagnostic and statistical manual for mental disorders (American Psychiatric Association, 2013) as a risk factor for panic, but an extensive literature suggests it is associated with a considerably broader array of psychopathology (Olatunji & Wolitzky-Taylor, 2009). In fact, anxiety sensitivity is one of the most well investigated, transdiagnostic risk factor constructs (e.g., Naragon-Gainey, 2010; Olatunji & Wolitzky-Taylor, 2009). The goal of this chapter is to summarize the literature with regard to anxiety sensitivity as a preventative strategy for a broad array of psychopathology including anxiety disorders, trauma disorders such as posttraumatic stress disorder (PTSD), and mood disorders including suicide. As our review will show, anxiety sensitivity has been implicated as a risk factor in each of these domains though some areas are more developed than others, and there is promising work to indicate that targeting anxiety sensitivity is likely to prevent the development of later psychopathology.

Anxiety sensitivity is an exceedingly well-researched construct that includes three meta-analytic reviews. Two of these reviews focus on anxiety sensitivity and anxiety and mood in adults (Naragon-Gainey, 2010; Olatunji & Wolitzky-Taylor, 2009) and one focuses on anxiety sensitivity in children (Noël & Francis, 2011). These reviews include scores of studies involving thousands of participants and essentially showed that anxiety sensitivity is consistently and robustly associated with anxiety, trauma, and mood psychopathology. Thus, we can fairly claim that anxiety sensitivity is indeed a transdiagnostic factor since it is associated with a broad array of psychopathology. However, this is a relatively narrow view of the concept of "risk."

The work of Kraemer and colleagues is useful to consider in the context of our discussion of the risk status of anxiety sensitivity. Kraemer et al. (1997) have proposed a framework that suggests there are different types of risk constructs and this model provides a series of "tests" to ascertain the nature of these risk variables. Criterion one of this framework is that two variables must be correlated. The second criterion of this framework requires that the risk factor (e.g., anxiety sensitivity) precedes an outcome (e.g., anxiety diagnosis). At this point, Kraemer makes a distinction in the conception of risk in terms of fixed versus malleable factors. A fixed risk factor is one that is relatively unchangeable such as demographic factors. On the other hand, malleable risk factors are those that can change and are critical to identify because of this property since it is informative regarding the possibility of preventative intervention. Finally, criterion four of the framework indicates that changes in the factor must yield changes in the outcome. If we can identify a factor (e.g., anxiety sensitivity) that affects outcomes when changed, then the construct is considered a causal risk factor within the Kraemer framework. In the context of the Kraemer framework, there is a rich history implicating anxiety sensitivity as a causal risk factor for anxiety and related disorders, suggesting it is an excellent target for prevention and intervention efforts.

Anxiety sensitivity intervention trials

One important line of work attesting to the viability of anxiety sensitivity as a preventative intervention target grew out of cognitive behavioral interventions for anxiety psychopathology. These studies in patient samples revealed that anxiety sensitivity is malleable via cognitive-behavioral interventions. For example, several investigations focused on panic disorder (PD) treatment have reported significant reductions in anxiety sensitivity following treatment (Barlow, Craske, Cerny, & Klosko, 1989; Westling & Öst, 1999). In a meta-analysis, Smits, Berry, Tart, and Powers (2008) summarized this literature indicating that CBT can substantially reduce anxiety sensitivity. In general, these studies suggest that cognitive behavioral approaches not only reduce anxiety sensitivity, but the changes in anxiety sensitivity are responsible for (i.e., mediate) symptomatic improvement. In conjunction with these findings, it is important to note that anxiety sensitivity can be elevated in preclinical or nonclinical samples (Telch, Lucas, & Nelson, 1989). As such, and consistent with Expectancy Theory (Reiss, 1991), the existence of nonclinical samples with elevated anxiety sensitivity suggests a population of individuals that would likely benefit from anxiety sensitivity mitigation. This work helped to inspire investigations focused on the reduction of anxiety sensitivity as a preventative intervention in nonclinical, at-risk samples

Anxiety sensitivity intervention strategies and effects

Efforts by multiple research teams over the past two decades have resulted in multiple anxiety sensitivity prevention protocols, primarily utilizing cognitive behavioral therapy techniques to target anxiety sensitivity. In review of the literature on anxiety sensitivity interventions, these interventions can be divided into categories based on their defining characteristics (see Table 1). Defining characteristics include psychoeducation, interoceptive exposure (IE), and cognitive bias modification (CBM). Psychoeducation involves providing corrective information about anxious sensations. IE involves inducing anxiety-related sensations, typically via IE challenge exercises used to treat PD (i.e., hyperventilation, straw breathing) to demonstrate that these sensations are not harmful. Exercise-based interventions are a special form of IE interventions, focusing primarily on the use of aerobic exercise as a natural intervention for anxious sensations. Finally, CBM approaches involve bottom-up targeting of

Table 1 Anxiety sensitivity mitigation interventions

Year Authors	Sample Studied	Randomized conditions	Anxiety sensitivity outcome findings	Risk outcome findings
Psychoeducation				
2017 Norr et al.	*Elevated anxiety sensitivity* 54 Undergraduates selected on the basis of ≥7 on ASI-3 cognitive score	Randomized to 35 min of computer-provided intervention: (1) psychoeducation, with a particular focus on dispelling myths about high anxiety, or (2) physical health education training control	Individuals in the active condition demonstrated significantly greater anxiety sensitivity reductions than the control condition as assessed immediately postintervention, with effects generally in the large range: total ($d=0.81$), cognitive ($d=0.79$), physical ($d=0.57$), and social subscale scores ($d=0.56$)	N/A
Exercise-based				
2004 Broman-Fulks et al.	*Elevated anxiety sensitivity* 54 Physically healthy participants scoring ≥25 on the ASI	Randomized to six 20-min sessions of: (1) high-intensity aerobic exercise, or (2) low-intensity aerobic exercise	Both groups improved, but group by time interaction showed faster reductions in the high intensity group. Also, 52% in the high-intensity group achieved at least a 1 standard deviation decrease in anxiety sensitivity scores, compared to 20% in the low-intensity group	N/A
2008 Broman-Fulks and Storey	*Elevated anxiety sensitivity* Nonclinical participants with elevated anxiety sensitivity scores (>26 on ASI-R)	Randomized to six 20-min sessions of: (1) aerobic exercise, or (2) a no-exercise control condition	Significantly lower anxiety sensitivity in the aerobic exercise condition relative to those nonexercise condition	N/A

Table 1 Anxiety sensitivity mitigation interventions—cont'd

Year Authors	Sample Studied	Randomized conditions	Anxiety sensitivity outcome findings	Risk outcome findings
2008 Smits et al.	*Elevated anxiety sensitivity* 60 Nonclinical participants with elevated anxiety sensitivity scores (ASI ≥25)	Randomized to one of three 2-week protocols: (1) six 20-min sessions of aerobic exercise, (2) identical aerobic exercise plus cognitive restructuring, or (3) or a waitlist control condition	The two exercise conditions had greater anxiety sensitivity reductions than the control condition, reflecting a very large effect size ($d=2.15$). the addition of cognitive restructuring to aerobic exercise did not significantly improve outcomes	Lower rates of mood/anxiety symptoms postintervention in the exercise conditions, compared to the control condition. These effects were mediated by anxiety sensitivity reductions
2015 Broman-Fulks et al.	*Unselected* 77 Physically healthy participants	Random assignment to a single, 20-min session of: (1) aerobic exercise, (2) resistance training, (3) rest control condition	The two exercise conditions demonstrated greater decreases in anxiety sensitivity than the rest condition	N/A
2015 LeBouthillier and Asmundson	41 Healthy adults	Single session of aerobic exercise versus stretching control	At the 7 days postintervention, effect sizes indicated advantages for the aerobic exercise condition over the control condition for ASI-3 Physical ($d=0.44$), Cognitive ($d=0.64$), total ($d=0.70$), and Social scores ($d=0.72$)	N/A
Psychoeducation + interoceptive exposure (IE) ± additional elements				
2001 Maltby partially reported in	*Elevated anxiety sensitivity* 62 Participants selected on the basis of a high-anxiety sensitivity score (ASI >23)	Participants were randomized to one of three conditions, each a single session of 45 min: (1) an	No significant differences in anxiety sensitivity between groups, but effect sizes were in the expected	At 1-year follow-up, a total of 23% of no-treatment participants, 5% of education participants, and

Continued

Table 1 Anxiety sensitivity mitigation interventions—cont'd

Year Authors	Sample Studied	Randomized conditions	Anxiety sensitivity outcome findings	Risk outcome findings
Maltby, Mayers, Allen, and Tolin (2005)		anxiety sensitivity reduction intervention, (2) an education-only intervention, and (3) a no-treatment control condition	direction: interoceptive exposure plus psychoeducation: $d=1.36$; Psychoeduction: $d=1.12$; no treatment: $d=0.90$	10% of anxiety sensitivity reduction participants met criteria for panic disorder 67% of no-treatment participants, 55% of education participants, and 52% of anxiety sensitivity reduction participants reported at least one panic attack in the past year
2001 Gardenswartz and Craske	*Elevated anxiety sensitivity* 120 College students at risk for developing panic disorder defined by having had a panic attack within 12 months and at least moderate levels of anxiety sensitivity (ASI scores of 16 or higher)	Participants were randomly assigned to either: (1) a 5-h group workshop consisting psychoeducation about the nature of PD, breathing retraining, cognitive restructuring, interoceptive exposure, instruction to expose in vivo to agoraphobic-type situations, and the assignment of homework, or (2) waitlist control group	Both groups showed similar anxiety sensitivity reductions	Those in the treated group were less likely to develop panic disorder during a 6-month follow-up
2007 Schmidt et al.	*Elevated anxiety sensitivity* 404 Participants scoring 1.5 *SD* above the nonclinical mean (sample mean of 17.0)	Randomization to a single session of: (1) anxiety sensitivity amelioration training (ASAT), or (2) a control condition that	Both conditions produced a reduction in anxiety sensitivity; however, the ASAT condition produced a significantly larger	A lower incidence of axis I disorders during the follow-up period (12–24 months later)

Table 1 Anxiety sensitivity mitigation interventions—cont'd

Year Authors	Sample Studied	Randomized conditions	Anxiety sensitivity outcome findings	Risk outcome findings
		provided general information on health and nutrition. ASAT consisted of a 30-min computer presentation on the nature of stress, anxiety sensitivity, myths about the harmfulness of physiological arousal, and repeated (hyperventilation) interceptive exposure; plus 10 min with an experimenter to answer questions	reduction in anxiety sensitivity than did the control condition (30% versus 17%, respectively) Anxiety sensitivity reduction was primarily due to a reduction in the physical subfactor, the social subfactor showed a small but significant reduction, and no reduction was evident for the cognitive subfactor	
2008 Feldner et al.	Smokers + elevated anxiety sensitivity 90 Individuals with high anxiety sensitivity and who smoked	Randomized to a 2-h session focused on (1) both increasing motivation to quit smoking and reducing anxiety sensitivity or (2) a health information control condition	At 6 month follow-up, those in the treatment condition showed reduced anxiety sensitivity	
2012 Keough and Schmidt	*Elevated anxiety sensitivity* 104 Undergraduates scoring 1.5 SD above the ASI mean (sample mean of 29.6)	Randomized to a single session of: (1) anxiety sensitivity education and reduction training (ASERT) or (2) health-focused control intervention. ASERT consisted of the	Significantly greater reductions in total and subscale ASI-3 scores in the ASERT relative to the control condition. The ASERT group showed close to 60% reduction at	Allan, Albanese, Short, Raines, and Schmidt (2015), Allan, Norr, Boffa, et al. (2015), Allan, Norr, Capron, et al. (2015), and Allan, Short, Albanese, Keough, and Schmidt

Continued

Table 1 Anxiety sensitivity mitigation interventions—cont'd

Year Authors	Sample Studied	Randomized conditions	Anxiety sensitivity outcome findings	Risk outcome findings
		ASAT components augmented by discussions with a therapist, additional IE targeting top fears, and guided home practice	1-month follow-up, with maintenance of the majority of gains at a 6-month follow-up	(2015) evaluated a subsample of participants experiencing a traumatic event and found ASERT reduced later PTSD symptoms through reductions in anxiety sensitivity. Norr, Allan, Macatee, Keough, and Schmidt (2014) evaluated the indirect effects of ASERT on worry, anxiety, and depression, through anxiety sensitivity and distress tolerance. The mediating effect was through reductions in anxiety sensitivity and not distress tolerance
2014 Schmidt et al.	*Elevated anxiety sensitivity* 108 Adults from the general community, scoring at or above the community sample mean on the ASI-3 (sample mean of 31.5)	Randomized to web applications: (1) 50–60 min cognitive anxiety sensitivity treatment (CAST) intervention, (2) or a health education control condition. CAST included psychoeducation, IE, and fears of losing control of	Anxiety sensitivity was substantially reduced at posttreatment and the group differences were maintained at one-month follow-up. The overall effects on total anxiety sensitivity were in the medium-to-large effect size range. Consistent with	Mitchell, Capron, Raines, and Schmidt (2014) evaluated a subsample of Veterans with PTSD and found that CAST reduced later PTSD symptoms

Table 1 Anxiety sensitivity mitigation interventions—cont'd

Year Authors	Sample Studied	Randomized conditions	Anxiety sensitivity outcome findings	Risk outcome findings
		emotions/thought processes as core components	expectation, the intervention resulted in significant reductions in anxiety sensitivity cognitive concerns, and there were also significant reductions in physical and social concerns	
2016 Schmidt et al.	Smokers + elevated anxiety sensitivity 526 Daily smokers (ASI-3 sample mean of 14.6)	Randomized to four 90-min sessions of: (1) 45 min focused on smoking cessation and 45 min of psychoeducation and IE [panic-smoking program (PSP)], or (2) standard smoking cessation protocol (SP)	Significantly greater reductions in total ASI-3 scores in PSP relative to SP during treatment. Although treatment effects were small, the PSP group maintained these gains through 1-year follow-up	Mediation analyses indicated that change in anxiety sensitivity during the intervention mediated the effects of the intervention on change in panic symptoms during the 1-year follow-up
Cognitive bias modification (CBM)				
2016 Capron and Schmidt	*Elevated anxiety sensitivity* 89 Undergraduate participants with elevated anxiety sensitivity (1.5SD above population mean; >10.7 on ASI-3)	Randomized to single-session benign interpretation bias training or a control condition	Significant lower ASI-3 scores for the active treatment at week 1 and month 1 follow-up	N/A
2015 Clerkin et al.	*Elevated anxiety sensitivity* 65 Participants selected on the basis of elevated anxiety sensitivity (>26.45 on the ASI)	Randomized to benign interpretation bias training or a control condition	Anxiety sensitivity scores decreased in both groups, with no time by group interaction	N/A

Continued

Table 1 Anxiety sensitivity mitigation interventions—cont'd

Year Authors	Sample Studied	Randomized conditions	Anxiety sensitivity outcome findings	Risk outcome findings
	and self report of a panic attack or limited symptom attack			
2013 MacDonald et al.	*Elevated anxiety sensitivity* 34 Community participants with elevated anxiety sensitivity	Randomized to benign interpretation bias training or a control condition	Only the active training condition showed reductions in anxiety sensitivity	
2010 Steinman and Teachman	*Elevated anxiety sensitivity* 75 Undergraduate selected based on 1SD > mean on ASI	Randomized to 1 of 3 cognitive bias modification (CBM) conditions: positive training (active), neutral training (control), and no training (control)	Positive training led to lower anxiety sensitivity (evaluated by posttraining ASI residual scores) than the two control conditions	
Psychoeducation + IE + CBM				
2017 Schmidt et al.	*Elevated anxiety sensitivity, Suicidal Ideation, Anxiety Pathology* 74 Community participants with (1) ASI-3 cognitive score 1 SD > mean, (2) current suicidal ideation, and (3) primary anxiety disorder or mood disorder with anxious distress specifier	Randomized to: (1) CAST + cognitive bias modification or (2) a health education control condition + sham cognitive bias modification	1-h intervention as well as at 1- and 4-month follow-ups. The anxiety sensitivity cognitive concerns subscale was reduced almost 50% in the active treatment condition compared to only about 10% in the control condition	Treatment-related change in anxiety sensitivity mediated change in later anxiety, depression, and suicidal ideation
2018 Schmidt et al. (unpublished manuscript)	*Elevated anxiety sensitivity, thwarted belongingness, or perceived burdensomeness* 304 Participants with levels of anxiety sensitivity	Randomized to: (1) Depression and Anxiety Risk Treatment for Suicide (DARTS) or to (2) a repeated contact control	Results indicated an immediate effect of condition on anxiety sensitivity postintervention at Session 1 with a 38.2%	Treatment-related change in anxiety sensitivity mediated change in suicidal ideation

Table 1 Anxiety sensitivity mitigation interventions—cont'd

Year Authors	Sample Studied	Randomized conditions	Anxiety sensitivity outcome findings	Risk outcome findings
	cognitive concerns, thwarted belongingness, or perceived burdensomeness at or above the community mean	condition. relative to CARS (above) DARTS provides the CAST intervention during session one and then provides two additional sessions of CBM	reduction in anxiety sensitivity for participants in the active conditions. This effect was maintained throughout the intervention period until Session 3 with a 43.1% reduction in anxiety sensitivity observed in the active anxiety sensitivity conditions. These effects held at month 1, month 3, and month 6	

maladaptive cognitive beliefs. In the following, we discuss interventions that involve one or more of these components in preventative interventions targeting anxiety sensitivity.

Psychoeducation and IE studies

Most recent studies target anxiety sensitivity through psychoeducation and IE elements, two components central to typical CBT-based anxiety treatments. The goal of these studies revolves around normalizing anxiety-related sensations by "teaching" intervention recipients that anxiety is normal, and in the vast majority of cases, not harmful. This is followed up by "showing" intervention recipients that explicitly eliciting these feared sensations does not lead to a catastrophic outcome. One early "proof of concept" study (Harrington, Telch, Abplanalp, Hamilton, & Austin, 1995) focused on reducing anxiety sensitivity rather than the effects of the intervention on psychopathology. Harrington et al. (1995) delivered a brief (three session) CBT-style intervention that included psychoeducation, IE, and diaphragmatic breathing. There was some evidence that the treatment significantly reduced anxiety sensitivity relative to a control group. Two later studies provide some evidence that reduction in anxiety sensitivity decreases risk for anxiety pathology, particularly PD and panic attacks. Maltby (2001, partially reported in Maltby et al., 2005) randomly assigned approximately 62 high anxiety sensitivity individuals [defined by an ASI (Reiss, Peterson, Gursky, & McNally, 1986) score >23] to one of three experimental conditions: an anxiety sensitivity reduction intervention, an education-only intervention, and a no-treatment control condition. Each intervention was conducted in a single session of approximately 45 min. Follow-up assessments were conducted up to 12 months posttreatment. Reductions in anxiety sensitivity were comparable across groups including the control group, but outcome findings were in the expected direction (though they failed to reach statistically significance due to low statistical power). At 1-year follow-up, a total of 23% of no-treatment participants, 5% of education participants, and 10% of anxiety sensitivity reduction participants met criteria for PD. In addition, 67% of no-treatment participants, 55% of education participants, and 52% of anxiety sensitivity reduction participants reported at least one panic attack in the past year. In another protocol that did not directly target anxiety sensitivity, Gardenswartz and Craske (2001) studied about 120 college students at risk for developing PD as indexed by having had a panic attack within 12 months and at least moderate levels of anxiety sensitivity (ASI scores ≥16). Participants were randomly assigned to either a waitlist control or a workshop group. The workshop consisted of one didactic 5-h group. Workshop components included psychoeducation about the nature of PD, breathing retraining, cognitive restructuring, IE, instruction to expose in vivo to agoraphobic-type situations, and the assignment of homework. Findings suggested that both groups showed similar anxiety sensitivity reductions, but those in the treated group were less likely to develop PD during a 6-month follow-up. In an integrated clinical trial focused on reducing anxiety sensitivity among smokers, Feldner, Zvolensky, Babson, Leen-Feldner, and Schmidt (2008) evaluated the feasibility and short-term efficacy of a panic prevention program that targeted two malleable risk factors for panic development: anxiety sensitivity and daily cigarette smoking. They recruited individuals with both high levels of anxiety sensitivity and current daily smoking ($n = 96$). Participants were randomly assigned to either a 2-h session focused on (1) both increasing motivation to quit smoking and reducing anxiety sensitivity or (2) a health information control condition of comparable length. Participants were followed for 6 months. Consistent with hypotheses, those in the treatment condition showed reduced anxiety sensitivity and this effect was maintained across the follow-up period.

Anxiety sensitivity amelioration training

Our group has also been very interested in anxiety sensitivity prevention and we have completed a number of clinical trials primarily utilizing psychoeducation and IE that we will summarize in this section. Our first study (Schmidt, Eggleston, et al., 2007; Schmidt, Maner, & Zvolensky, 2007) recruited an at-risk sample such that participants ($N = 404$) had to show elevated anxiety sensitivity defined by scores 1.5 SD above the nonclinical mean (sample mean = 17.0). Moreover, participants could not meet for an anxiety diagnosis. In this study, participants were randomly assigned to either the Anxiety Sensitivity Amelioration Training (ASAT) condition or a control condition that provided general information on health and nutrition. The ASAT condition consisted of a 30-min computer PowerPoint presentation followed by 10 min with an experimenter to answer questions. The presentation explored the following concepts: the nature of stress, anxiety sensitivity, myths about the harmfulness of physiological arousal, and IE. The IE component involved repeated hyperventilation trials to demonstrate that internal perturbations could result in the generation of fear and that repeated IE could reduce these fears. Results indicated that both conditions produced a reduction in anxiety sensitivity; however, the ASAT condition produced a significantly larger reduction in anxiety sensitivity than did the control condition (30% vs. 17%, respectively). The reduction in anxiety sensitivity was primarily due to a reduction in the physical anxiety sensitivity subfactor. The social subfactor showed a small but significant reduction, whereas the cognitive subfactor did not. This trial also included a lengthy 24-month follow-up period to evaluate the incidence of new diagnoses. In terms of the development of psychopathology, those in the ASAT condition showed a lower incidence of Axis I diagnoses (First, Spitzer, Gibbon, & Williams, 1994) during the follow-up period.

Anxiety sensitivity education and reduction training

The follow-up clinical trial represented an augmented version of ASAT that was developed in an attempt to increase its potency (Keough & Schmidt, 2012). The new protocol—termed anxiety sensitivity education and reduction training (ASERT)—included the same psychoeducational component delivered via Powerpoint and was bolstered in a number of ways. First, a trained therapist sat with participants during the presentation to help explain the material. Second, ASERT included more intensive

IE exercises by having participants complete a battery of IE and then the most fear-provoking IE was chosen for repeated exposure. Finally, ASERT had a more rigorous home-based component where participants were given more guidance and coaching as well as reminders to complete IE. As predicted, this more intensive intervention yielded a higher level of anxiety sensitivity reduction relative to ASAT, such that the active ASERT group showed close to 60% reduction at 1-month follow-up, and unlike ASAT, ASERT produced significant reductions in all three anxiety sensitivity components. A 6-month follow-up assessment indicated that the treatment group retained the majority of their anxiety sensitivity reduction. Despite the high level of anxiety sensitivity reduction, this study utilized a small sample of approximately 100 participants and limited follow-up and so was unable to assess whether change in anxiety sensitivity was associated with incidence of psychopathology post intervention

Panic/smoking prevention

The next clinical trial represented an expansion of the earlier Feldner et al. (2008) study and involved the application of an anxiety sensitivity intervention to smokers as a means of preventing panic attacks (Schmidt, Raines, Allan, & Zvolensky, 2016). From an intervention standpoint, empirical and theoretical work on smoking and panic problems suggests it may be fruitful to simultaneously and concurrently target these risk factors (i.e., anxiety sensitivity and smoking) in one overarching model to reduce panic problems while also stimulating cessation-oriented behavior (e.g., enhance motivation to quit). Because panic factors and smoking interact in clinically meaningful ways, addressing one of these factors without addressing the other in this same context may not result in optimal efficacy regarding intervention goals. For example, simply targeting the cognitive-based fear of anxiety (anxiety sensitivity) without a recognition of smoking among those who often manage affect by smoking neglects clinically relevant self-regulation processes (e.g., escape and avoidant coping for emotionally salient events). Alternatively, because anxiety sensitivity is related to poorer success in quitting smoking (Brown, Kahler, Zvolensky, Lejuez, & Ramsey, 2001), a failure to target this cognitive-based affective vulnerability may yield lower rates of success in cessation. Thus, smoking should theoretically be directly targeted within the context of clinical intervention for preventing panic attacks and PD.

The risk reduction program, implemented across two sites, targeted two well-established risk factors for the development of panic: smoking and anxiety sensitivity (Schmidt et al., 2016). All participants received a state-of-the-art smoking cessation intervention with approximately half randomized to the anxiety sensitivity reduction intervention termed Panic Smoking Program (PSP). The PSP protocol integrated the elements of a standardized smoking intervention including nicotine replacement therapy along with the key elements of cognitive-behavioral treatment of anxiety sensitivity and panic. The combined intervention was delivered over four 90-min sessions. Each 90-min session included 45 min focused on smoking cessation and 45 min of cognitive-behavioral treatment strategies for anxiety sensitivity and panic; however, these components were integrated in a manner that discusses the cyclical types of processes related to both factors (Zvolensky & Bernstein, 2005). Similar to ASAT and

ASERT, psychoeducation about the nature of stress and normalization of stress symptoms were key components to the protocol, which could be delivered in more detail due to the length of the intervention. In addition, participants were assessed on a variety of interoceptive exercises including hyperventilation and straw breathing. Participants were also asked to practice relevant interoceptive exercises outside of session. Over 500 smokers participated in the clinical trial, though there was substantial attrition during the 1 year follow-up period. Consistent with ASAT and ASERT, we also were able to significantly reduce anxiety sensitivity among smokers. Importantly, mediation analyses suggested that change in anxiety sensitivity during the intervention mediated the effects of the intervention on change in panic symptoms during the one-year follow-up.

Unlike ASAT and ASERT as well as other protocols designed to reduce anxiety sensitivity in which effect sizes were found to be medium to large (Broman-Fulks & Storey, 2008; Feldner et al., 2008; Keough & Schmidt, 2012; Schmidt, Eggleston, et al., 2007; Schmidt, Maner, et al., 2007), effect sizes for anxiety sensitivity reduction within the smoking panic prevention investigation were in the small range (Schmidt et al., 2016). These differences could be explained by a host of study specific factors, including relatively lower baseline levels of anxiety sensitivity among the smokers in this study. It is also possible that differences in the nature of the population across the various anxiety sensitivity trials contributed to these disparate findings such that smokers represent a more anxiety sensitivity-refractory group. Alternatively, it is also possible that the control condition may have acted somewhat as an active anxiety sensitivity intervention since all smokers were encouraged to practice fading nicotine consumption, which should have resulted in frequent exposure to nicotine withdrawal symptoms. This repeated smoking discontinuation could have subsequently lowered sensitivity to such sensations thereby attenuating overall effect sizes between conditions. In any case, this sample is interesting in that in stands in contrast with all of the other trials we will discuss in that we were only able to achieve a small effect size impact on anxiety sensitivity.

Cognitive anxiety sensitivity treatment

Although ASAT, ASERT, and PSP trials were primarily focused on anxiety and panic outcomes, some of our more recent work, including an ongoing clinical trial, has shifted the focus of our preventative efforts away from anxiety to another pressing public health problem: suicide. Although suicide is commonly associated with mood psychopathology, emerging evidence links suicide with anxiety. For example, PTSD is consistently linked with suicidal ideation and suicide attempt (Cougle, Keough, Riccardi, & Sachs-Ericsson, 2009; Sareen et al., 2007). Nock, Hwang, Sampson, and Kessler (2010) found that although many disorders predict suicidal ideation, PTSD was among very few conditions that predict which suicide ideators go on to make a suicide plan or attempt. Although major depressive disorder is often comorbid with PTSD and is also a predictor of suicidal behavior, PTSD but not depression was found to be uniquely associated with suicide attempts in a large female sample, after controlling for comorbidity and trauma history (Cougle, Resnick, & Kilpatrick, 2009).

We have argued that anxiety sensitivity may partially explain the associations between PTSD, a condition showing some of the highest levels of anxiety sensitivity (Taylor, Koch, & McNally, 1992) and suicidality (Schmidt, Zvolensky, & Maner, 2006). As we noted, anxiety sensitivity is composed of three subscales related to fears of the physical, social, and cognitive features of anxiety. The cognitive facet taps into concerns about losing control of emotion or thought processes (e.g., "It is important for me to stay in control of my emotions" and "When I am nervous, I worry that I might be mentally ill"). Emerging evidence suggests that elevation in the anxiety sensitivity cognitive dimension is relevant to suicide as it has been significantly related to suicidal ideation in patients with anxiety disorders (Schmidt, Woolaway-Bickel, & Bates, 2001) and negative mental health outcomes in a large sample of Air Force cadets (Schmidt, Lerew, & Jackson, 1999). More specifically, Schmidt et al. (2001) found associations between greater anxiety sensitivity and suicidal ideation in a sample of patients with PD, even after covarying mood disorder diagnosis and depression symptoms. Further, much of this association was attributable to the anxiety sensitivity cognitive concerns subscale. Consistent with this, we found that elevated anxiety sensitivity cognitive concerns were related to suicide attempts in an outpatient sample with PTSD symptomatology ($N = 128$). Moreover, high anxiety sensitivity cognitive concerns scores were prospectively associated with increased suicidal ideation for cadets undergoing basic training (Capron, Cougle, Ribeiro, Joiner, & Schmidt, 2012). Taken together, these findings suggest that suicide potential may be related to cognitive risk factors for anxiety, particularly among individuals with PTSD symptomatology.

The specific relationship between anxiety sensitivity and suicide can be illuminated by considering the role anxiety sensitivity plays in response to stress. The well-established anxiety sensitivity literature highlights the idea that anxiety sensitivity increases distress responses in the context of general stress and anxiety symptoms. An expansion of this idea would include the possibility that anxiety sensitivity predisposes some to show increased distress in the context of aversive physical and cognitive mood symptoms. Thus, we proposed a depression-distress amplification model of anxiety sensitivity (Capron, Norr, Macatee, & Schmidt, 2013) that provides a more specific mechanism for the development of suicide. In the depression-distress amplification model, suicidal ideation is considered a symptom of depression corresponding to the severity of the depression. Just as anxiety sensitivity increases distress responses in the context of uncomfortable physical sensations (Schmidt, Maner, et al., 2007), the depression-distress amplification model posits that anxiety sensitivity cognitive concerns amplify distress brought on by the uncomfortable sensations experienced in the context of emerging or existing dysphoria (e.g., lack of concentration, insomnia, anhedonia). Suicide risk increases as the distress caused by the amplified depression reaches more severe levels.

Given the association between anxiety sensitivity cognitive concerns and suicide, as well as the fact that the original ASAT/ASERT protocols focused primarily on anxiety sensitivity physical concerns, we were interested in adapting those protocols to focus more on exaggerated fears related to cognitive dyscontrol. Thus, we developed the Cognitive Anxiety Sensitivity Treatment (CAST) intervention. The protocol was designed along the same lines as ASAT and ASERT and retained much of the content, but the psychoeducation was expanded to include additional "myths" related to cognitive dyscontrol such as fears of racing thoughts, concentration difficulty, and the like as signaling imminent danger. It is also notable that the intervention was redesigned as a web application using more sophisticated software to allow for the use of audio and video presentations, as well as certain interactive features. The CAST intervention consists of 50 screens containing information. Audio narration runs throughout. There are four "quizzes" interspersed throughout the program in order to increase comprehension of important material. A quiz consists of one item (e.g., "Everyone has stress sensitivity") along with the option to respond true or false. Incorrect responses result in corrective information, and correct responses are reinforced (e.g., "That's right! You are correct"). In addition, participants are guided through 10 hyperventilation exercises using a videotape to help time inhalations. Following each trial, physical sensations and anxiety ratings were made and later graphed out for participants to show (hopefully) habituation. The protocol also included examples of four other IE exercises that participants review. Participants are encouraged to practice these exercises on their own in order to further address their stress sensitivity. The duration of CAST is approximately 50–60 min. In order to test the CAST protocol, we also developed a health education control condition that mimicked the earlier version delivered in ASAT. Similar to CAST, the health education condition was produced as a Web application and the content was expanded. The program covers the following topics: diet, alcohol, water consumption, exercise, sexual health, good hygiene, stress management, life organization, social support, positive outlook, and sleep.

Participants ($N = 108$) were recruited from the general community. The primary inclusionary criterion was some evidence of anxiety sensitivity indicated by scoring at or above the community sample mean on the Anxiety Sensitivity Index-3 (ASI-3; sample mean = 31.5; Taylor et al., 2007). Note that suicidal symptoms were not required for inclusion in this trial even though suicide was the primary outcome of interest. In terms of exclusionary criteria, similar to prior work (Schmidt & Joiner, 2002), participants were excluded if they demonstrated evidence of a significant medical illness that would prevent the completion of IE exercises. Participants were randomized to CAST or the control condition and assessed at posttreatment and a relatively brief (1 month) follow-up. Consistent with most of the prior trials, anxiety sensitivity was substantially reduced at posttreatment and the group differences were maintained at follow-up. The overall effects on total anxiety sensitivity were in the medium-to-large effect size range. Consistent with expectation, the intervention resulted in significant reductions in anxiety sensitivity cognitive concerns. However, there were also significant reductions in physical and social concerns.

Psychoeducation only

As discussed previously, Maltby (2001, reported in Maltby et al., 2005) compared an education-only intervention to an anxiety sensitivity reduction intervention and a no-treatment control group. They found reductions were comparable across all three conditions. Further, the lowest rates of PD at follow-up were for those in the education condition (5% vs. 10% for anxiety sensitivity reduction intervention and 23% in the no-treatment condition). In an effort to dismantle our protocol that focuses on both psychoeducation about the nature of anxiety sensitivity as well as IE, we have completed a small clinical trial in which participants received only the psychoeducational materials (i.e., no repeated hyperventilation). Norr, Gibby, and Schmidt (2017) recently reported on a randomized clinical trial where they delivered the educational portion of CAST versus health education control to a sample of high anxiety sensitivity individuals ($N=54$). Findings indicated that individuals receiving CAST displayed greater reductions in self-reported anxiety sensitivity with a medium-to-large effect size as well as less fear reactivity to the induction of anxiety sensitivity cognitive-relevant sensations through a behavioral challenge compared to those in the control condition. Further, fear reactivity to the challenge was mediated by reductions in self-reported anxiety sensitivity cognitive concerns. Although this study is limited by the sample size and a limited follow-up period, it does provide evidence that psychoeducation alone may be sufficient to substantially reduce anxiety sensitivity for some individuals. This is notable because IE is inherently aversive. Although we do find high levels of acceptability and tolerance of the full protocol (Short, Fuller, Norr, & Schmidt, 2017), utilizing an even briefer, and less aversive protocol would obviously be more ideal.

Exercise-based

Several studies utilize a specific form of IE, aerobic exercise, in treating anxiety sensitivity (Broman-Fulks & Storey, 2008; Smits et al., 2008). Broman-Fulks and Storey (2008) were the first to consider aerobic exercise as an intervention for anxiety sensitivity. Their rationale for this method of intervention is that aerobic exercise involves exposure to physiological cues similar to those experienced during anxiety reactions. Nonclinical participants with elevated anxiety sensitivity scores were randomly assigned to complete either six 20-min sessions of aerobic exercise or a no-exercise control condition. The results indicated that individuals assigned to the aerobic exercise condition reported significantly less anxiety sensitivity after exercising, relative to those in the nonexercise group.

Smits et al. (2008) compared a 2-week exercise protocol, a 2-week exercise protocol plus cognitive restructuring, and a waitlist control condition on reductions in anxiety sensitivity and anxious and depressed mood. A total of 60 nonclinical participants with elevated anxiety sensitivity (≥ 25 on the ASI; 50 were undergraduates participating for research credit and 10 were recruited from the community) were randomized to one of these three conditions. The exercise conditions comprised six 20-min exercise sessions completed over a two-week period as well as an initial 15-min videotaped rationale for the intervention. In addition, participants in the exercise + cognitive restructuring condition also were provided information regarding the importance of cognitive restructuring to enhance treatment effects and were asked to chart cognitive distortions regarding bodily sensations during the exercise protocol and reframed these cognitive distortions following the 20-min exercise. Although all three conditions showed declines in anxiety sensitivity, these declines were greater in the exercise conditions. Inclusion of cognitive restructuring did not improve on effects found in the exercise condition only. Further, examination of mood and anxiety symptoms postintervention revealed significant reductions favoring both exercise conditions, compared to the waitlist control condition.

Several recent studies have confirmed the efficacy of aerobic exercise interventions to reduce anxiety sensitivity and have also continued to explore the exact mechanism through which these effects occur. Broman-Fulks, Kelso, and Zawilinski (2015) compared a single session of aerobic exercise to a single resistance training condition, arguing that because resistance training exhibits anxiolytic properties (see O'Connor, Herring, & Caravalho, 2010) similar reductions in anxiety sensitivity should be found. Across a sample of 77 physically healthy young adults, similar anxiety sensitivity reductions were found in the aerobic exercise and resistance training conditions, although only those in the aerobic exercise condition demonstrated attenuated reactivity to a CO_2 challenge task. Further, effects of this intervention were specific to anxiety sensitivity, as there were no reductions in alternate risk factors (i.e., distress tolerance, discomfort intolerance, and state anxiety). LeBouthillier and Asmundson (2015) also found that reductions in anxiety sensitivity could be found in a single aerobic exercise session, compared to a placebo condition, in a sample of 41 healthy young adults. They also found no effects on intolerance of uncertainty, another cognitive risk factor for anxiety (Carleton, 2016).

CBM-based

A constellation of procedures known as CBM (MacLeod & Mathews, 2012) have also shown promise in the treatment of anxiety psychopathology by directly manipulating cognitive biases, including anxiety sensitivity, via computer-based protocols. Unlike CBT, CBM is designed to directly alter underlying cognitive processes that give rise to anxiogenic thinking (MacLeod & Mathews, 2012). Whereas studies demonstrate conflicting results about the efficacy of CBM (e.g., Cristea, Kok, & Cuijpers, 2015), those procedures designed to affect interpretation biases appear to be promising for anxiety (Beard, 2011; Hallion & Ruscio, 2011; MacLeod & Mathews, 2012). Interpretation bias in those with anxiety refers to selective information processing favoring negative/threatening interpretations of ambiguous information. CBM for interpretation bias (CBM-I; Beard & Amir, 2008) involves presenting individuals with ambiguous scenarios in order to train interpretative tendencies. Negative biases, or the tendency to make threatening interpretations, are then typically modified by reinforcing nonthreatening over threatening interpretations.

Several published studies have suggested that CBM-I can be effective for reducing anxiety sensitivity. In the first CBM-I study for anxiety sensitivity, Steinman and Teachman (2010) found a significant effect of positive CBM-I training on posttask anxiety sensitivity in undergraduates. Next, MacDonald, Koerner, and Antony (2013) found anxiety sensitivity could be reduced in a sample of community participants. More recently, Clerkin, Beard, Fisher, and Schofield (2015) found decreases on the Anxiety Sensitivity Index (ASI; Reiss et al., 1986) over two CBM-I sessions; though the group differences were only trending likely due to limited power. Finally, Capron and Schmidt (2016) tested a CBM-I protocol designed to address some of the methodological limitations of Clerkin et al. (2015). These limitations include a limited follow-up period and a lack of potency with regard to effects on symptom induction exercises. This study included the use of a larger sample, longer follow-up, increasing the number of CBM trials, as well as reinforcing "correct" responses (i.e., providing "correct" feedback) and punishing "incorrect" responses (i.e., providing "incorrect" feedback combined with an 85-db airhorn). Findings suggested that CBM-I produced substantial reductions in anxiety sensitivity among undergraduate participants that persisted through follow-up. In fact, the level of reduction (64% at follow-up) was larger than the ASERT intervention (Keough & Schmidt, 2012) that heretofore had yielded the greatest reductions in anxiety sensitivity (58% at follow-up). Results also revealed that individuals in the active condition reported significantly lower rates of panic responding to a straw-breathing challenge and change in IB significantly mediated the relationship between treatment condition and post-treatment anxiety sensitivity reductions.

Combined (psychoeducation + IE + CBM)

Despite promise of CBM approaches to psychopathology, there have been relatively few attempts to combine so-called bottom up (targeting unconscious, unintentional processing) CBM approaches with more "top down" (targeting conscious and intentional processing) CBT approaches, such as those that utilized in most existing anxiety sensitivity reduction protocols. Moreover, we are not aware of any published work that has combined CBM and CBT approaches for anxiety sensitivity. Therefore, we decided to extend work in this area is to determine the compatibility and potential synergy in the utilization of these brief, automated interventions.

Cognitive anxiety sensitivity treatment for suicide

Similar to our other protocols, the Cognitive Anxiety Sensitivity Treatment for Suicide (CATS) study was designed to advance knowledge regarding the mitigation of anxiety sensitivity using brief, one session computer delivered interventions, but in this case, we focused on a fairly severe clinical sample of 74 patients with cooccurring anxiety psychopathology and active suicidal ideation (Schmidt et al., 2016). Although not a prevention trial per se, this study provides preliminary evidence in support of the efficacy of these combined protocols when used in the context of prevention. The primary study hypothesis was that the combination of CAST plus CBM-I for anxiety sensitivity, compared with a health information control plus sham CBM-I condition, would yield greater reductions in overall anxiety sensitivity, as well as the anxiety sensitivity cognitive concerns subdimension. Consistent with the CAST trial (Schmidt, Capron, Raines, & Allan, 2014), we hypothesized that changes in anxiety sensitivity would result in indirect changes in symptoms, particularly suicidal ideation, during the follow-up interval. Participants ($N=74$) were randomized to the two treatment conditions and assessed immediately after the 1-h intervention as well as at 1- and 4-month follow-ups. Consistent with hypotheses as well as prior trials, participants in the active treatment showed significantly greater anxiety sensitivity reductions that were maintained through follow-up (effect sizes ranged from medium to large for the overall anxiety sensitivity and the anxiety sensitivity subscales). For example, the anxiety sensitivity cognitive concerns subscale was reduced almost 50% in the active treatment condition compared to only about 10% in the control condition. Importantly, mediation analyses suggested that changes in anxiety sensitivity-mediated change in suicidal ideation as well as anxiety and depression symptoms.

Depression and anxiety risk treatment for suicide

The Depression and Anxiety Risk Treatment for Suicide (DARTS) is the final clinical trial we will describe. DARTS is currently ongoing as we are collecting data from a long-term follow-up, but we have preliminary, unpublished data from posttreatment and short-term follow-up. DARTS was a somewhat more complex design in that it focused on replicating some of the prior work focused on anxiety sensitivity as well as extending our work on suicide risk reduction by developing a new intervention targeting interpersonal risk factors for suicide based on the Interpersonal Theory of suicide (Chu et al., 2017). Similar to CATS, DARTS combines a "top-down" psychoeducational intervention approach aimed at changing risk via conscious and deliberate cognitive evaluation with a "bottom-up" CBM approach that directly targets information processing biases relevant to risk. The DARTS protocol attempts to address three suicide-relevant risk targets including two risk factors related to the Interpersonal Theory of suicide (thwarted belongingness (TB), perceived burdensomeness (PB)) in addition to anxiety sensitivity. Approximately 300 participants ($N=304$) were enrolled in the DARTS trial and randomized to one of four conditions. The three active treatment conditions utilized a combined CBT/CBM approach to mitigate mood risk factors (TB/PB) or anxiety sensitivity or all three (combined) along with a repeated contact control. The anxiety sensitivity and combined conditions utilized the same combined CBM/CBT for anxiety sensitivity that was employed in CATS. However, in DARTS, we were also interested in delivering a more substantial "dose" so that participants received the CAST intervention during session one and then returned for two additional sessions of CBM-I for anxiety sensitivity. For purposes of this discussion, we will only focus on the treatment conditions that included the CBT/CBM for anxiety sensitivity. Results indicated an immediate effect of condition on anxiety sensitivity postintervention at Session 1 with a 38.2% reduction in anxiety sensitivity for participants in the active conditions. This effect was maintained throughout the intervention period until Session 3, with a 43.1% reduction in anxiety sensitivity observed in the active conditions. Intervention effects were in the medium range. Effects held at month 1, month 3, and month 6. At month 6, participants in the active condition maintained a 51.7% reduction in anxiety sensitivity, which is consistent with a slight strengthening of the effects over time. Also, we replicated our mediation effects from previous work in that treatment related change in anxiety sensitivity-mediated change in suicidal ideation.

Other notable outcomes from anxiety sensitivity intervention trials

We have also evaluated secondary outcomes from some of the clinical trials described earlier (CAST, CATS, and DARTS) and found that the intervention has positive effects on PTSD (Allan, Short, Albanese, et al., 2015; Short, Boffa, et al., 2017) as well as insomnia (Short, Allan, Raines, & Schmidt, 2015). For example, we utilized a subsample of trauma-exposed participants ($N = 63$) and showed that CAST produced a direct effect on posttraumatic stress symptoms at month one that was also mediated by changes in anxiety sensitivity cognitive concerns during the intervention period (Short, Boffa, et al., 2017). Similarly, Mitchell et al. (2014) evaluated a subsample of Veterans with PTSD and found that CAST reduced later PTSD symptoms. At this point, we have fairly consistent evidence that intervening on anxiety sensitivity will positively impact later panic, anxiety, and PTSD symptoms as well as suicidal ideation.

Recently, we have been interested in potential moderators of our anxiety sensitivity interventions. Based on studies conducted by our group and others, in which we found qualitatively distinct anxiety sensitivity classes, described as Normative, Moderate, and High anxiety sensitivity, we have recently begun examining whether anxiety sensitivity class status might moderate the efficacy of our brief anxiety sensitivity interventions (e.g., Schmidt & Allan, 2017). In Schmidt and Allan (2017), we explored anxiety sensitivity class status as a moderator of treatment effects for two published anxiety sensitivity intervention trials comparing CAST to a control condition. Linear regression was conducted, including preintervention anxiety sensitivity scores, treatment condition, anxiety sensitivity class, and the interaction between condition and anxiety sensitivity class as predictors of postintervention anxiety sensitivity. Results suggested an interaction such that for those in the Normative/Moderate anxiety sensitivity class CAST produced slight reductions in anxiety sensitivity compared to the control condition, whereas for those in the High anxiety sensitivity class CAST produced significantly larger reductions. Further, the effect size from pre- to postintervention and from preintervention to month 1 follow-up was large and stable for those in the High anxiety sensitivity class (pre to post $d = 1.15$, pre to month 1 $d = 0.92$) whereas the effect size for those in the Normative/Moderate anxiety sensitivity class was moderate pre to post ($d = 0.61$) and small and negative from preintervention to month 1 ($d = -0.13$). Study two compared the same two conditions in the CATS study (Schmidt, Norr, Allan, Raines, & Capron, 2017). There was again an interaction between condition and class ($P < 0.001$) such that no treatment effect was found in the Normative/Moderate anxiety sensitivity class ($B = 4.11$, $P = 0.11$), whereas a significant treatment effect was found in the High anxiety sensitivity class ($B = 15.58$, $P < 0.001$). Further, the effect size from pre- to postintervention and from preintervention to month 4 follow-up was again large in the High anxiety sensitivity class (pre to post $d = 1.15$, pre to month 4 $d = 0.96$) and was again moderate in the Normative/Moderate anxiety sensitivity class from pre- to postintervention ($d = 0.61$) and small from preintervention to month 4 follow-up ($d = 0.28$). In contrast to our expectations, we found greater and seemingly more stable reductions in anxiety sensitivity for those with the highest levels of anxiety sensitivity. These findings suggest that these brief treatments including preventive interventions may be most effective for people with the most severe levels of anxiety sensitivity.

Acceptability and dissemination

As researchers move forward with anxiety sensitivity interventions, acceptability and dissemination should be a major focus. We are interested in exploring avenues to disseminate CAST and other Web applications. Technology-based interventions have the potential to drastically increase the reach of preventative interventions by overcoming common barriers to treatment such as cost, accessibility, and convenience. In one recent study (Norr, Gibby, Fuller, Portero, & Schmidt, 2017), we assessed the reach, acceptability, and efficacy of CAST delivered for free online using Craigslist as an advertising platform. Participants ($N = 103$) accessed the treatment through a Craigslist advertisement posted in the "Community" page, under the "Volunteer" category. Results revealed that this strategy was effective in reaching individuals with significant self-reported anxiety and mood symptoms, those who report not currently receiving mental health treatment, and those in areas with likely lower access to mental health resources, though the overall response rate was quite low. Further, results demonstrate high levels of participant rated acceptability and efficacy in the reduction of psychiatric symptoms and impairment. These results provide preliminary evidence to suggest that CAST can be delivered effectively over the Internet to reach individuals in need of treatment.

Anxiety sensitivity and childhood anxiety psychopathology

A discussion of the role of anxiety sensitivity in prevention should certainly attend to work with anxiety sensitivity in children. As with adults, studies suggest anxiety sensitivity is broadly associated with a range of anxiety problems in children (see the meta-analytic review by Noël & Francis, 2011). For example, a behavior genetic analysis suggested that anxiety sensitivity at age 8 was broadly associated with most anxiety subtypes at age 10 (Waszczuk, Zavos, & Eley, 2013). The exact risk trajectories and contributors are not well researched, though anxiety sensitivity is partially heritable (Waszczuk et al., 2013), and some reports indicate that parental anxiety sensitivity is moderately associated with child anxiety sensitivity (Francis, 2014).

The preponderance of prevention work utilizing anxiety sensitivity as a prevention strategy has been conducted with adults, which is unfortunate given adolescence is a period of "core risk" period in terms of anxiety disorder onset (Beesdo, Knappe, & Pine, 2009; Cicchetti & Rogosch, 2002; Dahl, 2004; Paus, Keshavan, & Giedd,

2008). Clinical work with youth support the malleability of anxiety sensitivity (Ollendick, 1995; Pincus, Ehrenreich-May, Whitton, Mattis, & Barlow, 2010), inspiring the focus of anxiety sensitivity mitigation within the preventive intervention context. This section describes the adolescent adaption of our team's adult ASERT program and the two other lines of research that focus solely or partially on anxiety sensitivity reduction in preventive interventions among at-risk youth.

Adolescent anxiety sensitivity amelioration program

The Adolescent Anxiety Sensitivity Amelioration Program (AASAP) was adapted from our team's ASAT program (Schmidt et al., 2006) to be developmentally appropriate for and used with youth (Knapp, Feldner, Schmidt, Keough, & Leen-Feldner, 2018). High anxiety sensitivity youth aged 10–14 years ($N = 88$) plus one of their parents were recruited from the local community and randomly assigned to either the intervention condition or a general health information control condition. The intervention condition consisted of a single 50-min session of psychoeducation and experimenter-led IE session as well as parent-led IE homework. Whereas both conditions decreased in anxiety sensitivity levels across the intervention period, youth in the intervention condition evidenced significantly lower anxiety sensitivity levels at the 1-month follow-up period compared to youth in the control condition. A medium effect was observed for these 1-month anxiety sensitivity outcomes. Further, treatment-related change in anxiety sensitivity served as a significant mediator between intervention condition and panic and generalized anxiety symptoms after accounting for baseline symptom levels, suggesting that psychoeducation and IE exercises yield anxiety-related benefits through the indirect effects of reduced anxiety sensitivity. Interestingly, adolescents in the intervention condition evidenced decreased generalized anxiety symptoms, but not panic symptoms at 1-month after controlling for baseline levels.

Two other research groups have used anxiety sensitivity as a preventive intervention target with youth. First, Balle and Tortella-Feliu (2010) adapted the Australian FRIENDS anxiety prevention program to a six-session, school-based selective prevention program for high anxiety sensitivity youth (11–17 years) from the Balearic Islands. This study involved three groups of youth: (a) adolescents with elevated levels of anxiety sensitivity assigned to the intervention condition (prevention group), (b) adolescents with high anxiety sensitivity assigned to the waitlist condition (waitlist control group), and (c) adolescents who did not evidence elevated anxiety sensitivity assigned to an assessment-only condition (nonelevated anxiety sensitivity comparison group). The sessions focused on anxiety psychoeducation, emotion regulation strategies, and exposure exercises including IE. At postintervention, both the prevention group and waitlist control group evidenced decreases in anxiety sensitivity levels, each higher than the nonelevated anxiety sensitivity comparison group (whose anxiety sensitivity did not change from pre- to postintervention). Anxiety and depressive symptoms comparably decreased in both the prevention group and waitlist control group at postintervention, and symptom levels in both groups were similar to the scores in the nonelevated anxiety sensitivity comparison group. At the 6-month follow-up, the anxiety sensitivity levels of the prevention group were similar to those scores evidenced by the nonelevated anxiety sensitivity control group, and lower than the anxiety sensitivity scores in the waitlist control group; the anxiety and depressive scores were similar across all three groups.

Second, based on the "common factor" model of cooccurring substance use and mental health problems (Castellanos-Ryan & Conrod, 2012), Dr. Patricia Conrod and Dr. Sherry Stewart have conducted several trials in multiple countries targeting the four high-risk personality profiles of anxiety sensitivity, hopelessness, impulsivity, and sensation seeking in their program called PreVenture (Conrod, Stewart, Comeau, & Maclean, 2006), with a particular focus on the outcomes of substance use and related psychopathology. The anxiety sensitivity intervention module involves two 90-min sessions focused on combating catastrophic thinking and maladaptive coping strategies (e.g., substance use, truancy, etc.; Castellanos & Conrod, 2006). Results suggest the anxiety sensitivity module has promising effects for panic attack reduction at 6-month follow-up (Castellanos & Conrod, 2006), but not at the 2-year follow-up (O'Leary-Barrett et al., 2013).

Emerging data through these three series of studies support targeting anxiety sensitivity in the context of preventive interventions. Knapp et al. (2018) adolescent adaption of our team's adult ASERT program demonstrated that the brief, 50-min intervention and related homework reduced anxiety sensitivity at the 1-month follow-up period compared to an active control group, and that the reductions in anxiety sensitivity mediated the relation between intervention condition and 1-month symptoms of generalized anxiety and panic symptoms. The most promising observation in Balle and Tortella-Feliu (2010) was reduction in anxiety sensitivity at the 6-month follow-up period among the prevention group, that were similar to the levels observed in the nonelevated anxiety sensitivity comparison group and lower than the levels evidenced in the waitlist control condition. The PreVenture Program (Conrod et al., 2006) has shown promising reductions on panic attack outcomes; however, the changes in anxiety sensitivity postintervention and over the follow-up periods have yet to be published.

Implications for prevention

So what does the literature tell us in regard to targeting anxiety sensitivity as a prevention strategy for anxiety psychopathology? Using the risk factor framework delineated by Kraemer et al. (1997), a variable must demonstrate a correlation with the outcome of interest as well as precede these outcomes. An extensive literature partially summarized by two metaanalyses supports these ideas, though prospective studies are much more limited (Naragon-Gainey, 2010; Olatunji & Wolitzky-Taylor, 2009). Kraemer's next criterion focuses on the idea of the risk factor must be malleable, and as we have noted in the preceding sections, a number of studies indicate that anxiety sensitivity can be rapidly ameliorated (Schmidt et al., 2014; Schmidt et al., 2017; Schmidt, Eggleston, et al., 2007; Schmidt, Maner, et al., 2007). Critically, the last piece of the puzzle in Kraemer's framework is that manipulating the risk factor must lead to changes in the outcome. Indeed, several studies have demonstrated that reductions in anxiety sensitivity are associated with reductions in anxiety symptoms (Schmidt et al., 2014, 2017). However, this literature is limited in that we do not have compelling studies suggesting that reductions in anxiety sensitivity lead to reductions in specific anxiety diagnoses. Schmidt et al. (2014, 2017), for example, showed that reductions in anxiety sensitivity lead to reductions in anxiety symptoms and Schmidt et al. (2016) found that reducing anxiety sensitivity led to later reductions in panic attacks. Finally, Schmidt, Eggleston, et al. (2007) and Schmidt, Maner, et al. (2007) showed that reductions in anxiety sensitivity were associated with a lower incidence of all diagnoses during the following 2 years, the relatively low incidence of diagnoses does not allow us to conclusively say that reductions in anxiety sensitivity will lead to later reductions in phobic anxiety diagnoses. By and large, the data are consistent with the idea that anxiety sensitivity is a causal risk factor for anxiety psychopathology and is therefore an appropriate target as a preventative intervention. These findings are supported by the numerous studies we presented showing positive treatment effects with diverse treatment elements.

Despite myriad treatments for anxiety disorders (Chambless & Ollendick, 2001), anxiety disorders continue to result in substantial societal burden (Kessler, Chiu, Demler, & Walters, 2005) due to a number of factors including issues such as access, cost, and stigma. New models of treatment delivery, such as the Muñoz et al. (2016) Massive Open Online Intervention delivery model, which support the idea of making automated interventions such as the automated protocols described for anxiety sensitivity reduction freely available over the internet. Whereas the prevention of anxiety is complex, such interventions for anxiety sensitivity could have tremendous value in a stepped-care model of anxiety prevention and intervention.

These findings provide guidance for clinicians as well. First, given evidence presented in this chapter as well as other chapters in this book as well as the large amount of literature published, anxiety sensitivity is an important risk and maintenance factor clinicians should consider when patients are presenting with anxiety, but also when patients are presenting with depression, PTSD, insomnia, and suicidal ideation. Thus, clinicians should screen for anxiety sensitivity, using the ASI-3 given it has been well validated. Second, at the moment, there is limited evidence regarding which anxiety sensitivity intervention components are the most valuable. Interventions that have included psychoeducation, IE, CBM, or are exercise-based have all shown positive results in reducing anxiety sensitivity. Whereas there is some limited evidence that psychoeducation alone, CBM alone, or a single exercise session alone can reduce anxiety sensitivity as well as interventions including multiple components, it is unclear whether these findings would generalize across all populations. Currently, few moderators of treatment effectiveness have been considered, although there is preliminary evidence that our interventions utilizing psychoeducation and IE tend to show greater gains for those with more elevated anxiety sensitivity (Schmidt & Allan, 2017). Given the brief nature of these interventions, clinicians may consider using one or more of these interventions prior to more intensive treatment or as an adjunct to treatment.

Given the robust effects found, at least some treatment gain should be found regardless of the particular intervention selected. Finally, if clinicians were to consider these anxiety sensitivity-focused interventions as adjuncts to current treatment, it would be worth considering which aspects the current treatment lacks to guide the style of intervention chosen.

References

Achenbach, T. M., Howell, C. T., McConaughy, S. H., & Stanger, C. (1995). Six-year predictors of problems in a national sample: III. Transitions to young adult syndromes. *Journal of the American Academy of Child and Adolescent Psychiatry*, *34*(5), 658–669.

Allan, N. P., Albanese, B. J., Short, N. A., Raines, A. M., & Schmidt, N. B. (2015). Support for the general and specific bifactor model factors of anxiety sensitivity. *Personality and Individual Differences*, *74*, 78–83.

Allan, N. P., Norr, A. M., Boffa, J. W., Durmaz, D., Raines, A. M., & Schmidt, N. B. (2015). Examining the unique relations between anxiety sensitivity factors and suicidal ideation and past suicide attempts. *Psychiatry Research*, *228*(3), 441–447.

Allan, N. P., Norr, A. M., Capron, D. W., Raines, A. M., Zvolensky, M. J., & Schmidt, N. B. (2015). Specific associations between anxiety sensitivity dimensions and fear and distress dimensions of emotional distress disorders. *Journal of Psychopathology and Behavioral Assessment*, *37*(1), 67–78.

Allan, N. P., Short, N. A., Albanese, B. J., Keough, M. E., & Schmidt, N. B. (2015). Direct and mediating effects of an anxiety sensitivity intervention on posttraumatic stress disorder symptoms in trauma-exposed individuals. *Cognitive Behaviour Therapy*, *44*, 512–524.

American Academy of Child and Adolescent Psychiatry. (1990). Guidelines for the clinical evaluation for child and adolescent sexual abuse. Retrieved from https:/www.aacap.org/aacap/Policy_Statements/1990/Guidelines_for_the_Clinical_Evaluation_for_Child_and_Adolescent_Sexual_Abuse.aspx.

American Psychiatric Association (2013). *Diagnostic and statistical manual of mental disorders* (5th ed.). Arlington, VA: American Psychiatric Publishing.

Balle, M., & Tortella-Feliu, M. (2010). Efficacy of a brief school-based program for selective prevention of childhood anxiety. *Anxiety, Stress, and Coping*, *23*(1), 71–85. https://doi.org/10.1080/10615800802590652.

Barlow, D. H., Craske, M. G., Cerny, J. A., & Klosko, J. S. (1989). Behavioral treatment of panic disorder. *Behavior Therapy*, *20*(2), 261–282.

Beard, C. (2011). Cognitive bias modification for anxiety: current evidence and future directions. *Expert Review of Neurotherapeutics*, *11*(2), 299–311.

Beard, C., & Amir, N. (2008). A multi-session interpretation modification program: changes in interpretation and social anxiety symptoms. *Behaviour Research and Therapy*, *46*(10), 1135–1141.

Beesdo, K., Knappe, S., & Pine, D. (2009). Anxiety and anxiety disorders in children and adolescents: developmental issues and implications for DSM-V. *The Psychiatric Clinics of North America*, *32*(3), 483–524. https://doi.org/10.1016/j.psc.2009.06.002.

Broman-Fulks, J. J., & Storey, K. M. (2008). Evaluation of a brief aerobic exercise intervention for high anxiety sensitivity. *Anxiety, Stress, and Coping*, *21*(2), 117–128.

Broman-Fulks, J. J., Kelso, K., & Zawilinski, L. (2015). Effects of a single bout of aerobic exercise versus resistance training on cognitive vulnerabilities for anxiety disorders. *Cognitive Behaviour Therapy*, *44*(4), 240–251.

Brown, R. A., Kahler, C. W., Zvolensky, M. J., Lejuez, C. W., & Ramsey, S. E. (2001). Anxiety sensitivity: relationship to negative affect smoking and smoking cessation in smokers with past major depressive disorder. *Addictive Behaviors*, *26*(6), 887–899.

Capron, D. W., Cougle, J. R., Ribeiro, J. D., Joiner, T. E., & Schmidt, N. B. (2012). An interactive model of anxiety sensitivity relevant to suicide attempt history and future suicidal ideation. *Journal of Psychiatric Research*, *46*(2), 174–180. https://doi.org/10.1016/j.jpsychires.2011.10.009.

Capron, D. W., Norr, A. M., Macatee, R. J., & Schmidt, N. B. (2013). Distress tolerance and anxiety sensitivity cognitive concerns: testing the incremental contributions of affect dysregulation constructs on suicidal ideation and suicide attempt. *Behavior Therapy*, *44*(3), 349–358.

Capron, D. W., & Schmidt, N. B. (2016). Development and evaluation of a novel computer-delivered anxiety sensitivity intervention. *Behaviour Research and Therapy*, *81*, 47–55.

Castellanos, N., & Conrod, P. (2006). Brief interventions targeting personality risk factors for adolescent substance misuse reduce depression, panic and risk-taking behaviours. *Journal of Mental Health*, *15*, 645–658.

Castellanos-Ryan, N., & Conrod, P. J. (2012). Personality and substance misuse: evidence for a four factor model of vulnerability. J. Vester, K. Brady, E. Strain, M. Galanter, & P. J. Conrod (Eds.), *Drug abuse and addiction in medical illness*. Vols. 1–2. New York, NY: Humana/Spring Press.

Chambless, D. L., & Ollendick, T. H. (2001). Empirically supported psychological interventions: controversies and evidence. *Annual Review of Psychology*, *52*(1), 685–716.

Chu, C., Buchman-Schmitt, J. M., Stanley, I. H., Hom, M. A., Tucker, R. P., Hagan, C. R., … Joiner, T. E., Jr. (2017). The interpersonal theory of suicide: a systematic review and meta-analysis of a decade of cross-national research. *Psychological Bulletin*, *143*(12), 1313.

Cicchetti, D., & Rogosch, F. A. (2002). A developmental psychopathology perspective on adolescence. *Journal of Consulting and Clinical Psychology*, *70*, 6–20. https://doi.org/10.1037/0022-006X.70.1.6.

Clerkin, E. M., Beard, C., Fisher, C. R., & Schofield, C. A. (2015). An attempt to target anxiety sensitivity via cognitive bias modification. *PLoS One*. *10*(2)https://doi.org/10.1371/journal.pone.0114578.

Conrod, P. J., Stewart, S. H., Comeau, N., & Maclean, A. M. (2006). Efficacy of cognitive–behavioral interventions targeting personality risk factors for youth alcohol misuse. *Journal of Clinical Child and Adolescent Psychology*, *35*(4), 550–563.

Cougle, J. R., Keough, M. E., Riccardi, C. J., & Sachs-Ericsson, N. (2009). Anxiety disorders and suicidality in the National Comorbidity Survey-Replication. *Journal of Psychiatric Research*, *43*(9), 825–829. https://doi.org/10.1037/0021-843x.110.4.585.

Cougle, J. R., Resnick, H., & Kilpatrick, D. G. (2009). PTSD, depression, and their comorbidity in relation to suicidality: cross-sectional and prospective analyses of a national probability sample of women. *Depression and Anxiety*, *26*(12), 1151–1157. https://doi.org/10.1002/da.20621.

Carleton, R. N. (2016). Into the unknown: A review and synthesis of contemporary models involving uncertainty. *Journal of Anxiety Disorders*, *39*, 30–43.

Cristea, I. A., Kok, R. N., & Cuijpers, P. (2015). Efficacy of cognitive bias modification interventions in anxiety and depression: meta-analysis. *The British Journal of Psychiatry*, *206* (1), 7–16.

Dahl, R. E. (2004). Adolescent brain development: a period of vulnerabilities and opportunities. Keynote address. *Annals of the New York Academy of Sciences*, *1021*, 1–22. https://doi.org/10.1196/annals.1308.001.

Feldner, M. T., & Zvolensky, M. J. (2004). Prevention of anxiety psychopathology: a critical review of the empirical literature. *Clinical Psychology: Science and Practice, 11*(4), 405–424.

Feldner, M. T., Zvolensky, M. J., Babson, K., Leen-Feldner, E. W., & Schmidt, N. B. (2008). An integrated approach to panic prevention targeting the empirically supported risk factors of smoking and anxiety sensitivity: theoretical basis and evidence from a pilot project evaluating feasibility and short-term efficacy. *Journal of Anxiety Disorders, 22*(7), 1227–1243.

Ferdinand, R. F., & Verhulst, F. C. (1995). Psychopathology from adolescence into young adulthood: an 8-year follow-up study. *The American Journal of Psychiatry, 152*(11), 1586.

First, M. B., Spitzer, R. L., Gibbon, M., & Williams, J. B. (1994). *Structured clinical interview for axis I DSM-IV disorders.* New York: Biometrics Research.

Francis, S. E. (2014). The role of parental anxiety sensitivity in parent reports of child anxiety in treatment seeking families. *Clinical Child Psychology and Psychiatry, 19*(1), 111–124.

Gardenswartz, C. A., & Craske, M. G. (2001). Prevention of panic disorder. *Behavior Therapy, 32*(4), 725–737.

Hallion, L. S., & Ruscio, A. M. (2011). A meta-analysis of the effect of cognitive bias modification on anxiety and depression. *Psychological Bulletin, 137*(6), 940–958.

Harrington, P. J., Telch, M. J., Abplanalp, B., Hamilton, A. C., & Austin, U. T. (1995). Lowering anxiety sensitivity in nonclinical subjects: preliminary evidence for a panic prevention program. In: *Vol. 29. Proceedings of the Association for Advancement of Behavior Therapy* (p. 192).

Holden, E. W., & Black, M. M. (1999). Theory and concepts of prevention science as applied to clinical psychology. *Clinical Psychology Review, 19*(4), 391–401.

Kellam, S. G., & Rebok, G. W. (1992). Building developmental and etiological theory through epidemiologically based preventive intervention trials. In J. McCord & R. E. Tremblay (Eds.), *Preventing antisocial behavior: Interventions from birth through adolescence* (pp. 162–195). New York: Guilford Press.

Keough, M. E., & Schmidt, N. B. (2012). Refinement of a brief anxiety sensitivity reduction intervention. *Journal of Consulting and Clinical Psychology, 80*, 766–772.

Kessler, R. C., Chiu, W. T., Demler, O., & Walters, E. E. (2005). Prevalence, severity, and comorbidity of 12-month DSM-IV disorders in the National Comorbidity Survey replication. *Archives of General Psychiatry, 62*(6), 617–627.

Knapp, A. A., Feldner, M. T., Schmidt, N. B., Keough, M. E., & Leen-Feldner, E. W. (2018). *Test of an adolescent anxiety sensitivity amelioration program (AASAP) for at-risk youth.* (Manuscript under review).

Kraemer, H. C., Kazdin, A. E., Offord, D. R., Kessler, R. C., Jensen, P. S., & Kupfer, D. J. (1997). Coming to terms with the terms of risk. *Archives of General Psychiatry, 54*(4), 337–343.

LeBouthillier, D. M., & Asmundson, G. J. (2015). A single bout of aerobic exercise reduces anxiety sensitivity but not intolerance of uncertainty or distress tolerance: A randomized controlled trial. *Cognitive Behaviour Therapy, 44*(4), 252–263.

MacDonald, E. M., Koerner, N., & Antony, M. M. (2013). Modification of interpretive bias: impact on anxiety sensitivity, information processing and response to induced bodily sensations. *Cognitive Therapy and Research, 37*(4), 860–871.

MacLeod, C., & Mathews, A. (2012). Cognitive bias modification approaches to anxiety. *Annual Review of Clinical Psychology, 8*(1), 189–217.

Maltby, N. A. (2001). *Evaluation of a brief preventative treatment for panic disorder.* (Doctoral dissertation). Retrieved from: opencommons.uconn. (AAI3025035).

Maltby, N., Mayers, M. F., Allen, G. J., & Tolin, D. F. (2005). Anxiety sensitivity: stability in prospective research. *Journal of Anxiety Disorders*, *19*(6), 708–716.

Mitchell, M. A., Capron, D. W., Raines, A. M., & Schmidt, N. B. (2014). Reduction of cognitive concerns of anxiety sensitivity is uniquely associated with reduction of PTSD and depressive symptoms: a comparison of civilians and veterans. *Journal of Psychiatric Research*, *48*, 25–31.

Muñoz, R. F., Bunge, E. L., Chen, K., Schueller, S. M., Bravin, J. I., Shaughnessy, E. A., & Pérez-Stable, E. J. (2016). Massive open online interventions: a novel model for delivering behavioral-health services worldwide. *Clinical Psychological Science*, *4*(2), 194–205.

Naragon-Gainey, K. (2010). Meta-analysis of the relations of anxiety sensitivity to the depressive and anxiety disorders. *Psychological Bulletin*, *136*(1), 128.

Nock, M. K., Hwang, I., Sampson, N. A., & Kessler, R. C. (2010). Mental disorders, comorbidity and suicidal behavior: results from the National Comorbidity Survey replication. *Molecular Psychiatry*, *15*(8), 868–876.

Noël, V. A., & Francis, S. E. (2011). A meta-analytic review of the role of child anxiety sensitivity in child anxiety. *Journal of Abnormal Child Psychology*, *39*(5), 721–733.

Norr, A. M., Allan, N. P., Macatee, R. J., Keough, M. E., & Schmidt, N. B. (2014). The effects of an anxiety sensitivity intervention on anxiety, depression, and worry: mediation through affect tolerances. *Behaviour Research and Therapy*, *59*, 12–19.

Norr, A. M., Gibby, B. A., Fuller, K. L., Portero, A. K., & Schmidt, N. B. (2017). Online dissemination of the Cognitive Anxiety Sensitivity Treatment (CAST) using Craigslist: a pilot study. *Cognitive Therapy and Research*, *41*, 600–609.

Norr, A. M., Gibby, B. A., & Schmidt, N. B. (2017). Is computerized psychoeducation sufficient to reduce anxiety sensitivity in an at-risk sample? A randomized trial. *Journal of Affective Disorders*, *212*, 48–55.

O'Connor, P. J., Herring, M. P., & Caravalho, A. (2010). Mental health benefits of strength training in adults. *American Journal of Lifestyle Medicine*, *4*(5), 377–396.

Olatunji, B. O., & Wolitzky-Taylor, K. B. (2009). Anxiety sensitivity and the anxiety disorders: a meta-analytic review and synthesis. *Psychological Bulletin*, *135*(6), 974–999.

O'Leary-Barrett, M., Topper, L., Al-Khudhairy, N., Pihl, R. O., Castellanos-Ryan, N., Mackie, C. J., & Conrod, P. J. (2013). Two-year impact of personality-targeted, teacher-delivered interventions on youth internalizing and externalizing problems: A cluster-randomized trial. *Journal of the American Academy of Child & Adolescent Psychiatry*, *52*(9), 911–920.

Ollendick, T. H. (1995). Cognitive behavioral treatment of panic disorders with agoraphobia in adolescents: a multiple baseline design analysis. *Behavior Therapy*, *26*, 517–531. https://doi.org/10.1016/S0005-7894(05)80098-X.

Paus, T., Keshavan, M., & Giedd, J. N. (2008). Why do many psychiatric disorders emerge during adolescence? *Nature Reviews Neuroscience*, *9*, 947–957. https://doi.org/10.1038/nrn2513.

Pincus, D. B., Ehrenreich-May, J., Whitton, S. W., Mattis, S. G., & Barlow, D. H. (2010). Cognitive-behavioral treatment of panic disorder in adolescence. *Journal of Clinical Child & Adolescent Psychology*, *39*(5), 638–649. https://doi.org/10.1080/15374416.2010.501288.

Pine, D. S., Cohen, P., Gurley, D., Brook, J., & Ma, Y. (1998). The risk for early-adulthood anxiety and depressive disorders in adolescents with anxiety and depressive disorders. *Archives of General Psychiatry*, *55*(1), 56–64.

Reiss, S. (1991). Expectancy model of fear, anxiety, and panic. *Clinical Psychology Review*, *11*(2), 141–153.

Reiss, S., Peterson, R. A., Gursky, D. M., & McNally, R. J. (1986). Anxiety sensitivity, anxiety frequency and the prediction of fearfulness. *Behaviour Research and Therapy*, *24*(1), 1–8.
Sareen, J., Cox, B. J., Stein, M. B., Afifi, T. O., Fleet, C., & Asmundson, G. J. G. (2007). Physical and mental comorbidity, disability, and suicidal behavior associated with posttraumatic stress disorder in a large community sample. *Psychosomatic Medicine*, *69*(3), 242–248.
Schmidt, N. B., & Allan, N. P. (2017, November). Validating factor mixture modeling-derived anxiety sensitivity cut scores through response to brief interventions [Chair]. In: N. P. Allan (Ed.), *Data-driven approaches to exploring heterogeneity in response to treatments for mood and anxiety disorders. Oral presentation at the 51st annual convention of the association for behavioral and cognitive therapies, San Diego, CA.*
Schmidt, N. B., Capron, D. W., Raines, A. M., & Allan, N. P. (2014). Randomized clinical trial evaluating the efficacy of a brief intervention targeting anxiety sensitivity cognitive concerns. *Journal of Consulting and Clinical Psychology*, *82*, 1023–1033.
Schmidt, N. B., Eggleston, A. M., Woolaway-Bickel, K., Fitzpatrick, K. K., Vasey, M. W., & Richey, J. A. (2007). Anxiety sensitivity amelioration training (ASAT): a longitudinal primary prevention program targeting cognitive vulnerability. *Journal of Anxiety Disorders*, *21*, 302–319.
Schmidt, N. B., & Joiner, T. E. (2002). Structure of the Anxiety Sensitivity Index psychometrics and factor structure in a community sample. *Journal of Anxiety Disorders*, *16*(1), 33–49.
Schmidt, N. B., Lerew, D. R., & Jackson, R. J. (1999). Prospective evaluation of anxiety sensitivity in the pathogenesis of panic: replication and extension. *Journal of Abnormal Psychology*, *108*(3), 532–537. https://doi.org/10.1037/0021-843x.108.3.532.
Schmidt, N. B., Maner, J. K., & Zvolensky, M. J. (2007). Reactivity to challenge with carbon dioxide as a prospective predictor of panic attacks. *Psychiatry Research*, *151*(1), 173–176.
Schmidt, N. B., Norr, A. M., Allan, N. P., Raines, A. M., & Capron, D. W. (2017). A randomized clinical trial targeting anxiety sensitivity for patients with suicidal ideation. *Journal of Consulting and Clinical Psychology*, *85*, 595–610.
Schmidt, N. B., Raines, A. M., Allan, N. P., & Zvolensky, M. J. (2016). Anxiety sensitivity risk reduction in smokers: a randomized controlled trial examining effects on panic. *Behaviour Research and Therapy*, *77*, 138–146.
Schmidt, N. B., Woolaway-Bickel, K., & Bates, M. (2001). Evaluating panic-specific factors in the relationship between suicide and panic disorder. *Behaviour Research and Therapy*, *39*(6), 635–649. https://doi.org/10.1016/s0005-7967(00)00034-6.
Schmidt, N. B., Zvolensky, M. J., & Maner, J. K. (2006). Anxiety sensitivity: prospective prediction of panic attacks and axis I pathology. *Journal of Psychiatric Research*, *40*(8), 691–699. https://doi.org/10.1016/j.jpsychires.2006.07.009.
Short, N. A., Allan, N. P., Raines, A. M., & Schmidt, N. B. (2015). The effects of an anxiety sensitivity intervention on insomnia symptoms. *Sleep Medicine*, *16*, 152–159.
Short, N. A., Boffa, J. W., Norr, A. M., Albanese, B. J., Allan, N. P., & Schmidt, N. B. (2017). A randomized clinical trial investigating the direct and indirect effects of an anxiety sensitivity intervention on posttraumatic stress symptoms: a replication and extension. *Journal of Traumatic Stress*, *30*, 296–303.
Short, N. A., Fuller, K., Norr, A. M., & Schmidt, N. B. (2017). Acceptability of a brief computer-based intervention targeting anxiety sensitivity cognitive concerns. *Cognitive Behaviour Therapy*, *46*, 250–274.
Smits, J. A., Berry, A. C., Tart, C. D., & Powers, M. B. (2008). The efficacy of cognitive-behavioral interventions for reducing anxiety sensitivity: a meta-analytic review. *Behaviour Research and Therapy*, *46*(9), 1047–1054.

Steinman, S. A., & Teachman, B. A. (2010). Modifying interpretations among individuals high in anxiety sensitivity. *Journal of Anxiety Disorders*, *24*(1), 71–78.

Taylor, S., Koch, W. J., & McNally, R. J. (1992). How does anxiety sensitivity vary across the anxiety disorders? *Journal of Anxiety Disorders*, *6*(3), 249–259.

Taylor, S., Zvolensky, M. J., Cox, B. J., Deacon, B., Heimberg, R. G., Ledley, D. R., … Cardenas, S. J. (2007). Robust dimensions of anxiety sensitivity: development and initial validation of the Anxiety Sensitivity Index-3. *Psychological Assessment*, *19*(2), 176–188.

Telch, M. J., Lucas, J. A., & Nelson, P. (1989). Nonclinical panic in college students: an investigation of prevalence and symptomatology. *Journal of Abnormal Psychology*, *98*(3), 300.

Waszczuk, M., Zavos, H., & Eley, T. (2013). Genetic and environmental influences on relationship between anxiety sensitivity and anxiety subscales in children. *Journal of Anxiety Disorders*, *27*(5), 475–484.

Westling, B. E., & Öst, L. G. (1999). Brief cognitive behaviour therapy of panic disorder. *Scandinavian Journal of Behaviour Therapy*, *28*(2), 49–57.

Zvolensky, M. J., & Bernstein, A. (2005). Cigarette smoking and panic psychopathology. *Current Directions in Psychological Science*, *14*(6), 301–305.

Further reading

Allan, N. P., Capron, D. W., Raines, A. M., & Schmidt, N. B. (2014). Unique relations among anxiety sensitivity factors and anxiety, depression, and suicidal ideation. *Journal of Anxiety Disorders*, *28*(2), 266–275.

Allan, N. P., Korte, K. J., Capron, D. W., Raines, A. M., & Schmidt, N. B. (2014). Factor mixture modeling of anxiety sensitivity: a three-class structure. *Psychological Assessment*, *26*(4), 1184.

Allan, N. P., MacPherson, L., Young, K. C., Lejuez, C. W., & Schmidt, N. B. (2014). Examining the latent structure of anxiety sensitivity in adolescents using factor mixture modeling. *Psychological Assessment*, *26*(3), 741.

Allan, N. P., Raines, A. M., Capron, D. W., Norr, A. M., Zvolensky, M. J., & Schmidt, N. B. (2014). Identification of anxiety sensitivity classes and clinical cut-scores in a sample of adult smokers: results from a factor mixture model. *Journal of Anxiety Disorders*, *28*(7), 696–703.

Allan, N. P., Saulnier, K. G., Cooper, D., Oglesby, M. E., & Schmidt, N. B. (2018). *Niacin biological challenge: a paradigm to evaluate social concerns.* (Submitted for publication).

Amir, N., Beard, C., Burns, M., & Bomyea, J. (2009). Attention modification program in individuals with generalized anxiety disorder. *Journal of Abnormal Psychology*, *118*(1), 28–33.

Amir, N., Beard, C., Taylor, C. T., Klumpp, H., Elias, J., Bums, M., & Chen, X. (2009). Attention training in individuals with generalized social phobia: a randomized controlled trial. *Journal of Consulting and Clinical Psychology*, *77*(5), 961–973.

Amir, N., Weber, G., Beard, C., Bomyea, J., & Taylor, C. T. (2008). The effect of a single-session attention modification program on response to a public-speaking challenge in socially anxious individuals. *Journal of Abnormal Psychology*, *117*(4), 860–868.

Asmundson, G. J., Weeks, J. W., Carleton, R. N., Thibodeau, M. A., & Fetzner, M. G. (2011). Revisiting the latent structure of the anxiety sensitivity construct: more evidence of dimensionality. *Journal of Anxiety Disorders*, *25*(1), 138–147.

Bernstein, A., Stickle, T. R., & Schmidt, N. B. (2013). Factor mixture model of anxiety sensitivity and anxiety psychopathology vulnerability. *Journal of Affective Disorders, 149*(1), 406–417.

Bernstein, A., Stickle, T. R., Zvolensky, M. J., Taylor, S., Abramowitz, J., & Stewart, S. (2010). Dimensional, categorical, or dimensional-categories: testing the latent structure of anxiety sensitivity among adults using factor-mixture modeling. *Behavior Therapy, 41*(4), 515–529.

Bernstein, A., Zvolensky, M. J., Stewart, S., & Comeau, N. (2007). Taxometric and factor analytic models of anxiety sensitivity among youth: exploring the latent structure of anxiety psychopathology vulnerability. *Behavior Therapy, 38*(3), 269–283.

Bernstein, A., Zvolensky, M. J., Stewart, S. H., Comeau, M. N., & Leen-Feldner, E. W. (2006). Anxiety sensitivity taxonicity across gender among youth. *Behaviour Research and Therapy, 44*(5), 679–698.

Capron, D. W., Norr, A. M., Albanese, B. J., & Schmidt, N. B. (2017). Fear reactivity to cognitive dyscontrol via novel head-mounted display perceptual illusion exercises. *Journal of Affective Disorders, 217*, 138–143.

Ebesutani, C., McLeish, A. C., Luberto, C. M., Young, J., & Maack, D. J. (2014). A bifactor model of anxiety sensitivity: analysis of the Anxiety Sensitivity Index-3. *Journal of Psychopathology and Behavioral Assessment, 36*(3), 452–464.

Krueger, R. F. (1999). The structure of common mental disorders. *Archives of General Psychiatry, 56*(10), 921–926.

MacLeod, C., Mathews, A., & Tata, P. (1986). Attentional bias in emotional disorders. *Journal of Abnormal Psychology, 95*(1), 15.

Mathews, A., & Mackintosh, B. (2000). Induced emotional interpretation bias and anxiety. *Journal of Abnormal Psychology, 109*(4), 602–615.

Meehl, P. E. (1999). Clarifications about taxometric method. *Applied and Preventive Psychology, 8*(3), 165–174.

National Advisory Mental Health Council Workgroup on Mental Disorders Prevention Research (1998). *Priorities for prevention research at NIMH (NIH Publication No. 98-4321)*. Rockville, MD: NIMH.

Pastötter, B., Schicker, S., Niedernhuber, J., & Bäuml, K.-H. T. (2011). Retrieval during learning facilitates subsequent memory encoding. *Journal of Experimental Psychology: Learning, Memory, and Cognition, 37*(2), 287.

Reise, S. P. (2012). The rediscovery of bifactor measurement models. *Multivariate Behavioral Research, 47*(5), 667–696.

Reiss, S., & McNally, R. (1985). Expectancy model of fear. In S. Reiss & R. R. Bootzin (Eds.), *Theoretical issues in behavior therapy inside*. San Diego, CA: Academic Press.

Salemink, E., van den Hout, M., & Kindt, M. (2007). Trained interpretive bias: validity and effects on anxiety. *Journal of Behavior Therapy and Experimental Psychiatry, 38*(2), 212–224.

Salemink, E., van den Hout, M., & Kindt, M. (2009). Effects of positive interpretive bias modification in highly anxious individuals. *Journal of Anxiety Disorders, 23*(5), 676–683.

Schmidt, N. B. (1999). Examination of differential anxiety sensitivities in panic disorder: a test of anxiety sensitivity subdomains predicting fearful responding to a 35% CO_2 challenge. *Cognitive Therapy and Research, 23*(1), 3–20.

Schmidt, N. B., Kotov, R., Lerew, D. R., Joiner, T. E., & Ialongo, N. S. (2005). Evaluating latent discontinuity in cognitive vulnerability to panic: a taxometric investigation. *Cognitive Therapy and Research, 29*(6), 673–690.

Schmidt, N. B., Richey, J. A., Buckner, J. D., & Timpano, K. R. (2009). Attention training for generalized social anxiety disorder. *Journal of Abnormal Psychology*, *118*(1), 5–14.

Seeley, J. R., Kosty, D. B., Farmer, R. F., & Lewinsohn, P. M. (2011). The modeling of internalizing disorders on the basis of patterns of lifetime comorbidity: associations with psychosocial functioning and psychiatric disorders among first-degree relatives. *Journal of Abnormal Psychology*, *120*(2), 308.

Vollebergh, W. A., Iedema, J., Bijl, R. V., de Graaf, R., Smit, F., & Ormel, J. (2001). The structure and stability of common mental disorders: the NEMESIS study. *Archives of General Psychiatry*, *58*(6), 597–603.

Watson, D. (2005). Rethinking the mood and anxiety disorders: a quantitative hierarchical model for DSM-V. *Journal of Abnormal Psychology*, *114*(4), 522.

Wheaton, M. G., Deacon, B. J., McGrath, P. B., Berman, N. C., & Abramowitz, J. S. (2012). Dimensions of anxiety sensitivity in the anxiety disorders: evaluation of the ASI-3. *Journal of Anxiety Disorders*, *26*(3), 401–408.

Zinbarg, R. E., Barlow, D. H., & Brown, T. A. (1997). Hierarchical structure and general factor saturation of the Anxiety Sensitivity Index: evidence and implications. *Psychological Assessment*, *9*(3), 277–284.

Zinbarg, R. E., Brown, T. A., Barlow, D. H., & Rapee, R. M. (2001). Anxiety sensitivity, panic, and depressed mood: a reanalysis teasing apart the contributions of the two levels in the hierarchical structure of the Anxiety Sensitivity Index. *Journal of Abnormal Psychology*, *110*(3), 372.

Anxiety sensitivity and your clinical practice

9

Michael W. Otto, Jasper A.J. Smits†, Hayley E. Fitzgerald*, Mark B. Powers‡, Scarlett O. Baird†*

*Boston University, Boston, MA, United States, †The University of Texas at Austin, Austin, TX, United States, ‡Baylor University Medical Center, Dallas, TX, United States

Chapter Outline

There may come a time when patients ask for treatment for anxiety sensitivity by name, given evidence that the concept of anxiety sensitivity is expanding into the more popular literature. In 2016, anxiety sensitivity appeared by name in both the *Huffington Post* and the *Scientific American*, with such titles as: "Anxiety sensitivity' is real. Here's how to know if your're caught in this spiral," and "What is anxiety sensitivity, and do I have it?" These titles aptly underscore the importance of anxiety sensitivity to a striking range of psychiatric disorders, medical conditions, and maladaptive coping responses; and reflects the importance of targeting anxiety sensitivity as part of the treatment of anxiety and related disorders (Chapter 5) or the prevention of/early intervention for disorders with at-risk cohorts (Chapter 4).

As we wrote at the outset of this book (Chapter 1), we believe the link between anxiety sensitivity and these disorders and conditions is due to the role of anxiety sensitivity as an amplifying factor: increasing the degree of distress and disability in response to somatic sensations and emotional experiences. Although anxiety sensitivity is most focused on the somatic and cognitive symptoms associated with anxiety,

The Clinician's Guide to Anxiety Sensitivity Treatment and Assessment. https://doi.org/10.1016/B978-0-12-813495-5.00009-7

anxiety sensitivity fuels catastrophic interpretations of a broader set of symptoms as exemplified by associations of anxiety sensitivity with catastrophic interpretations of pain (Ocañez, McHugh, & Otto, 2010), greater perceived difficulty quitting smoking (Langdon, Farris, Hogan, Grover, & Zvolensky, 2016; Zvolensky, Stewart, Vujanovic, Gavric, & Steeves, 2009), and with hypochondriacal concerns/health anxiety more generally (Otto, Demopulos, McLean, Pollack, & Fava, 1998; Otto, Pollack, Sachs, & Rosenbaum, 1992; Wright, Lebell, & Carleton, 2016). In addition, we believe that measures of anxiety sensitivity have enjoyed particularly strong prediction relative to other measures of distress (in)tolerance because it focuses on *anxious responses* to symptoms rather than merely the experience of anxiety-related symptoms. For example, as witnessed by the Anxiety Sensitivity Index-3 (ASI-3), a total of 10 items involve "worry" about a symptom, 4 items assess being "scared" in relation to a symptom, and 2 items about responding with "fear" to a symptom. This is at the heart of the amplification effect: elevated scores on anxiety sensitivity measures involve anxious responses to internal events. It is being scared, worried, and fearful about symptoms that drives individuals to desire to rapidly terminate these sensations by escape, avoidance, or the use of maladaptive coping responses such as drug use or mood-induced eating (Otto et al., 2016).

Given these associations between anxiety sensitivity and multiple dysfunctional habits, just what is a clinician to do when high anxiety sensitivity is detected in a patient? In the following sections, we provide answers to these questions in context of patient with any of a number of conditions with documented role for anxiety sensitivity. We start with a review of cut-points for considering intervention with elevated anxiety sensitivity, provide a brief review of intervention strategies for anxiety sensitivity, and then exemplify anxiety sensitivity intervention issues in the context of select conditions.

What anxiety sensitivity scores indicate the need for intervention?

Measures of anxiety sensitivity provide an index of where an individual falls on a continuum of concerns about anxiety-related sensations, and we know that higher scores have a stronger relationship with psychopathology, distress, and disability. Yet, the question of whether there is a point on that continuum that signifies the transition between *normative* and *unhealthy* anxiety sensitivity remains unclear. Taxometric analyses are analytic strategies used to investigate whether a construct is better modeled as a category or a dimension. These analyses have indicated that anxiety sensitivity may be more effectively conceptualized as a categorical rather than a continuous variable (Bernstein, Zvolensky, Kotov, et al., 2006; Bernstein et al., 2007; Bernstein, Zvolensky, Stewart, Comeau, & Leen-Feldner, 2006), supporting the notion that a cut-point for scores in the unhealthy range could be determined. However, at the time of this writing, the literature has yet to converge on a consistent cut-point, particularly given that anxiety sensitivity cut-points may function differentially in different subpopulations (e.g., a cut-point the prediction of maladaptive patterns in those with anxiety disorders vs. a cut-point to identify risk for engagement in negative health behaviors in otherwise healthy individuals). Also, the meaning of a particular anxiety sensitivity score may be different depending on the degree of internal stimuli to which the individual is subjected (Smits, Tart, Rosenfield, & Zvolensky, 2011). That is, if anxiety sensitivity is best conceived of as an amplifying factor, then the degree of distress and disability associated with anxiety sensitivity will also depend on the degree of stress, sadness, or aversive physical stimulation to which the individual is subjected. This raises challenges for the clinician who has to decide when anxiety sensitivity needs to be targeted in its own right. As such, with increasing internal stimulation, it may be relevant to intervene with even moderate anxiety sensitivity elevations, whereas under less extreme circumstances, high anxiety sensitivity scores may serve as the best cut score for intervention.

With these complexities in mind, let's consider what we know at present about cut-point scores for determining unhealthy anxiety sensitivity. As informed by Chapter 2, researchers have often used informal standards to identify individuals who have moderate and high elevations in anxiety sensitivity, as measured by the ASI. For example, a score of 25 on the original ASI has been recommended as a cut-point for elevated anxiety sensitivity (Peterson & Plehn, 1999). In addition to this general guidance, the ASI-3 has undergone more formal evaluation of cut-point scores in the context of select studies. For example, research has indicated that almost 4/5ths of individuals can be considered as scoring in the normative class of the ASI-3 as distinguished by a cut-score of 17 (Allan, Korte, Capron, Raines, & Schmidt, 2014; Allan, Raines, et al., 2014). Furthermore, a cut-score of 23 distinguishes the approximately 5% of individuals in the high-anxiety sensitivity class from the remainder of the individuals in the moderate-anxiety sensitivity Class. Accordingly, interventions targeting anxiety sensitivity could easily be considered appropriate for individuals with ASI-3 scores above 17, and deemed very important for those scoring 23 and above.

How to intervene with elevated anxiety sensitivity

Interventions for anxiety sensitivity differ dramatically in the degree of clinician and patient effort, with psychoeducation representing a low-effort strategy and a full program of interoceptive exposure (as operationalized in the treatment for those with panic disorder, e.g., Otto et al., 2012; Otto & Pollack, 2009) on the other. Between these extremes are cognitive restructuring, cognitive bias modification, mindfulness, and exercise-based interventions. The choice of which interventions to use is based on both the intensity as well as the interactability of the anxiety sensitivity. That is, there are a variety of conditions where fears of somatic sensations of anxiety can be maintained or exacerbated by associated disorder features. Panic disorder and post-traumatic stress disorder (PTSD) provide prototypic examples. Both of these disorders have been identified as having the highest elevations in anxiety sensitivity (Naragon-Gainey, 2010; Olatunji & Wolitzky-Taylor, 2009), and in many ways panic disorder represents the endpoint of the anxiety sensitivity amplification effect: symptoms of anxiety sensations have become so intense that the emergence of a feared sensation cues a next panic episode (McNally, 2002). In addition to the wealth of evidence that anxiety sensitivity serves as a risk factor for both panic disorder and PTSD, there is also evidence of reverse causality in terms of the maintenance or exacerbation of anxiety sensitivity. For example, in panic disorder, ongoing panic episodes may keep fears of symptoms alive through sensitizing individuals to the distress associated with symptoms (McNally, 2002).

In part because interoceptive exposure has been used so successfully to decrease anxiety sensitivity in the context of treatment of both panic disorder and PTSD (Smits, Berry, Tart, & Powers, 2008), and effective interoceptive-exposure based treatment can be honed to 5 sessions (Otto et al., 2012), we think of interoceptive exposure as a core tool for challenging elevations in anxiety sensitivity. Yet, surveys have shown that fewer than 1 in 5 clinicians use interoceptive exposure for panic disorder, social anxiety, obsessive-compulsive disorder (OCD), and PTSD (Hipol & Deacon, 2012). Accordingly, in addition to the extensive coverage of interoceptive exposure in this book (see also Smits, Powers, & Otto, in press), we want to underscore additional applications of interoceptive exposure, followed by alternative interventions to interoceptive exposure. Our first example concerns the role of anxiety sensitivity and interoceptive exposure for the treatment of PTSD.

Attending to anxiety sensitivity in PTSD

Wald and associates observed that individuals with a greater inability to tolerate the anxious arousal that accompanies trauma memories, had greater difficulty engaging in trauma-related imaginal exposure (Wald & Taylor, 2010; Wald, Taylor, Chiri, & Sica, 2010). We have further characterized this difficulty as follows, arguing that it is important clinically to be:

> *... alert to the way in which symptoms may "fold back upon themselves" in the context of exposure sessions. Exposure to traumatic material induces autonomic arousal (e.g., rapid heart rate, muscle tension, flushing) in patients, and may also induce feelings of dissociation. These feelings may be interpreted as threatening in their own right (e.g., "I am about to lose control," "I'll go crazy if I keep this up"); more significantly, they may be experienced as additional cues of the original trauma (at which time the patients may have experienced autonomic arousal, dissociation, and/or fears of loss of control or death). This rush of additional, interoceptive cues of the trauma may lead the patients to feel that the trauma is going to happen again, or that they cannot tolerate the memories. This experience may increase the patients' sense that trauma-related memories are uncontrollable, unpredictable, and dangerous; thus, it may lead to increased cognitive avoidance*
>
> *(Otto, Penava, Pollock, & Smoller, 1996; p. 236).*

Accordingly, we have recommended use of interoceptive exposure as a regular feature of CBT for PTSD (Otto et al., 1996; Smits et al., in press), arguing that: (1) emotional and somatic sensations are an expected part of trauma memories (response components) as elucidated by the fear network theory (Foa & Kozak, 1986); (2) these sensations can serve the dual function of being a trauma cue ("I felt this way during the shooting") and a strategy for engaging the fear network (using fear sensations); (3) the elevated anxiety sensitivity in patients with PTSD is likely to be a factor in both cognitive and behavioral avoidance patterns. There is evidence that even a single-session focus on anxiety sensitivity in PTSD can bring benefits. For example, Mitchell and associates (Mitchell, Capron, Raines, & Schmidt, 2014) investigated a single session intervention with psychoeducation and interoceptive exposure to target ASI-cognitive concerns. They targeted this intervention to a sample of civilians and veterans with elevated ASI-cognitive concerns. They found that reduction in ASI-cognitive concerns was associated with reduction in PTSD and depressive symptoms (Mitchell et al., 2014). Also, given the substantial link between PTSD and substance overuse, and the importance of elevated anxiety sensitivity for both of these disorders, anxiety sensitivity has the potential to be the linking therapeutic target between these comorbid disorders (Vujanovic et al., 2018).

Intervening on anxiety sensitivity across cultures

Interoceptive exposure may also play a more central role in the treatment of PTSD when anxiety sensitivity is intensified by culture-specific interpretations of symptoms as has been documented for Cambodian survivors of the Cambodian genocide (Otto & Hinton, 2006). For example, culture-specific interpretation of neck tightness/soreness as the blockage of a vapor-like "*Wind*" may be seen as heralding impending death via rupture of blood vessels. Likewise, fatigue may reflect energy depletion of *Wind* to the point of heart attack and death, or limb coolness or joint pain may reflect *Wind* blockage and indicate possible imminent loss of limb. These catastrophic interpretations of symptoms were central enough to the fears and disability surrounding PTSD in a Cambodian-American sample that we assessed these concerns with a culture-specific additions to the ASI (Otto et al., 2003), and specifically targeted these concerns with interoceptive exposure procedures delivered in a culturally sensitive manner:

> *We explicitly did not challenge the concept of* Wind *or its [culture-specific] treatment (with the "cupping" or "coining" procedures discussed by Hinton & Otto, 2006), but introduced an alternate label and explanation for these symptoms and acknowledged that at times these symptoms may "mimic" (provide a false alarm for) the apparent effects of* Wind. *We helped patients discriminate anxiety symptoms from their* Wind-*related fears by: (a) predicting the conditions under which anxiety symptoms would arise (i.e., in relation to trauma cues), and (b) providing patients with repeated demonstrations of an alternative account of symptoms, using in-session symptom provocation (first with interoceptive exposure, and later in treatment, with limited discussions of trauma cues) as a tool. By talking about the syndrome of PTSD early in treatment, and then providing experiences that could help patients reinterpret the meaning of symptoms (as trauma-related anxiety responses vs.* Wind*), we helped patients consider an alternative account of the etiology and meaning of symptoms and the interventions appropriate for these symptoms. We then relied on treatment benefits to help solidify this conceptualization. This process is consistent with the idea*

> *that although the labeling and accounting of trauma-related symptoms may differ by culture, identification of these symptoms as a syndrome has more universal acceptance across cultures*
>
> *(Breslau, 2004; Young, 1995).*

Overall, our culturally adapted treatment for PTSD in Cambodian refugees resulted in large improvements in core PTSD reexperiencing and avoidance symptoms, moderate changes in hyperarousal symptoms, and dramatic improvements in the ASI and the culture specific anxiety sensitivity items, respectively (Otto et al., 2003).

Interoceptive exposure for residual symptoms

Anxiety sensitivity has functioned as a broad predictor of relapse in anxiety treatment programs (Taylor, Jakubovski, & Bloch, 2015), and tracking of anxiety sensitivity may have particular importance for judging the adequacy of psychosocial treatment as well as pharmacologic treatments. For example, although medication treatment can reduce anxiety sensitivity as part of reductions in anticipatory anxiety, negative cognitions, and panic frequency (Simon et al., 2004), this is not necessarily the case. Indeed, investigators have documented that taking benzodiazepine, particularly taking benzodiazepines on an as needed (prn) basis, may lead to enhanced anxiety sensitivity over time and may impair response to alternative treatment (Fava et al., 1994; Westra, Stewart, & Conrad, 2002). Moreover, we have hypothesized that residual anxiety sensitivity elevations in patients treated for panic disorder is a major risk factor for the failure to successfully discontinuing benzodiazepine and antidepressant treatment (Otto, Hong, & Safren, 2002; Whittal, Otto, & Hong, 2001). Treating the fear of anxiety symptoms is at the core of our approach to aiding individuals with benzodiazepine discontinuation while maintaining or extending treatment response (Otto et al., 1993; Otto et al., 2010). Cognitive-restructuring and interoceptive exposure is central to these interventions, with both aimed at helping individuals reinterpret and relax with the presence of these symptoms regardless of whether they are due to benzodiazepine withdrawal or the reemergence of panic disorder (Otto & Pollack, 2009). Indeed, Bruce and colleagues (Bruce, Spiegel, & Hegel, 1999) have shown that the failure to adequately reduce anxiety sensitivity in treatment predicts future relapse. In sum, consideration of residual elevations in anxiety sensitivity and targeting treatment to these concerns can be considered both a relapse prevention strategy and an element of treatment aimed at helping patients successfully discontinue their antianxiety medications.

Considering the link between anxiety sensitivity and interpersonal attachment

Anxiety sensitivity reductions may also aid engagement in other interactions where avoidance of emotional content restricts adaptive behavior. For example, as one of our patients with panic disorder progressed in interoceptive exposure, he noted an increasing ability to be comfortable with his own emotional experiences well beyond his fears of panic symptoms. He then reported improved interactions and enhanced feelings of closeness with his teenage son. Upon discussion he was able to link his increasing tolerance of unexpected emotions to the ability to better remain in conversations with his son. In short, teenage sons can evoke emotions in their father, and improved tolerance of these emotions means that there is less reason to terminate such interactions prematurely with anger or other avoidance strategies. Reflections on this clinical observation can be found in investigations showing a relation between anxiety sensitivity and attachment in both the context of panic treatment (Zalaznik, Weiss, & Huppert, 2017) and unselected samples (Watt, Gallagher, Couture, Wells, & MacLean, 2016). ASI subscales have also been associated with specific parenting styles (Timpano, Carbonella, Keuough, & Schmidt, 2015).

Health applications and anxiety sensitivity

Perhaps it is most efficient to point out that anxiety sensitivity is linked to the top three preventable causes of disease and death in the United States: (1) tobacco use, (2) poor diet and physical inactivity (obesity), and (3) alcohol overuse (Institute of Medicine, 2001). Understanding the scope of these effects has clear public health significance. Chapter 7 details the strong relation between anxiety sensitivity and smoking, suggesting novel integrated treatment strategies. As we noted in Chapter 1, anxiety sensitivity predicts both exercise avoidance and mood-induced eating (Hearon, Quatromoni, Mascoop, & Otto, 2014) providing a concerning "1:2 punch" to the two pillars of obesity control. Concerning alcohol use, anxiety sensitivity guides coping motives for drinking (Paulus et al., 2017). Coping motives themselves are proximal determinants of alcohol use and abuse (Cooper, Frone, Russell, & Mudar, 1995). Moreover, anxiety sensitivity preceded the emergence of alcohol use disorder in a longitudinal study (Schmidt, Bucker, & Keough, 2007), and likewise changes in anxiety sensitivity have been linked to beneficial alcohol treatment outcomes (Wolitzky-Taylor et al., 2018). These findings support the consideration of anxiety sensitivity in both prevention and intervention programs for alcohol use disorder. Likewise, because of the anxiety sensitivity-coping motives relation that is evident in other drug use patterns (e.g., marijuana use; Buckner et al., 2011; Smits, Bonn-Miller, Tart, Irons, & Zvolensky, 2011), and the observation that anxiety sensitivity results in illicit drug craving in response to negative mood induction (Stathopoulou, Pollack, & Otto, 2018), targeting anxiety sensitivity is relevant across substance use disorders.

As we step from these top-three health conditions to other health challenges, there is strong emphasis for the role of anxiety sensitivity in increasing health disability by either reducing engagement in positive health behaviors or by enhancing disability and avoidance (Horenstein, Potter, & Heimberg, 2018; Otto et al., 2016). As we noted at the outset of this book, Horenstein and colleagues (Horenstein et al., 2018) identified 160 studies of the association of anxiety sensitivity to pain, cardiac, respiratory, and gastrointestinal symptoms and disorders. The significance of these broad-based linkages is that anxiety sensitivity can serve as an additional treatment target to potentially reduce disability in those with fears of symptoms (Otto & Smits, in press). This is especially important when other medical options are limited, so that anxiety sensitivity can emerge as "comorbid treatable trait" to enhance the care of disorders when the efficacy for other medical targets is limited (for discussion of this issue for asthma see Tay & Hew, 2018).

How much interoceptive exposure is needed?

There is evidence that even ultra-brief treatments (e.g., five 90-min sessions of interoceptive-exposure-based CBT) can treat panic disorder and associated elevations in anxiety sensitivity (Otto et al., 2012). But outside the disorders with the highest elevation in anxiety sensitivity—panic disorder and PTSD—what is the evidence for more minimal interventions for anxiety sensitivity? In Chapter 4, Schmidt and associates make clear that a variety of strategies can be applied to anxiety sensitivity reduction in a prevention model. For example, brief one-session interoceptive exposure has been shown to be helpful for individuals with high anxiety sensitivity who were not otherwise treatment seeking (Keough & Schmidt, 2012). In this study, Specifically, Keough and Schmidt (2012) devoted a single 50-min session to psychoeducation (aided by a slide presentation) followed by several interoceptive exposure exercises to assess their fear of arousal sensations The most fear-producing exercise was subsequently selected for repeated exposure until the participant's associated distress reaching minimal self-report ratings. Participants were asked to complete interoceptive exposure practice every day for the next month and were given monitoring forms to track their adherence. This program resulted in significant and sustained reductions on the ASI (i.e., from a mean score of 29.4 to a mean score of 16.1 1 week later), that remained low at a 6-month follow-up.

Exercise is another strategy that has been used and studied as a method to reduce anxiety sensitivity. Engaging in aerobic exercise naturally exposes individuals to feared bodily sensations, thus providing them with an opportunity to habituate and gain corrective learning about the outcomes of experiencing those sensations (i.e., learning that feelings such as muscle tension, sweating, and increased heart rate may be uncomfortable, but are nonthreatening; Asmundson et al., 2013; Smits, Berry, Rosenfield, et al., 2008; Smits et al., 2016; Smits, Powers, Berry, & Otto, 2007; Zvolensky et al., 2018).

In our work testing exercise as an intervention for augmenting smoking cessation in individuals with elevated anxiety sensitivity (Smits et al., 2016), we have found that we can facilitate engagement in exercise for this purpose when we, at the onset of the program, provide patients with brief education on (1) the nature of the relation between anxiety sensitivity, stress, and smoking and (2) the principle that repeated bouts of exercise can serve to provide interoceptive exposure practice, helping patients reestablish a sense of safety around somatic arousal.

In terms of ease of clinical intervention, it appears that exercise alone does most of the heavy lifting for treatment response. That is, in the Smits and associates study (Smits, Berry, Rosenfield, et al., 2008) referenced earlier, it had been assumed that adding cognitive restructuring to the brief exercise intervention would lead to even more powerful effects on anxiety sensitivity. But it did not; exercise plus cognitive restructuring did not outperform exercise alone in changing anxiety sensitivity (Smits, Berry, Rosenfield, et al., 2008).

Cognitive restructuring and psychoeducation

As we have noted, surveys have shown that fewer than 1 in 5 clinicians use interoceptive exposure for anxiety-related disorders (Hipol & Deacon, 2012), and hence may also be reluctant to use interoceptive exposure in the applications we noted earlier. Accordingly, we will briefly review other interventions useful for reducing anxiety sensitivity to complement the comprehensive treatment of this issue discussed in other chapters in this book.

Cognitive restructuring for anxiety sensitivity represents an intensification of psychoeducation to focus on logical analysis of catastrophic interpretations of symptoms. In Chapter 5, Taylor and associates provide an extensive discussion on cognitive restructuring specifically as it applies to anxiety sensitivity, and include information on component strategies such as: (1) empirical disputes, (2) challenging beliefs by reviewing the sensations, and (3) and challenging the components (probability and cost) of catastrophic beliefs. In many applications, cognitive restructuring is used in conjunctions with exposure (Smits, Berry, Rosenfield, et al., 2008). At the current state of research, we do not have a very good estimate of the efficacy of cognitive restructuring alone for anxiety sensitivity, but we do have evidence that psychoeducation alone can help in some circumstances. Psychoeducation for anxiety sensitivity involves the provision of information to dispel myths about the dangers of anxiety disorder. In psychoeducation, the concept of anxiety sensitivity is defined, information may be provided on the onset of elevated anxiety sensitivity (e.g., the development of a conditioned fear to these sensations), and the provision of specific instruction that anxiety sensations are not dangerous. There is promising evidence that a computerized psychoeducation with these elements can reduce symptoms in a nonpatient sample. Specifically, Norr, Gibby, and Schmidt (2017) found that a 35-min computerized program utilizing video animation, audio narration, and interactive features such as brief quizzes can significantly reduce ASI scores.

Cognitive bias modification

This intervention requires specialty computer programs, but once obtained, computerized cognitive bias modification (CBM) can provide a cost-efficient (in terms of clinician effort) approach to changing anxiety sensitivity. Anxiety tends to lead individuals to favor making negative or threatening interpretations when presented with ambiguous information. This specific cognitive bias has been referred to an interpretation bias (Beard & Amir, 2008). CBM focusing on interpretation bias (CBM-I; Beard & Amir, 2008) involves computerized training procedures to retrain this tendency by repeatedly reinforcing nonthreatening interpretations of ambiguous cues.

CBM-I to reduce anxiety sensitivity have been investigated in multiple randomized controlled studies. As reviewed and summarized in Chapter 5, there have been several studies that have shown CBM-I to be efficacious in reducing anxiety sensitivity (Capron & Schmidt, 2016; Clerkin, Beard, Fisher, & Schofield, 2015; MacDonald, Koerner, & Antony, 2013; Steinman & Teachman, 2010), making this an empirically supported option for those with the right computer setup.

Mindfulness training

Mindfulness training—systematically learning to pay attention to the present moment in a meaningful and nonjudgmental way so that the present moment can be approached with compassion, openness, acceptance, and curiosity (Kabat-Zinn, 1994)—is associated with reliable benefits to cognitive and emotional reactivity and a variety of health benefits (Gu, Strauss, Bond, & Cavanagh, 2015; Schumer, Lindsay, & Creswell, 2018). Also, preliminary research has demonstrated that mindfulness and anxiety sensitivity are negatively correlated (McKee, Zvolensky, Solomon, Bernstein, & Leen-Feldner, 2007; Waszczuk et al., 2015). Mindfulness training may include both cognitive restructuring effects and (low level) interoceptive exposure components (Baer, 2003). For example, in the application of mindfulness to chronic pain patients, individuals are encouraged to practice nonjudgmentally observing their pain sensations and disidentifying from specific interpretations of pain as part of broader training that "thoughts are just thoughts" and may not bear a tight relationship to experience (Baer, 2003; Bernstein et al., 2015). This disidentification from the meaning of thoughts may act to decatastrophize anxiety-related concerns. Likewise, the act of continued sitting regardless of the internal content (ranging from discomfort from sitting to acute or chronic pain) may function as lower-level interoceptive exposure (Kabat-Zinn, 1982).

An interactive model between mindfulness and anxiety sensitivity has also been proposed, with the idea that mindfulness may have the power to "dampen" the negative toll that anxiety sensitivity has on an individual (Vujanovic, Zvolensky, Bernstein, Feldner, & McLeish, 2007). Specifically, in this study of 248 participants, the interactive effects of anxiety sensitivity and mindfulness significantly predicted some, but not all, panic-relevant symptoms. Specifically, the interaction predicted anxious arousal and agoraphobic cognitions in combination of high levels of anxiety sensitivity and low levels of mindfulness yielding the highest prediction.

Given the preliminary nature of mindfulness and anxiety sensitivity findings, mindfulness cannot be recommended as a treatment for anxiety sensitivity, especially given that interoceptive exposure and cognitive interventions appear to offer a much more focused and efficient approach. Nonetheless, given the popularity of mindfulness interventions, it seems important for clinicians to consider how such training could be tasked more directly to reducing anxiety sensitivity in those needing such treatment.

Summary

As we search for the right strategies to help our patients achieve their goals, we consider the mechanistic targets or factors that we know to maintain their problems. In this book, the authors have made a compelling case for considering anxiety sensitivity such as target for many of the problems and goals that we see in clinical practice. The beauty of anxiety sensitivity as a transdiagnostic treatment target is that (1) elevations in anxiety sensitivity and changes with intervention are easy to measure and (2) there are a number of relatively easy-to-implement interventions available to modify anxiety sensitivity. Our aim for this book was to provide a resource for clinicians who wish to integrate anxiety sensitivity assessment and treatment with the approaches they use in their practice. We hope that by providing guidance on assessment, case formulation, and the intervention strategies across different presenting problems and populations, this book has achieved its aim and can facilitate the desire to optimize the efficiency and effectiveness of interventions.

References

Allan, N. P., Korte, K. J., Capron, D. W., Raines, A. M., & Schmidt, N. B. (2014). Factor mixture modeling of anxiety sensitivity: a three-class structure. *Psychological Assessment*, *26*(4), 1184.

Allan, N. P., Raines, A. M., Capron, D. W., Norr, A. M., Zvolensky, M. J., & Schmidt, N. B. (2014). Identification of anxiety sensitivity classes and clinical cut-scores in a sample of adult smokers: results from a factor mixture model. *Journal of Anxiety Disorders*, *28*(7), 696–703.

Asmundson, G. J., Fetzner, M. G., DeBoer, L. B., Powers, M. B., Otto, M. W., & Smits, J. A. (2013). Let's get physical: a contemporary review of the anxiolytic effects of exercise for anxiety and its disorders. *Depression and Anxiety*, *30*(4), 362–373.

Baer, R. A. (2003). Mindfulness training as a clinical intervention: a conceptual and empirical review. *Clinical Psychology: Science and Practice*, *10*, 125–143.

Beard, C., & Amir, N. (2008). A multi-session interpretation modification program: changes in interpretation and social anxiety symptoms. *Behaviour Research and Therapy*, *46*(10), 1135–1141.

Bernstein, A., Hadash, Y., Lichtash, Y., Tanay, G., Shepherd, K., & Fresco, D. M. (2015). Decentering and related constructs: a critical review and metacognitive processes model. *Perspectives in Psychological Science*, *10*, 599–617.

Bernstein, A., Zvolensky, M. J., Kotov, R., Arrindell, W. A., Taylor, S., Sandin, B., … Schmidt, N. B. (2006). Taxonicity of anxiety sensitivity: a multinational analysis. *Journal of Anxiety Disorders*, *20*(1), 1–22.

Bernstein, A., Zvolensky, M. J., Norton, P. J., Schmidt, N. B., Taylor, S., Forsyth, J. P., … Cox, B. (2007). Taxometric and factor analytic models of anxiety sensitivity: integrating approaches to latent structural research. *Psychological Assessment*, *19*(1), 74–87.

Bernstein, A., Zvolensky, M. J., Stewart, S. H., Comeau, M. N., & Leen-Feldner, E. W. (2006). Anxiety sensitivity taxonicity across gender among youth. *Behaviour Research and Therapy*, *44*(5), 679–698.

Breslau, J. (2004). Cultures of trauma: anthropological views of posttraumatic stress disorders in international health. *Culture, Medicine & Psychiatry*, *28*(2), 113–126.

Bruce, T. J., Spiegel, D. A., & Hegel, M. T. (1999). Cognitive-behavioral therapy helps prevent relapse and recurrence of panic disorder following alprazolam discontinuation: a long-term follow-up of the Peoria and Dartmouth studies. *Journal of Consulting and Clinical Psychology*, *67*(1), 151–160.

Buckner, J. D., Zvolensky, M. J., Smits, J. A. J., Norton, P. J., Crosby, R. D., Wonderlich, S. A., & Schmidt, N. B. (2011). Anxiety sensitivity and marijuana use: an analysis from ecological momentary assessment. *Depression and Anxiety*, *28*(5), 420–426.

Capron, D. W., & Schmidt, N. B. (2016). Development and evaluation of a novel computer-delivered anxiety sensitivity intervention. *Behaviour Research and Therapy*, *81*, 47–55.

Clerkin, E. M., Beard, C., Fisher, C. R., & Schofield, C. A. (2015). An attempt to target anxiety sensitivity via cognitive bias modification. *PLoS One*, *10*(2).

Cooper, M. L., Frone, M. R., Russell, M., & Mudar, P. (1995). Drinking to regulate positive and negative emotions: a motivational model of alcohol use. *Journal of Personality and Social Psychology*, *69*(5), 990–1005.

Fava, G. A., Grandi, S., Belluardo, P., Savron, G., Raffi, A. R., Conti, S., & Saviotti, F. M. (1994). Benzodiazepines and anxiety sensitivity in panic disorder. *Progress in Neuro-Psychopharmacology & Biological Psychiatry*, *18*(7), 1163–1168.

Foa, E. B., & Kozak, M. J. (1986). Emotional processing of fear: exposure to corrective information. *Psychological Bulletin*, *99*(1), 20–35.

Gu, J., Strauss, C., Bond, R., & Cavanagh, K. (2015). How do mindfulness-based cognitive therapy and mindfulness-based stress reduction improve mental health and wellbeing? A systematic review and meta-analysis of mediation studies. *Clinical Psychology Review*, *37*, 1–12.

Hearon, B. A., Quatromoni, P. A., Mascoop, J. L., & Otto, M. W. (2014). The role of anxiety sensitivity in daily physical activity and eating behavior. *Eating Behaviors*, *15*(2), 255–258.

Hinton, D. E., & Otto, M. W. (2006). Symptom presentation and symptom meaning among traumatized Cambodian refugees; relevance to a somatically focused cognitive-behavior therapy. *Cognitive and Behavioral Practice*, *13*, 249–260.

Hipol, L. J., & Deacon, B. J. (2012). Dissemination of evidence-based practices for anxiety disorders in Wyoming: a survey of practicing psychotherapists. *Behavior Modification*, *37*(2), 170–188.

Horenstein, A., Potter, C. M., & Heimberg, R. G. (2018). How does anxiety sensitivity increase risks for chronic medical conditions. *Clinical Psychology: Science and Practice*, *25*(3), e12248. https://doi.org/10.1111/cpsp.12248.

Institute of Medicine (2001). *Health and behavior: The interplay of biological, behavioral, and societal influences*. Washington, DC: The National Academies Press.

Kabat-Zinn, J. (1982). An outpatient program in behavioral medicine for chronic pain patients based on the practice of mindfulness meditation: theoretical considerations and preliminary results. *General Hospital Psychiatry*, *4*, 33–47.

Kabat-Zinn, J. (1994). *Wherever you go, there you are: Mindfulness meditation in everyday life*. New York: Hyperion.

Keough, M. E., & Schmidt, N. B. (2012). Refinement of a brief anxiety sensitivity reduction intervention. *Journal of Consulting and Clinical Psychology*, *80*, 766–772.

Langdon, K. J., Farris, S. G., Hogan, J. B. D., Grover, K. W., & Zvolensky, M. J. (2016). Anxiety sensitivity in relation to quit day dropout among adult daily smokers recruited to participate in a self-guided cessation attempt. *Addictive Behavior*, *58*, 12–15.

MacDonald, E. M., Koerner, N., & Antony, M. M. (2013). Modification of interpretive bias: impact on anxiety sensitivity, information processing and response to induced bodily sensations. *Cognitive Therapy and Research*, *37*(4), 860–871.

McKee, L., Zvolensky, M. J., Solomon, S. E., Bernstein, A., & Leen-Feldner, E. (2007). Emotional-vulnerability and mindfulness: a preliminary test of associations among negative affectivity, anxiety sensitivity, and mindfulness skills. *Cognitive Behaviour Therapy*, *36* (2), 91–101.

McNally, R. J. (2002). Anxiety sensitivity and panic disorder. *Biological Psychiatry*, *52*(10), 938–946.

Mitchell, M. A., Capron, D. W., Raines, A. M., & Schmidt, N. B. (2014). Reduction of cognitive concerns of anxiety sensitivity is uniquely associated with reduction of PTSD and depressive symptoms: a comparison of civilians and veterans. *Journal of Psychiatric Research*, *48*, 25–31.

Naragon-Gainey, K. (2010). Meta-analysis of the relations of anxiety sensitivity to the depressive and anxiety disorders. *Psychological Bulletin*, *136*, 128–150.

Norr, A. M., Gibby, B. A., & Schmidt, N. B. (2017). Is computerized psychoeducation sufficient to reduce anxiety sensitivity in an at-risk sample?: a randomized trial. *Journal of Affective Disorders*, *212*, 48–55.

Ocañez, K. S., McHugh, R. K., & Otto, M. W. (2010). A meta-analytic review of the association between anxiety sensitivity and pain. *Depression and Anxiety*, *27*, 760–767.

Olatunji, B. O., & Wolitzky-Taylor, K. B. (2009). Anxiety sensitivity and the anxiety disorders: a meta-analytic review and synthesis. *Psychological Bulletin*, *135*, 974–999.

Otto, M. W., Demopulos, C. M., McLean, N. E., Pollack, M. H., & Fava, M. (1998). Additional findings on the association between anxiety sensitivity and hypochondriacal concerns: examination of patients with major depression. *Journal of Anxiety Disorders*, *12*(3), 225–232.

Otto, M. W., Eastman, A., Lo, S., Hearon, B. A., Bickel, W. K., Zvolensky, M., … Doan, S. N. (2016). Anxiety sensitivity and working memory capacity: risk factors and targets for health behavior promotion. *Clinical Psychology Review*, *4*, 967–978.

Otto, M. W., & Hinton, D. E. (2006). Modifying exposure-based CBT for Cambodian refugees with posttraumatic stress disorder. *Cognitive and Behavioral Practice*, *13*(4), 261–270.

Otto, M. W., Hinton, D., Korbly, N. B., Chea, A., Phalnarith, B., Gershuny, B. S., & Pollack, M. H. (2003). Treatment of pharmacotherapy-refractory posttraumatic stress disorder among Cambodian refugees: a pilot study of combination treatment with cognitive-behavior therapy vs. sertraline alone. *Behaviour Research and Therapy*, *41*, 1271–1276.

Otto, M. W., Hong, J. J., & Safren, S. A. (2002). Benzodiazepine discontinuation difficulties in panic disorder: conceptual model and outcome for cognitive-behavior therapy. *Current Pharmaceutical Design*, *8*, 75–80.

Otto, M. W., McHugh, R. K., Simon, N. M., Farach, F. J., Worthington, J. J., & Pollack, M. H. (2010). Efficacy of CBT for benzodiazepine discontinuation in patients with panic disorder: further evaluation. *Behaviour Research and Therapy*, *48*, 720–727.

Otto, M. W., Penava, S. J., Pollock, R. A., & Smoller, J. W. (1996). Cognitive-behavioral and pharmacologic perspectives on the treatment of post-traumatic stress disorder. In M. H. Pollack, M. W. Otto, & J. F. Rosenbaum (Eds.), *Challenges in clinical practice: Pharmacologic and psychosocial strategies* (pp. 219–260). New York: The Guilford Press.

Otto, M. W., & Pollack, M. H. (2009). *Stopping anxiety medication* (Therapist guide, 2nd ed.). New York, NY: Oxford University Press.

Otto, M. W., Pollack, M. H., Sachs, G. S., Reiter, S. R., Meltzer-Brody, S., & Rosenbaum, J. F. (1993). Discontinuation of benzodiazepine treatment: efficacy of cognitive-behavior therapy for patients with panic disorder. *American Journal of Psychiatry*, *150*, 1485–1490.

Otto, M. W., Pollack, M. H., Sachs, G. S., & Rosenbaum, J. F. (1992). Hypochondriacal concerns, anxiety sensitivity, and panic disorder. *Journal of Anxiety Disorders*, *6*, 93–104.

Otto, M. W., & Smits, J. A. J. (2018). Anxiety sensitivity, health behaviors, and the prevention and treatment of medical illness. *Clinical Psychology: Science and Practice*, *25*(3), e12253. https://doi.org/10.1111/cpsp.12253.

Otto, M. W., Tolin, D. F., Nations, K. R., Utschig, A. C., Rothbaum, B. O., Hofmann, S. G., & Smits, J. A. (2012). Five sessions and counting: considering ultra-brief treatment for panic disorder. *Depression and Anxiety*, *29*(6), 465–470.

Paulus, D. J., Valadka, J., Businelle, M. S., Gallagher, M. W., Viana, A. G., Schmidt, N. B., & Zvolensky, M. J. (2017). Emotion dysregulation explains association between anxiety sensitivity and hazardous drinking and drinking motives among adult treatment-seeking smokers. *Psychology of Addictive Behaviors: Journal of the Society of Psychologists in Addictive Behaviors*, *31*(2), 189–199.

Peterson, R. A., & Plehn, K. (1999). Measuring anxiety sensitivity. In *Anxiety sensitivity: Theory, research, and treatment of the fear of anxiety* (pp. 61–81). Mahwah, NJ: Lawrence Erlbaum Associates Publishers.

Schmidt, N. B., Bucker, J. D., & Keough, M. E. (2007). Anxiety sensitivity as a prospective predictor of alcohol use disorders. *Behavior Modification*, *31*(2), 202–219.

Schumer, M. C., Lindsay, E. K., & Creswell, J. D. (2018). Brief mindfulness training for negative affectivity: a systematic review and meta-analysis. *Journal of Consulting and Clinical Psychology*, *86*(7), 569–583.

Simon, N. M., Otto, M. W., Smits, J. A., Nicolaou, D. C., Reese, H. E., & Pollack, M. H. (2004). Changes in anxiety sensitivity with pharmacotherapy for panic disorder. *Journal of Psychiatric Research*, *38*(5), 491–495.

Smits, J. A. J., Berry, A. C., Rosenfield, D., Powers, M. B., Behar, E., & Otto, M. W. (2008). Reducing anxiety sensitivity with exercise. *Depression and Anxiety*, *25*(8), 689–699.

Smits, J. A. J., Berry, A. C., Tart, C. D., & Powers, M. B. (2008). The efficacy of cognitive-behavioral interventions for reducing anxiety sensitivity: a meta-analytic review. *Behaviour Research and Therapy*, *46*(9), 1047–1054.

Smits, J. A. J., Bonn-Miller, M. O., Tart, C. D., Irons, J. G., & Zvolensky, M. J. (2011). Anxiety sensitivity as a mediator of the relationship between moderate-intensity exercise and coping-oriented marijuana use motives. *The American Journal on Addictions*, *20*(2), 113–119.

Smits, J. A. J., Powers, M. B., Berry, A. C., & Otto, M. W. (2007). Translating empirically supported strategies into accessible interventions: the potential utility of exercise for the treatment of panic disorder. *Cognitive and Behavioral Practice*, *14*(4), 364–374.

Smits, J. A. J., Powers, M. B., & Otto, M. W. (in press). *Personalized exposure therapy: A person-centered transdiagnostic approach*. New York, NY: Oxford University Press.

Smits, J. A. J., Tart, C. D., Rosenfield, D., & Zvolensky, M. J. (2011). The interplay between physical activity and anxiety sensitivity in fearful responding to CO_2 challenge. *Psychosomatic Medicine*, *73*(6), 498–503.

Smits, J. A. J., Zvolensky, M. J., Davis, M. L., Rosenfield, D., Marcus, B. H., Church, T. S., … Brown, R. A. (2016). The efficacy of vigorous-intensity exercise as an aid to smoking cessation in adults with high anxiety sensitivity: a randomized controlled trial. *Psychosomatic Medicine*, *78*(3), 354–364.

Stathopoulou, G., Pollack, M. H., & Otto, M. W. (2018). Anxiety sensitivity moderates drug cravings in response to induced negative affect in opioid dependent outpatients. *Addictive Behaviors*, *84*, 75–78.

Steinman, S. A., & Teachman, B. A. (2010). Modifying interpretations among individuals high in anxiety sensitivity. *Journal of Anxiety Disorders*, *24*(1), 71–78.

Tay, T. R., & Hew, M. (2018). Comorbid "treatable traits" in difficult asthma: current evidence and clinical evaluation. *Allergy*, *73*(7), 1369–1382.

Taylor, J. H., Jakubovski, E., & Bloch, M. H. (2015). Predictors of anxiety recurrence in the coordinated anxiety learning and management (CALM) trial. *Journal of Psychiatric Research*, *65*, 154–165.

Timpano, K. R., Carbonella, J. Y., Keuough, M., & Schmidt, N. B. (2015). Anxiety sensitivity: an examination of the relationship with authoritarian, authoritative, and permissive parental styles. *Journal of Cognitive Psychotherapy*, *29*(2), 95–105.

Vujanovic, A. A., Farris, S. G., Bartlett, B. A., Lyons, R. C., Haller, M., Colvonen, P. J., & Norman, S. B. (2018). Anxiety sensitivity in the association between posttraumatic stress and substance use disorders: a systematic review. *Clinical Psychology Review*, *62*, 37–55.

Vujanovic, A. A., Zvolensky, M. J., Bernstein, A., Feldner, A. T., & McLeish, A. C. (2007). A test of the interactive effects of anxiety sensitivity and mindfulness in the prediction of anxious arousal, agoraphobic cognitions, and body vigilance. *Behaviour Research and Therapy*, *45*, 1393–1400.

Wald, J., & Taylor, S. (2010). Implementation and outcome of combining interoceptive exposure with trauma-related exposure therapy in a patient with combat-related posttraumatic stress disorder. *Clinical Case Studies*, *9*, 243–259.

Wald, J., Taylor, S., Chiri, L., & Sica, C. (2010). Posttraumatic stress disorder and chronic pain arising from motor vehicle accidents: efficacy of interoceptive exposure plus trauma-related exposure therapy. *Cognitive Behaviour Therapy*, *39*(2), 104–113.

Waszczuk, M. A., Zavos, H. M., Antonova, E., Haworth, C. M., Plomin, R., & Eley, T. C. (2015). A multivariate twin study of trait mindfulness, depressive symptoms, and anxiety sensitivity. *Depression and Anxiety*, *32*, 254–261.

Watt, M. C., Gallagher, C. E., Couture, M. E., Wells, R., & MacLean, K. (2016). Anxiety sensitivity mediates relations between attachment and aggression differently by gender. *Journal of Interpersonal Violence*, 1–20. https://doi.org/10.1177/0886260516683173.

Westra, H. A., Stewart, S. H., & Conrad, B. E. (2002). Naturalistic manner of benzodiazepine use and cognitive behavioral therapy outcome in panic disorder with agoraphobia. *Journal of Anxiety Disorders*, *16*(3), 233–246.

Whittal, M. L., Otto, M. W., & Hong, J. J. (2001). Cognitive-behavior therapy for discontinuation of SSRI treatment of panic disorder: a case series. *Behavior Research and Therapy*, *39*, 939–945.

Wolitzky-Taylor, K., Drazdowski, T. K., Niles, A., Roy-Byrne, P., Ries, R., Rawson, R., & Craske, M. G. (2018). Change in anxiety sensitivity and substance use coping motives as putative mediators of treatment efficacy among substance users. *Behaviour Research and Therapy*, *107*, 34–41.

Wright, K. D., Lebell, M. A., & Carleton, R. N. (2016). Intolerance of uncertainty, anxiety sensitivity, health anxiety, and anxiety disorder symptoms in youth. *Journal of Anxiety Disorders*, *41*, 35–42.

Young, A. (1995). Reasons and causes for post-traumatic stress disorder. *Transcultural Psychiatric Research Review*, *32*, 287–298.

Zalaznik, D., Weiss, M., & Huppert, J. D. (2017). Improvement in adult anxious and avoidant attachment during cognitive behavioral therapy for panic disorder. *Psychotherapy Research*, *22*, 1–17.

Zvolensky, M. J., Rosenfield, D., Garey, L., Kauffman, B. Y., Langdon, K. J., Powers, M. B., … Smits, J. A. J. (2018). Does exercise aid smoking cessation through reductions in anxiety sensitivity and dysphoria? *Health Psychology*, *37*(7), 647–657.

Zvolensky, M. J., Stewart, S. H., Vujanovic, A. A., Gavric, D., & Steeves, D. (2009). Anxiety sensitivity and anxiety and depressive symptoms in the prediction of early smoking lapse and relapse during smoking cessation treatment. *Nicotine & Tobacco Research*, *11*(3), 323–331.

Index

Note: Page numbers followed by *f* indicate figures, *t* indicate tables, and *b* indicate boxes.

MIX
Papier | Fördert gute Waldnutzung
FSC® C083411

Kolibri 360 GmbH
Ferdinand-Jühlke-Straße 7
99095 Erfurt, Deutschland
produktsicherheit@kolibri360.de